THE FIRST TEN YEARS OF
AMERICAN COMMUNISM

Report of a participant

by

JAMES P. CANNON

PATHFINDER
New York   London   Montreal   Sydney

Copyright © 1962 by James P. Cannon
All rights reserved

ISBN 978-0-87348-353-7
Library of Congress Catalog Card Number 73-88411
Manufactured in the United States of America

First edition published by Lyle Stuart, Inc., 1962
First Pathfinder edition, 1973
Fifteenth printing, 2024

COVER PHOTO: Communist Party-led demonstration of unemployed workers in New York City in 1922.

BACK COVER PHOTO: James P. Cannon, 1935.

PATHFINDER
www.pathfinderpress.com
Email: pathfinder@pathfinderpress.com

THE FIRST TEN YEARS OF AMERICAN COMMUNISM
Report of a participant

Contents

Preface by Theodore Draper	9
Acknowledgments	15
Introduction	19

Part 1: Letters to a historian

My thesis	45
Four ways of viewing the early Communist Party	49
The first years—the underground party	52
Fraina—the founder	58
The early leadership	64
Origin of the policy on the labor party	73
More on the labor party policy	77
The 'American question' at the Fourth Congress of the Comintern	80
The reshaping of the leadership after the legalization of the party	92
The Pepper regime	98
Overthrow of the Pepper regime	105
Notes on the Third Party Convention	118
The pre-war Socialist Party	120
The pre-war anarchists	122
The pre-war left wing	126
Foster in World War I	131
Foster and Browder	135
Lovestone and Bittelman	143
The Foster-Cannon group	146
Browder's role	157
Fourth Plenum of the Comintern—1924	159

After the 1924 elections	161
1925: The 'Parity Commission' and the 'cable from Moscow'	164
'Party life' in the twenties	172
The Passaic strike	175
The overriding issue in the factional struggle of 1925–1928	180
After 1925: Permanent factionalism	184
International Labor Defense	198
1927: From Ruthenberg to Lovestone	206
Notes and sidelights on the year 1927	217
The Lovestone regime	227
A note on Zinoviev	231
Some people in the party	233
Before the Sixth Congress of the Comintern	242
Lovestone's troubles in Moscow	250
Stalin's devious design	252
At the Sixth World Congress of the Comintern	254
On critics and criticism	268
The 'Third Period'	269
Foster's last stand	271
Foster and the later Stalinists	272
Spector's role	273
Our trial for 'Trotskyism'	276
On 'The Birth of American Trotskyism'	278
The Negro question	282

Part 2: The Russian Revolution and the American Negro movement 285

Part 3: The forerunners
Eugene V. Debs and the socialist movement of his time	305
The IWW—The great anticipation	341

Part 4: A critical review of Theodore Draper's history

1. 'The Roots of American Communism'   381
2. 'American Communism and Soviet Russia'   397

Index   407

Preface

BY THEODORE DRAPER

Many years ago, or so it seems, when I first thought of getting in touch with Jim Cannon to ask him for his cooperation in what was still only an early stage of a history of American communism, I did not have much hope that he would agree. I could think of several reasons why he might be less than enthusiastic about the idea. I had never met him, and I saw no reason why he should trust me. I tentatively confided my intention of asking him anyway to some mutual acquaintances who had known Jim, and they were unanimously and vociferously certain that he would have none of me.

Nevertheless, I decided to try. If he refused, it would be on his head, not mine. A letter came back from James P. Cannon; it met my proposal more than half way. Still, I could not be sure until I had sent him the first questions and received his answers. I spent several days preparing the initial inquisition. At this point, the reader may be interested in the "methodology" of this historical venture.

Traditionally, the historian does not "create" his source material; he finds it ready-made in some concrete form. He looks for documents, memoirs, letters, and the like. But the subject of contemporary history cannot be treated in the traditional way, and this is especially true of the communist movement. (Some historians regard with suspicion anything written about events after 1789, and the real purists seem to draw a line at about the Renaissance.) Communist documents can be peculiarly opaque; one often gets out of them no more than one brings to them. Above all, however, an entire class of traditional historical material is almost entirely lacking—personal recollections and interpretations in the form of biographies, autobiographies, letters, diaries. Some of these exist, to be sure, but on examination they prove to be interesting and informative only as long as they are not dealing with the communist movement. For example, the official biography of Charles E. Ruthenberg stops just about the time Ruthenberg became a communist leader. Memoirs by ex-communists vary in content, but too many of them are basically motivated by the desire to tell why the writer decided to break with the communist movement rather than what he did in it.

Thus the historian of communism is faced with a peculiar problem: if he wishes to make use of memoirs by leading figures in his story, he may have to go out to get them. The historian cannot wait passively for such material to come to him; he must assume an active role in creating it. In my case, the assumption of this function was especially tempting because so many of the leading figures of the early period had left the party, some of them many years ago, and no longer needed to respond on the basis of loyalty and discipline. Also, they represented such different views, then and now, that nothing I could write would possibly satisfy all of them or, indeed, any one of them. Time was fleeting, and I decided to make the effort, at first without too much reason for optimism. And I was keenly aware of the risks in such an enterprise.

The events themselves had occurred thirty and more years ago. The passage of time, the fallibility of memory, and the human predilection for self-justification were obvious pitfalls. Could they be avoided? The answer, I think, is that there are no absolute safeguards—but there are no absolute safeguards built into old documents, either. The historian of contemporary history resorts to what may be called "direct contact" not as a substitute for documentary sources but as a supplement to them. Documentation retains all its old authenticity and takes precedence—where it exists in sufficient quantity and quality. Indeed, only a mastery of the available documents makes possible fruitful interviewing or letters. The historian who merely asks, "What happened?" about an event already thirty or more years old is doomed to disappointment and worse—deception. The task is far more difficult and complex.

Before I wrote Jim Cannon a single letter, I tried to learn as much as possible about him and his role in the communist movement from the available material. I did so for several reasons. I wanted to ask only those questions which I could not answer in any other way. I also wished to pose questions in such a way that it would be clear how much I already knew. Therefore, I carefully set the stage for each question by reconstructing the situation out of which the question had arisen. This necessitated letters on my part easily as long and detailed as those I received. But these letters, which sometimes took me a week to compose, were well worth the trouble. They forced me to organize the existing material as far as it would go and to clarify in my own mind just what it was I wanted to know. On the other side, they stimulated the memory and reawakened the past. And they also implied that any answers would have to be compatible with a body of acknowledged facts and documentary evidence.

In the case of Jim Cannon, I did not meet him personally until a very late stage of our correspondence. I rather preferred it that way; distance and impersonality gave the relationship an objectivity which it might otherwise have lacked in the same degree. At first, his letters were such as anyone might write in reply to a stranger's demands. But soon, I noticed a most significant change. They became more formal, better organized, each a little gem of its kind.

After a while, I realized that Jim was well on his way to writing an autobiography—the first and perhaps the only one we will ever have from an old-timer in the American communist movement. Official American communists have published so-called autobiographies, but they have been largely spurious. Cannon's letters are the real thing. I feel that students of the American labor movement in general and the American communist movement in particular will cherish them for years to come.

And why? Because, I suppose, enough time had passed so that the old wars and old enemies were no longer to be fought but to be understood. A man looked back at what may have been the richest and most painful period of his long life, and he reflected on people and events with a mature humanity and compassionate candor that might not have been possible before. I do not know what else of Cannon's writings will survive the test of time, but I am sure that this book will. It transcends pettiness, partisanship, and personalities. It is a "remembrance of things past" that may well be its author's greatest gift to the movement which has been his life's work.

And I can testify that he has remembered phenomenally well. One occasion stands out in my mind. The event had happened thirty-five years earlier. Only two people, one of them Jim Cannon, were involved. Both had given me their versions, and they could not be made to fit together. After I received Jim's letter on this incident, I went back to the other person and simply read him Jim's account without telling him the source. After I finished, he shook his head and said: "Yes, I think that is how it was. I must have been mistaken." Jim proved to be right on several such occasions, and I learned from repeated experiences that his memory excelled by far that of his contemporaries with whom I have dealt in the same way.

For a long time, I wondered why Jim Cannon's memory of events in the Nineteen-Twenties was so superior to that of all the others. Was it simply some inherent trait of mind? Rereading some of these letters, I came to the conclusion that it was something more. Unlike other communist leaders of his generation, Jim Cannon *wanted* to remember. This portion of his life still lives for him because he has not killed it within himself, and I am happy that I had some part in luring him into making it live for others.

Theodore Draper
NEW YORK
FEBRUARY 3, 1961

Acknowledgments

This book about the first ten years of American communism, as its subtitle indicates, is the testimony of a participant written from memory. Originally, I did not plan to write these extensive recollections and comments. I was prodded into it.

In February 1954, I received a letter from Theodore Draper stating that he was working on a history of the American communist movement, and wanted to check his findings with various people who had been present in the early period. He asked if I would be willing to "discuss some problems and go over some material" relating to the first ten years. I was occupied with other work at the time but I thought it would be easy to answer a few questions, and I accepted his proposal rather light-heartedly.

That's the way it started. I didn't have the faintest idea of where it was going to end; for I greatly underestimated the seriousness of this historian's approach to his task and his persistence in tracking down every possible source of information and opinion about the material he had turned up in his exhaustive research, and the problems of interpretation he had encountered.

Draper's first questions called for far more extensive answers than I had at first contemplated. My first answers then prompted him to submit a new set of questions. And that was still only the beginning. More questions and answers dealing with matters of fact and opinion, with several personal interviews sandwiched in between, were exchanged over a three-year period until the publication of his first volume, *The Roots of American Communism,* in 1957. Then the question-answer correspondence was resumed and continued for another three years, until the publication of his second volume, *American Communism and Soviet Russia,* in 1960.

Under Draper's persistent, probing questioning I was impelled, step by step, to write down a fairly complete record of my recollections as a participant and eyewitness of the first ten years of American communism; my opinions of its historical significance; my appraisals of the people concerned, as I remembered them; and even to write a summary report of the radical movement in America before the First World War in which I had also taken part.

The bulk of the material in this book—Part I, Letters to a Historian—consists of letters written to Draper in reply to questions posed by him. All the other sections, including the Introduction, which deal with specific questions in self-contained articles, were by-products of the correspondence with Draper and were more or less directly inspired by it.

Our six-year correspondence, as I see it, was a good example of loyal collaboration on both sides to set the record straight despite basic differences of opinion and interpretation. Part 4, A Critical Review of Theodore Draper's History, gives my version of our points of agreement and disagreement.

I am gratefully indebted to three comrades—Jeanne Morgan, Reba Hansen and Julia Houdek—who did all the hard work of typing and re-typing and other technical jobs connected with this enterprise because they believed in it; and to Rose Karsner, who lived through all the tough struggles of the old days, and then lived them over again with me as they were remembered and reported here.

A large part of the material in this collection was originally published in the magazine *Fourth International* and its successor, *International Socialist Review.*

J.P.C.
LOS ANGELES
DECEMBER 1, 1961

Introduction

THE FIRST TEN YEARS IN PERSPECTIVE

I

The Communist Party, as it stands today, is undoubtedly the most friendless party in the history of American radicalism, and this unpopularity is by no means confined to reactionary ruling circles which are fiercely persecuting the party incident to the cold war. The party is despised and rejected by the workers too, and not only by the ignorant and the backward. For the first time, a party faces persecution without the moral support and sympathy of even the more progressive workers who have traditionally extended their solidarity to any party or group hounded by the ruling powers.

In its later evolution the Communist Party has written such a consistent record of cynical treachery and lying deception that few can believe it was ever any different. A quarter of a century of Stalinism has worked mightily to obliterate the honorable record of American communism in its pioneer days.

Yet the party wrote such a chapter too, and the young militants of the new generation ought to know about it and claim it for their own. It belongs to them. The first six years of American communism—1918–1923—represent a heroic period from which all future revolutionary movements in this country will be the lineal descendants. There is no getting away from that. The revolutionist who would deny it is simply renouncing his own ancestry. That's where he came from, and without it he would not be.

The Communist Party did not change its nature and its

color overnight. Between its early years of integrity and its later corruption there was a transition period of the transformation of the once revolutionary organization into its opposite. This transition period, which began in the last half of the Twenties, is the subject of this inquiry.

The degeneration of the Communist Party of the United States in this fateful period did not happen by accident. It had profound causes which must be considered in their entirety. The same can be said of the struggle for the regeneration of American communism which began in 1928.

A complex of external factors, upon which the party tried to operate, also operated upon the party and eventually determined its course. Different problems—posed by national and international developments—confronted the party in the different stages of its evolution. Different influences—national and international—predominated at different times. The actions of the party leaders must be related to their context of time and circumstance. Only from this point of view can one approach an understanding of the party's retrogressive transformation. The rest is only malicious gossip or special pleading, which presents a mystery without a clue.

II

The history of the first ten years of American communism properly falls into three distinct periods. These three periods may be summarized as follows:

From *1917 to 1919* the life of the left wing of the Socialist Party—out of which the first troops of American communism were assembled—was governed primarily by international events and influences. Two "outside" factors, namely, the First World War and the Russian Revolution, created the issues which deepened the division between the left and the right in the American SP; and the theoretical formulation of these issues by the Russian Bolsheviks and the Comintern gave the left wing its program.

The factional struggle of this period occurred along clearly defined lines of political principle. The left wing, which had previously fought as a theoretically uncertain and somewhat heterogeneous minority, was armed with the great ideas of the Bolsheviks and unified on a new foundation. The left wing as a whole clashed with the traditional leadership of the SP over the most basic issues of doctrine, as they had been put to the test in the war and the Russian Revolution.

Leaving aside all the mistakes and excesses of the left-wing leaders, personal antagonisms engendered in the fight, etc., the lines of principle which separated them from the old leadership of the Socialist Party were clearly drawn. The split of 1919, resulting in the formal constitution of the communist movement as an independent party, was a split over *international* issues of *principle* in the broadest and clearest sense of the term.

III

The period from *1920 to 1923* presents a different picture. After the split with the right socialists, the left wing was preoccupied with differences and divisions in its own ranks, and the issues of factional struggle were different. *National* considerations dominated the life of the young communist movement at this time.

The big questions in dispute in this period—Americanization, legalization, trade-union work, labor party, leadership—were specifically *American* questions. The issues of internal controversy were not matters of *principle*—since all factions supported the program of Bolshevism and all acknowledged allegiance to the Comintern—but of *tactics*.

Nevertheless, the political nature of the differences in that period stands out very clearly above all secondary questions of personal antagonisms, rivalries, etc. The *international* factor—the Comintern—appears in this period as a helpful advisor in the settlement of *national* questions. The American party was throwing up its own indigenous leadership and fighting out its own battles with the help of the Comintern, rather than, as in the preceding period, simply reflecting and re-enacting the international fight on American grounds.

IV

The years *1924 to 1928* stand out as the great dividing line between progress and regression in the evolution of the Communist Party of the United States.

Prior to that time national conditions, on the whole, had favored the consolidation of a revolutionary party, even though a small one, and the process was greatly aided by the powerful inspiration of the Russian Revolution and the friendly intervention of the Comintern in matters of doctrine and policy. The party, like all other parties, had developed in the course of internal struggles. The issues of these struggles, as written in the record, stand out in retrospect sharp and clear. Everything that happened in those earlier periods makes political sense and is easily comprehensible. The record explains itself.

The evolution of the party in the last half of the Twenties must appear as a puzzle to the student who tries to decipher the formal record of this period; for the record was in part falsified even while it was being made, and has been even more falsified in later accounts. In these years real differences between the factions over national policy actually narrowed down, and they were usually able to agree on common resolutions, but the faction fight raged fiercer than ever.

Something went wrong, and the party began to gyrate crazily like a mechanism out of control. The purposeful and self-explanatory internal struggles of temporary factions in the earlier periods, by which the party was propelled forward in spite of all mistakes and inadequacies of the participants, gave place to a "power fight" of permanent factions struggling blindly for supremacy or survival in a form of political gang warfare.

People who had started out to fight for communism began to lose sight of their goal. Factionalism, which in earlier times had been a means to an end, became an end in itself. Allegiance to communism and to the party gave way, gradually and imperceptibly, to allegiance to the faction-gang. There could be no winners in this crazy game, which—unknown to the participants at the time—was destined to find its eventual solution in a three-way split and a new beginning.

V

What threw the machine out of control? That is the question. Stories told about the unsightly squabbles and scandals of that time of troubles, whether true or false, which leave unanswered the question of basic causes, are mere descriptions which explain nothing and properly come under the heading of gossip.

Such gossip represents the individual participants in the events of that period as masters of their own fate. This gives them too much credit—or too much blame. The party leaders did not operate in circumstances of their own making. Their actions were far less significant than the forces that acted upon them. To be sure, they were communists, committed to the service of a great cause. By that fact, they were superior to others of their generation who limited themselves to small aims. But they were neither gods nor devils, and they were not able to make history according to their will. They were not even able to stick to their original design.

The story of the Communist Party in the different stages of its evolution is a story of different people, even though some of the names are the same—a story of people who changed. In examining the record of the early days one must try to see the people as they were then, and not as they became after the passage of time and many pressures had wrought their changes. The period of party history under review was a time of change—in the party and in the people who headed it.

In order to understand what happened to them it is necessary to recognize what was happening in the world at large and how they were affected by it. Like many before them and after them, they who had set out to change the world were imperceptibly changed by it. They meant well—with possible exceptions. Their fault, which was their undoing, was that they did not fully recognize the forces operating upon them.

This made it all the easier for objective factors in the national and international situation of the time, which proved to be weightier than their will, to convert most of them into instruments—at first unconsciously—of a course which contradicted their original design and which eventually brought the majority of them, by different routes, into the camp of renegacy.

VI

It has long since become fashionable for ex-communists, repenting of the idealistic follies and courageous excesses of their youth—along with others who lack this distinction—to attribute all the evils and misfortunes which befell the native left-wing movement to "Moscow domination" exerted through the Communist International. From this it is implied that everything would have been all right with American radicalism if it had followed a policy of isolationism and rejected the "outside influences" of the outside world.

At the same time, without noticing the contradiction, the representatives of this school of thought—if you want to call it that—fervently recommend a "One World" policy of internationalism to American imperialism, whose virtues they have belatedly discovered and which some of them serve as unofficial advisors, and even, in some cases, as direct agents.

There is no doubt that the Russian Communist Party, itself corrupted into conservatism under Stalin, transmitted its own corruption to the other parties of the Comintern which looked to it for leadership. But that's only part of the story. There were other influences working to sap the revolutionary integrity of the party—right here at home. It took more than outside influences—from Russia or anywhere else—to ruin the Communist Party of the United States.

As a matter of fact, in the modern world, internationalism is not an outside influence at all. The whole is not foreign to its parts. America, especially since 1914, has been a part of the "One World" and a very big part indeed. In reacting to events in other countries, America also reacts upon them. There is no such thing as "the international situation" outside and apart from this country. And the American communist movement, in all its reactions to international influences, was never free from the simultaneous influence of its national environment.

The causal factors which brought the Communist Party into being in the first place were both national and international. The same holds true for its later evolution at every stage. American communism, at the moment of its birth, represented a fusion of the Russian Revolution with a native movement of American radicalism. It is not correct to say that "everything came from Russia." The ideas of the Russian Revolution needed a given social environment to take root in, and receptive people to cultivate them; as far as we know, the Russian Revolution did not create a Communist Party on the moon.

International events and ideas were the predominating influence in bringing the American Communist Party into existence, but these events and ideas needed human instruments. These were provided by the native movement of American revolutionists which had grown up before the Russian Revolution out of the class struggle in the United States.

VII

These two combined national and international factors likewise operated interactively on the American Communist Party in the later transition period of its gradual degeneration, which began in the middle of the Twenties and was virtually completed by the end of the decade. At that conjuncture the deadening conservatism of American life, induced by the unprecedented boom of post-war American capitalism, coinciding with the reactionary swing in Russia, caught the infant movement of American communism from two sides, as in a vise from which it could not escape.

In this period the reactionary Russian influence, transmitted through the Comintern, wrought unmitigated evil in the American party. There is plenty of evidence of that. But here again it is false to ascribe all responsibility to the Russians, as an outside and uncontrolled force, for they, in turn, were powerfully influenced by the evolution of American capitalism. The American boom of that period, carrying European capitalism with it to a new stabilization after the post-war crisis and revolutionary upsurge, was the prime influence generating the mood of retreat to national reformism, and therewith the rise of Stalinism in Russia.

At the same time, the astounding vitality of expanding American capitalism seemed to close off all perspectives for a revolutionary movement in this country. As the wave of labor radicalism was pushed back by the ascending prosperity, the party began to run into difficulties on all fronts.

All the get-rich-quick schemes of Pepperite adventurism, all the "high politics" of bluff and make-believe, had blown up in disaster. Even the previous achievements of solid work began to crumble away. The trade-union successes, which had piled up so impressively in the preceding period, were turned into a series of defeats which became a virtual rout, while the Gompers "red hunt" rode triumphantly from one end of the labor movement to the other. The poor showing of the party in the presidential election of 1924 testified most convincingly to the party's isolation.

All the bright prospects which had fired the ambition of the party leaders to build a mass party of American communism in a short time, by a series of forced marches, had gone glimmering by the time the party picked up the pieces after the election campaign of 1924. And the worst was yet to come.

It was a time for the party to re-examine its prospects in the light of basic doctrine and to settle down for a siege; to recognize the new, unfavorable situation in the country, but not to mistake it for permanence. The party needed then a serious theoretical schooling, and a historical perspective upon which to base a confident and patient work of preparation for the future. But that was precisely what was lacking.

The great crisis of the Thirties, with its limitless possibilities for the revolutionary party, was just around the corner, but the party leaders could not see it. They spoke about it, from old habit, but they began to doubt it. The degeneration of the party as a revolutionary organization definitely began already then, and partly for this reason. When the crisis finally arrived—pretty much on schedule according to the Marxist prognosis—the party was no longer the same party.

VIII

The party needed then such ideological and political help from the Comintern as it had previously received in the time of Lenin and Trotsky—when the purpose of its intervention had been, in truth and in fact, to help the young American communists to build the party of the American revolution. But that was lacking too. The Comintern itself, following the Russian party, was sliding down into national reformism, dragging all the other parties with it.

The dimming of international revolutionary perspectives, and the loss of confidence in the capacity of the working class to transform society in the advanced countries, had motivated the retreat to national reformism in the Soviet Union and the wish to come to terms with world capitalism; to "coexist" with it; and to settle for "Socialism in One Country," which implicitly signified a renunciation of the program of international revolution.

The acceptance of this theory by the other Communist parties in the capitalist countries, prepared by their own weariness and loss of historical perspective, implicitly signified their renunciation of the revolutionary program in their own countries. At the same time, it gave them—for consolation—an ersatz program which enabled them to save face in making the transition to reformism, and to pretend to themselves and others that they were still fighting for "socialism"—in another country.

A more efficient way of cutting the revolutionary guts out of the Communist parties in the capitalist countries could not have been devised. This anti-Leninist theory of "Socialism in One Country" and "coexistence" with capitalism in all other countries, transformed the Soviet bureaucracy into the most effectively conservative, anti-revolutionary force in the world, and debased the Communist parties in the capitalist countries from agencies of revolution into border guards of the Soviet Union and pressure groups in the service of its foreign policy.

Comintern intervention in the affairs of the American party, under this new and revised program, only aggravated the difficulties of its national situation and confounded the confusion.

IX

The party was influenced from two sides—nationally and internationally—and this time adversely in each case. Its decline and degeneration in this period, no less than its earlier rise, must be accounted for primarily, not by national or international factors alone, but by the two together. These combined influences, at this time working for conservatism, bore down with crushing weight on the still infant Communist Party of the United States.

It was difficult to be a working revolutionist in America in those days, to sustain the agitation that brought no response, to repeat the slogans which found no echo. The party leaders were not crudely corrupted by personal benefits of the general prosperity; but they were affected indirectly by the sea of indifference around them.

"Moscow domination" did indeed play an evil role in this unhappy time, but it did not operate in a vacuum. All the conditions of American life in the late Twenties, pressing in on the unprepared infant party, sapped the fighting faith of the party cadres, including the central leaders, and set them up for the Russian blows. The party became receptive to the ideas of Stalinism, which were saturated with conservatism, because the party cadres themselves were unconsciously yielding to their own conservative environment.

Some of the original leaders became Stalinists, and as such, have made an occupation of betraying the American workers in the interests of the Kremlin bureaucracy. Others made their way in stages, over the bridge of

Stalinism, into the direct service of American imperialism. Others fell by the wayside. That did not happen all at once. It was a long, complicated and involved process. It took time. But once the process got fairly started, time worked inexorably to demoralize its victims and turn them into traitors.

I believe the corruption of the pioneer cadres of American communism—by its wholesale scope, by the extremes it called forth of self-repudiation and of treachery to a noble cause once espoused—is the most disgraceful and the most terrible chapter in American history. Never has a movement of social idealism suffered such a moral catastrophe, such a rotting away of its human material. Still, it must be recognized that—apart from its depth and scope—there is nothing really new or strange in this ugly spectacle of men and ideals devoured by time and circumstance.

By and large, that is the story of the gradual evolution of all backsliders in the history of the labor movement, from the early leaders of British labor reformism who had once belonged to the First International with Marx and Engels, to the latest CIO functionary, grown worldly-wise and fat around the ears, who will tell you, with shyly proud self-deprecation, that he "used to be a socialist himself."

This materialistic analysis of the ugly transformation of the pioneer leaders of American communism deprives them of their halo, which did not fit them in the first place, and also frees them from judgment by demonology. It simply shows them in their true light as human, capable of error and default under pressure. They stood up better and longer than others of their generation, but in the end they too succumbed to the pressures of their time. There is tragedy in their downfall, if the wretched renunciation of youthful allegiance to a great ideal deserves that name. But there is no mystery about it.

X

The degeneration of the Communist Party did not swallow up everybody in its ranks. A small minority revolted against Stalinism without capitulating to American imperialism. There were reasons for that too.

Those gossips who explain the degeneration of the majority as the natural result of their personal traits and delinquencies, or as the logical outcome of immoral communism, are puzzled by this apparent deviation from the rule. They are at a loss to explain why a few of the original communists became neither Stalinist flunkeys nor government informers, but remained what they had been and continued the struggle for the revolutionary program under the leadership of Trotsky and the Russian Opposition.

The moralistic judges have been especially puzzled by the circumstance that I was among them; was, in fact, the initiator; and—still more inexplicably—have held consistently to that position in 25 years of struggle. These noble commentators on the doings and motivations of others never fail to point out that I was mixed up in all the factional alley-fights of the party, without any pretensions to non-partisan holiness, then or afterward, and that I have neglected to offer any apologies or make any confessions—and on this point they do not lie. How then, they ask, could such a person "come out for Trotsky" after he was completely defeated, expelled, and isolated in exile in far away Alma Ata?

That question has really intrigued the kibitzers, and there has been no lack of speculation as to the causes for my action. In my reading of the political tradepapers, which is part of my routine, I have seen my revolt against the Stalinized Comintern in 1928 variously described as a "mistake," an "accident" and a "mystery"—the mistake, accident or mystery being why a communist faction fighter of the Twenties who, like all the others, fought to win, should deliberately align himself with a "lost cause"—and stick to it.

There was no mystery about it, and it was neither an accident nor a mistake. In the first chapters of my *History of American Trotskyism,* I have already told the truth about the circumstances surrounding my action in 1928 and the reasons for it. These reasons seemed to me to be correct and logical at the time as the simple duty of a communist—which I was, and am—and 25 years of reflection, combined with unceasing struggle to implement my decision, have not changed my opinion.

When I read Trotsky's "Criticism of the Draft Program" at the Sixth Congress of the Comintern in 1928, I was convinced at once—and for good—that the theory of "Socialism in One Country" was basically anti-revolutionary and that Trotsky and the Russian Opposition represented the true program of the revolution—the original Marxist program. What else could I do but support them? And what difference did it make that they were a small minority, defeated, expelled and exiled? It was a question of principle. This may be Greek to the philistine, but it is not an "accident" for a communist to act on principle, once it becomes clear to him. It is a matter of course.

My decision to support Trotsky and the Left Opposition in 1928, and to break with all the factions in the Communist Party over that issue, was not a sudden "conversion" on my part; and neither was my earlier decision in 1917 to support the Russian Revolution and the Bolsheviks and to leave the IWW behind.

Each time I remained what I had started out to be in my youth—a revolutionist against capitalism. The Russian Revolution and the Bolsheviks in the first instance, and the heroic struggle of the Left Opposition in the second, taught me some things I hadn't known before and hadn't been able to figure out for myself. They made me a better and more effective fighter for my own cause. But they did not basically change me into something I hadn't been before. They did not "convert" me to the revolution; I was a revolutionist to start with.

XI

I have nothing more to say about that. But here, following my exposition of the basic causes which brought about the degeneration of the Communist Party, I will undertake to explain why the initiators and organizers of the revolt and the new beginning came—and had to come—from the same party which, in its majority, had succumbed to external pressures; and why, therefore, the revolutionary movement of the present and the future must recognize its ancestral origin in this party.

Objective circumstances are powerful, but not all-powerful. The status quo in normal times works to compel conformity, but this law is not automatic and does not work universally. Otherwise, there would never be any rebels and dissenters, no human agencies preparing social changes, and the world would never move forward.

There are exceptions, and the exceptions become revolutionists long before the great majority recognize the necessity and the certainty of social change. These exceptions are the historically conscious elements, the vanguard of the class who make up the vanguard party. The act of becoming a revolutionist and joining the revolutionary party is a conscious act of revolt against objective circumstances of the moment and the expression of a will to change them.

But in revolting against their social environment and striving to change it, revolutionists nevertheless still remain a part of the environment and subject to its influences and pressures. It has happened more than once in history that unfavorable turns of the conjuncture and postponement of the expected revolution, combined with tiredness and loss of vision in the dull routine of living from day to day, have tended to make conservative even the cadres of the revolutionary party and prepare their degeneration.

On the basis of a long historical experience, it can be written down as a law that revolutionary cadres, who revolt against their social environment and organize parties to lead a revolution, can—if the revolution is too long delayed—themselves degenerate under the continuing influences and pressures of this same environment.

This was the case with the pre-war German Social Democracy whose original leaders had been the immediate disciples of Marx. The same thing occurred in the Communist Party of Russia, whose leaders had been taught by Lenin. It happened again—with a big push and pull from the Russians—in the Communist Party of the United States, whose leaders lacked the benefit of systematic theoretical instruction and who had, in addition, to work in the most unfavorable social environment in the richest and most conservative country in the world.

XII

But the same historical experience also shows that there are exceptions to this law too. The exceptions are the

Marxists who remain Marxists, the revolutionists who remain faithful to the banner. The basic ideas of Marxism, upon which alone a revolutionary party can be constructed, are continuous in their application and have been for a hundred years. The ideas of Marxism, which create revolutionary parties, are stronger than the parties they create, and never fail to survive their downfall. They never fail to find representatives in the old organizations to lead the work of reconstruction.

These are the continuators of the tradition, the defenders of the orthodox doctrine. The task of the uncorrupted revolutionists, obliged by circumstances to start the work of organizational reconstruction, has never been to proclaim a new revelation—there has been no lack of such Messiahs, and they have all been lost in the shuffle—but to reinstate the old program and bring it up to date.

They have never sought to destroy and cast out the positive values and achievements of the old organizations, but to conserve them and build upon them. They have never addressed their first appeals to the void and sought to recruit a non-descript army out of people unidentified and unknown. On the contrary, they have always sought—and found—the initiating cadres of the new organization in the old.

This was demonstrated when the Second International, which collapsed so ignominiously in the First World War, nevertheless provided the forces, out of its own ranks, for the new parties and the new International. Some socialists remained socialists; not everybody capitulated and betrayed. From the Russian party, in the first place, from the German party, and from every other Socialist Party in the entire world, uncorrupted socialists, who simply remained true to themselves, stood up against the degeneration of the old organizations and began to build the new. Even the Socialist Party of the United States, that ugly duckling of the Second International, which really wasn't much of a party, furnished cadres not undeserving of mention in this honorable company.

The same thing happened in almost exactly the same way—according to the same laws and the same exceptions to the laws—in the case of the Communist International. The degeneration of the leading cadres of the Russian party, and of all the other parties of the Comintern, including the American party, followed the same general pattern and was induced by the same basic causes as the degeneration of the Second International. The great majority of the leading cadres of the Russian party, and of all the other parties of the Comintern, betrayed the program.

But not all. Once again the old organizations provided the forces, out of their own ranks, to begin the determined struggle for the old program. Again, the Russian party provided the leaders, and again all the other parties in the International provided supporting cadres. Even the Communist Party of the United States, with all its handicaps of ignorance and inexperience, with all its faults of unfinished youth and premature senility, furnished its quota of uncorrupted communists for the new struggle and the new beginning.

XIII

Those who see a "mystery" or an "accident" in this origin of the revolutionary party of the present and the future, who ask why and how it was possible for the original banner-bearers to come from the Communist Party of the late Twenties, which has been described here so unsparingly, really ought to be answered with another question:

Where else could they come from?

The struggle for the regeneration of American communism was a task for people capable of understanding the responsibilities and hazards of their undertaking and prepared by their past to stand up to them. Where else could such people be found at the end of the first decade of American communism outside its ranks?

Certainly not from the Socialist Party or the IWW, not to mention the Socialist Labor Party and the Proletarian Party of pretentious pundits. By 1928 these organizations were hollow shells of futility, sucked dry of all revolutionary juice. By 1928, when the big fight started, all the organized revolutionists—that is to say, all those who professed allegiance to socialism and were willing to do something about it—were organized in the Communist Party, and nowhere else.

It may be that there were other people, outside all parties, in the United States in the year 1928, who were better informed in matters of theoretical doctrine and more qualified by intellect and character, than those who came forward to lead the struggle out of the rough-and-tumble faction fights of the Communist Party. I cannot deny it because I have no way of knowing. But I do know that if there were such people, they remained in hiding, and no clue to their whereabouts has been discovered till this day. They didn't show up for the battle, as they had also failed to show up for the previous work and struggles of American communism which had sifted out and tested the people for the new responsibility.

These hypothetically superior forces were not committed; as the French say, they were not "engaged." And therefore they did not count. Abstentionists never count when responsibilities and hazards are involved. The fight had to be started by those who were on hand and ready.

The fulfillment of the assignment by some previously unknown and uncommitted people—some strange Men from Nowhere—would indeed have been a mystery and an accident.

The original Trotskyists in the United States, the initiating nucleus of the revolutionary party of the future victory, came from the Communist Party because the Communist Party—and the Communist Party alone—contained the human material prepared by the past for the work of reconstruction. There were, and could be, no other volunteers for the burden and the hazard, no other candidates for the honor—to call the thing by the right name.

XIV

Long experience has shown that economic conditions, which produce revolutionary movements in the first place and largely regulate the tempo of their growth, can also, in changed circumstances, halt their progress and push them back. Individuals on both sides of the class struggle can do only so much, for they are required to operate within this general framework. It would be well to keep this in mind if one is to make head or tail of the ups and downs of early American communism and see something in the process besides personal delinquencies, quarrels and accidents.

The current witch hunt in the United States is apparently motivated by the theory that a revolutionary movement is created by the will of conspirators, and conversely, that it can be eliminated by police measures. This assumption finds little support in the history of the first ten years of the Communist Party in this country.

The American radical movement, in all its branches,

was fiercely persecuted during the war and post-war period (1917–1920). Vigilante raids on radical meetings were the order of the day. Practically all the prominent leaders were indicted. Thousands were arrested. Whole shiploads of foreign-born radicals were deported. Hundreds were imprisoned.

It took tough people to stand up against all that, but the pioneer communists were pretty tough, as the record shows. The persecution cut down the numerical strength of the movement, but did not break its basic cadres. The party emerged from the underground at the end of 1921 with a strong morale and with a leadership tested in the process of natural selection, including the test of persecution.

The quick recovery of American economy after the crisis of 1921, and the beginning of the long boom, was accompanied by a relaxation of the political tension and a virtual suspension of police action against the radicals. That did not help the revolutionary party, far from it. That's when it began to run into real trouble.

The prosperity, which appeared to push revolutionary perspectives far into the future, dealt heavier blows to the party than the earlier persecution. The persecution had cut down its numerical strength, but its cadres remained intact and self-confident. The prosperity sapped the confidence of the cadres in the revolutionary future. Persecution inflicted wounds on the body of the party, but the drawn-out prosperity of the Twenties killed its soul.

Across the sea the same basic objective factor—the new stabilization of European capitalism sparked by the American boom—had similarly affected the ruling majority of the Russian party, and through them, the Comintern; and the conservative Comintern brought a heavy retrogressive influence to bear on the American party which had already begun to acquire the senile disease of conservatism before its youth was spent.

This is the true setting within which the history of the party in the last half of the Twenties must be studied. There is an instructive lesson here for our present times too. From the whole experience we can conclude that the present slump of American radicalism is due more to the long prosperity than to the witch hunt, and that a new economic crisis will set the stage for a revival of the movement, with or without the witch hunt.

We can also expect that the new revival will find more worthy leaders, who have learned from the mistakes of their ancestors to stand up against an unfavorable conjuncture and keep the historical perspective clear. This perspective reads: The stability of American capitalism is only the transient appearance of things; the revolution of the American workers is the true reality.

PART 1
Letters to a historian

Top: (Left) Louis Fraina in Moscow in 1920. (Right) Benjamin Gitlow in 1928.
Bottom: Max Eastman, James P. Cannon, and William D. Haywood in Moscow in 1922.

My thesis

MARCH 2, 1954

I received your letter stating that you are working on a history of the American communist movement. I am interested in your project and am willing to give you all the help I can.

Your task will not be easy, for you will be traveling in an undiscovered country where most of the visible road signs are painted upside down and point in the wrong directions. All the reports that I have come across, both from the renegades and from the official apologists, are slanted and falsified. The objective historian will have to keep up a double guard in searching for the truth among all the conflicting reports.

The Stalinists are not only the most systematic and dedicated liars that history has yet produced; they have also won the flattering compliment of imitation from the professional anti-communists. The history of American communism is one subject on which different liars, for different reasons in each case, have had a field day.

However, most of the essential facts are matters of record. The trouble begins with the interpretation; and I doubt very much whether a historian, even with the best will in the world, could render a true report and make the facts understandable without a correct explanation of what happened and why.

As you already know, I have touched on the pioneer

days of American communism in my book, *The History of American Trotskyism*. During the past year I have made other references to this period in connection with the current discussion in our movement. The party resolution on "American Stalinism and Our Attitude Toward It," which appeared in the May–June, 1953, issue of *Fourth International*, was written by me.

I speak there also of the early period of the Communist Party, and have made other references in other articles and letters published in the course of our discussion. All this material can be made available to you. I intend to return to the subject again at greater length later on, for I am of the definite opinion that an understanding of the pioneer days of American communism is essential to the education of the new generation of American revolutionists.

My writings on the early history of American communism are mainly designed to illustrate my basic thesis, which as far as I know, has not been expounded by anyone else. This thesis can be briefly stated as follows:

The Communist Party originally was a revolutionary organization. All the original leaders of the early Communist Party, who later split into three permanent factions within the party, *began* as American revolutionists with a perspective of revolution in this country. Otherwise, they wouldn't have been in the movement in the first place and wouldn't have split with the reformist socialists to organize the Communist Party.

Even if it is maintained that some of these leaders were careerists—a contention their later evolution tends to support—it still remains to be explained why they sought careers in the communist movement and not in the business or professional worlds, or in bourgeois politics, or in the trade-union officialdom. Opportunities in these fields were open to at least some of them, and were deliberately cast aside at the time.

In my opinion, the course of the leaders of American communism in its pioneer days, a course which entailed deprivations, hazards and penalties, can be explained only by the assumption that they were revolutionists to begin with; and that even the careerists among them believed in the future of the workers' revolution in America and wished to ally themselves with this future.

It is needless to add that the rank and file of the party, who had no personal interests to serve, were animated by revolutionary convictions. By that I mean, they were believers in the perspective of revolution in this country, for I do not know any other kind of revolutionists.

The American Communist Party did not begin with Stalinism. The Stalinization of the party was rather the end result of a process of degeneration which began during the long boom of the Twenties. The protracted prosperity of that period, which came to be taken for permanence by the great mass of American people of all classes, did not fail to affect the Communist Party itself. It softened up the leading cadres of that party, and undermined their original confidence in the perspectives of a revolution in this country. This prepared them, eventually, for an easy acceptance of the Stalinist theory of "socialism in one country."

For those who accepted this theory, Russia, as the "one country" of the victorious revolution, became a substitute for the American revolution. Thereafter, the Communist Party in this country adopted as its primary task the "defense of the Soviet Union" by pressure methods of one kind or another on American foreign policy, without any perspective of a revolution of their own. All the subsequent twists and turns of Communist policy in the

United States, which appears so irrational to others, had this central motivation—the subordination of the struggle for a revolution in the United States to the "defense" of a revolution in another country.

That explains the frenzied radicalism of the party in the first years of the economic crisis of the Thirties, when American foreign policy was hostile to the Soviet diplomacy; the reconciliation with Roosevelt after he recognized the Soviet Union and oriented toward a diplomatic rapprochement with the Kremlin; the split with Roosevelt during the Stalin-Hitler pact; and the later fervent reconciliation and the unrestrained jingoism of the American Stalinists when Washington allied itself with the Kremlin in the war.

The present policy of the Communist Party, its subordination of the class struggle to a pacifistic "peace" campaign, and its decision to ally itself at all costs with the Democratic Party, has the same consistent motivation as all the previous turns of policy.

The degeneration of the Communist Party began when it abandoned the perspective of revolution in this country, and converted itself into a pressure group and cheering squad for the Stalinist bureaucracy in Russia—which it mistakenly took to be the custodian of a revolution "in another country."

I shouldn't neglect to add the final point of my thesis: The degeneration of the Communist Party is not to be explained by the summary conclusion that the leaders were a pack of scoundrels to begin with; although a considerable percentage of them—those who became Stalinists as well as those who became renegades—turned out eventually to be scoundrels of championship caliber; but by the circumstance that they fell victim to a false theory and a false perspective.

What happened to the Communist Party would happen without fail to any other party, including our own, if it should abandon its struggle for a social revolution in this country, as the realistic perspective of our epoch, and degrade itself to the role of sympathizer of revolutions in other countries.

I firmly believe that American revolutionists should indeed sympathize with revolutions in other lands, and try to help them in every way they can. But the best way to do that is to build a party with a confident perspective of a revolution in this country.

Without that perspective, a Communist or Socialist party belies its name. It ceases to be a help and becomes a hindrance to the revolutionary workers' cause in its own country. And its sympathy for other revolutions isn't worth much either.

That, in my opinion, is the true and correct explanation of the Rise and Fall of the American Communist Party.

Four ways of viewing the early Communist Party

JULY 20, 1954

I enclose a manuscript* which attempts to explain the transformation of the Communist Party in the last half of the Twenties and gives my view of the basic causes. You will note that I have left out all reference to the various incidents and turns of events which you inquired about

---

* Republished as the Introduction to this volume.

in your letters dealing with this time. I will answer these questions separately, as well as I can from memory. But the more I thought about this period, the more it became clear to me that the factual story can be meaningful only if it is placed within a framework of interpretation.

As I see it, there are at least four ways to approach a history of the Communist Party in this period, leaving out the official CP version, which isn't worth mentioning:

(1) It can be described as a dark conspiracy of spies and "infiltrators." (This theme has already been pretty well exploited.)

(2) It can be told as a story of the doings and misdoings of more or less interesting people who fought like hell about nothing and finally knocked themselves out.

(3) It can be written as an item of curiosa about an odd lot of screwballs who operated in a world of their own, outside the main stream of American life and exerted no influence upon it; something like the books about the various utopian colonies, which from time to time occupy the attention of various professors, Ph.D. thesis writers and others who are interested in things remote from the work-a-day world.

(4) Or, one can treat the evolution of the CP in its first decade as a vital part of American history, which was destined to have a strong influence on the course of events in the next two decades.

This last is my point of view. The historian who wants to write a serious work, regardless of his own opinion of communism, will probably have to consider this approach to the subject. Otherwise, why bother with it?

The historical importance of the first ten years of American communism, particularly the latter half of this decade, really comes out when one gets into the New Deal era and attempts to explain the various factors which contributed to Roosevelt's astounding success in steering American capitalism through the crisis and the Second World War *without any substantial opposition on his left.*

My own opinion is that Roosevelt was the best political leader crisis-racked American capitalism could possibly have found at the time; and that his best helper—I would go farther and say his *indispensable* helper—was the Communist Party. The CP did not consist, as the current popular version has it, of the Ware-Chambers groups of spies who infiltrated some Washington offices and filched out a few secret documents. That was a mere detail in a side-show tent.

The CP itself operated during the Roosevelt regime as a first-class force in support of Roosevelt in the broad arena of politics and the labor movement. It played a major role first in promoting the expansion of a new labor movement and then in helping Roosevelt to domesticate it, to blunt its radical-revolutionary edge, and to convert it into his most solid base of support in both domestic and foreign policy.

Furthermore, the Communist Party had to be prepared for this role by the gradual and subtle, but all the more effective and irreversible transformation it went through precisely in the five years preceding the outbreak of the crisis.

Things might very well have happened differently. Let us assume that the CP had developed in the last half of the Twenties as a party of the Leninist type; that it had retained the strongest leaders of that time and they had remained communists and, in the meantime, had learned to work together as a team; that the party had used its near-monopolistic leadership of the new mass upsurge of labor militancy to impose upon the new union movement a genuine class-struggle policy.

Assume that the CP had contested with Lewis-Hillman-Murray in the struggle for leadership of the new union movement instead of abdicating to them for reasons of foreign policy; that the new union movement under communist influence had launched a radical labor party instead of submerging in the Rooseveltian People's Front in the Democratic Party; that the CP and the big segment of the labor movement which it influenced had opposed the war instead of becoming its most ardent and most reliable supporters.

All that is just about what a genuine Communist Party would have done. What would American history in the Roosevelt era have looked like in that case? It certainly would have been different. And it is not in the least visionary to imagine that such a different course was possible. The key to the whole situation was the evolution of the CP in the last half of the Twenties.

That, in my opinion, removes the study of early communism from an exercise in speculation about a bizarre cult and places it right where it belongs—in the main stream of *American* history.

The first years—the underground party

APRIL 21, 1954

I am very sorry that I delayed so long in answering your letter of March 5. This has not been due to lack of interest in your project or unwillingness to help you in any way I can. The trouble is that I am working on a rather full schedule which I have not been able to interrupt long enough to answer your questions adequately. I take them far too seriously to give offhand answers. Some of the questions require considerable time for thought and recollection of matters which have been long buried in memory.

I will undertake to answer all your questions as fully as I can, although I will not be able to do this all at once. Here I will make a beginning and will undertake to send you other comments later.

I attended the National Conference of the Socialist Party Left Wing in New York in May 1919 as a delegate from Kansas City. I did not attend the Party Convention in September of that year, which resulted in the split and the formation of the two Communist Parties. The reasons which motivated my non-attendance at this Convention were soon flooded out by events, but they seemed important to me at the time and still do. Perhaps they are worth stating.

The Left Wing Conference was my first introduction to the New York atmosphere and my first view of the dominating role of the foreign-language groups. I was in agreement with the Left Wing program, but I was appalled by the tactical unrealism of the language-federation leaders, represented there in the first place by Hourwich. Their manifest determination to speed up the split of the Socialist Party convinced me that they weren't really living in this country and didn't know or care about the state of mind of the Socialist Party membership outside New York at that time.

I was afraid that a premature split would run far ahead of the readiness of the rank and file in many sections of the country. For that reason, I was strongly opposed to any procedure which might precipitate it. Reed, Gitlow, etc., whom I first met at this Conference, impressed me as far more realistic. They were also more informed and concerned about the industrial labor movement, which was my major interest. I identified myself with their group, which later emerged as the Communist Labor Party.

My failure to be a delegate to the Chicago Convention in September followed from my opposition to a premature split and, because of that, my insistence on respecting party legality in the factional struggle. The party constitution at that time, as I recall, required that delegates to a National Convention be party members for a certain number of years. I did not strictly qualify under this provision, and did not wish to appear at the Convention as a contested delegate. My previous activity had been in the IWW; I only joined the Socialist Party in 1918, after the Russian Revolution and the rise of the left wing. For that reason, I declined the nomination as delegate and the election went to another comrade who was legally qualified under the party constitution.

In the light of later events this exaggerated "legalism" may appear as a quixotic reason for failing to attend the historic Convention. But that's the way it was, and I still think I was right. The precipitate split cut the left wing off from thousands of radical socialists who were revolutionary in their sentiments but not yet ready to follow the left wing in a split. They didn't stay with the right wing either. They just dropped out in discouragement over the split, and nearly all of them were lost to the movement.

Of course, the right-wing leaders were bent on a split too, and it probably could not have been prevented in any case. But it might have been delayed if the left-wing leadership had followed a more careful tactic, had shown more respect for party legalism and more patience and respect for those thousands of party members who were sympathetic to the Russian Revolution but had yet to be convinced of the necessity for a new party. The Communist Party was born in Chicago as a result of an unnecessary, or at any rate a premature, Caesarian operation, which weakened and nearly killed the child at birth. There is an important lesson in this experience which I have not seen mentioned elsewhere. Splits are sometimes unavoidable, but unprepared splits can do more harm than good.

Faced with the accomplished fact of the split, indeed of the double split, which brought two Communist Parties into existence—despite our wishes to the contrary—the Kansas City Local of the Socialist Party followed political lines and aligned itself with the Communist Labor Party. This was the direct continuation of the informal alliance I had made with the Reed-Gitlow group at the National Left Wing Conference in New York four months previously.

I attended the underground Convention in Bridgeman, Michigan, in the spring of 1920, where the Communist Labor Party united with the Ruthenberg faction of the Communist Party to form the United Communist Party. At that Convention I was elected to the Central Committee, and was assigned as organizer of the St. Louis–Southern Illinois district of the party. After a number of months in this post, working mainly among the coal miners of Southern Illinois, I was appointed editor of the *Toiler* and moved to Cleveland to take up the new post. A few months later I was called to New York and remained there as a resident member of the Central Committee.

I soon became convinced that the party could not survive in a completely underground existence where we were cut off from the labor movement and the real life of the country in general. But there were still two Communist Parties in existence and they were exhausting themselves in the underground factional struggle. The final unification of forces at a unity convention in the spring of 1921 brought a new leadership to the fore. Ruthenberg and Gitlow were in prison at that time, and several other previous members of the Central Committee failed of re-election. Lovestone and Weinstone were elected to the Central Committee at this Convention, and Bittelman was co-opted soon after.

We began a determined struggle for a step-by-step legalization of the movement. I was perhaps more determined than the others on the eventual complete legalization of the party; but this had to wait for some experimental tests.

We took a series of steps to test out legal possibilities. The first of these was the formation of a number of legal branches under the name of the American Labor Alliance. These groups sponsored the first election campaign of the Communist movement by nominating Gitlow for mayor of New York in that year. We also began to conduct forums and lectures under the name of the Labor Alliance.

Meantime, a belated left wing of the Socialist Party, headed by Salutsky (Hardman), Engdahl, Olgin, etc., had seceded from the Socialist Party and formed the Workers Council. I was one of the Communist Party representatives on the committee named to negotiate with this group for the joint formation of a legal party, which finally came into existence in late December 1921.

It is not true and could not be true, as Melech Epstein says, in his *Jewish Labor in the U.S.A.*, that a promise was made to disband the underground party and that this promise was broken. We were absolutely without authority to make such an agreement at that time. We were supported by a majority of the Communist Party in our proposal to unite with the Workers Council group in the formation of a legal party, with the distinct understanding that the underground party would be maintained. In fact, the paper of the Communist Party published at that time contained articles explaining how we conceived the functioning of both a legal and an illegal party and the relations between them.

The Workers Council group knew all about that. It is true that they wanted a single legal party without any underground organization. But they knew very well that we were in no position at that time to promise that. It is quite possible and even probable that they counted, as I did, on the logic of developments to assure the predominance of the legal party and the eventual liquidation of the underground organization as unnecessary in the political circumstances of the time. This proved to be correct, but another year's experience, plus the friendly help of the Communist International, were necessary to bring this about.

We had several meetings with the Workers Council people in the Joint Negotiating Committee. I do not recall any great difficulties, since both sides were eager for the unification. The Workers Council delegates were most concerned about being swallowed up and steam-rollered by the Communist Party majority. This difficulty was overcome by many organizational concessions which we made. They were accorded representation in the Convention and on the new National Committee far beyond their numerical strength. These concessions were easily made on our part, since we wanted to create the impression of a big unification to attract unaffiliated radicals, and the Workers Council group had a number of prominent and capable people whom the new party could use most advantageously.

The Convention which launched the Workers Party was quite successful and harmonious, and it gave a big impulse to the development of the movement. Max Eastman wrote a sympathetic and perspicacious account of the Convention in the *Liberator* of January or February 1923, which you may check for references. As you note, I was the keynote speaker at the Convention and was elected Chairman of the National Committee by agreement of both sides. Perhaps some special considerations accounted for this agreement. I was a sort of symbol of the "Western-American" orientation which it was deemed necessary to emphasize. Besides that, I have no doubt that the Workers Council people considered me to be more of a "liquidator" than some of the other Communist Party leaders—an impression which was not entirely unfounded.

In answer to your question, I would say that the political cooperation between me and Lovestone was the main driving force in all these party developments of the year 1921. Bittelman and Weinstone were also very effective in the collaboration. In fact, we worked quite effectively as a team in that period, considering the fact that we all came into the leadership cold, without much previous experience to go by. The overriding political consideration—the imperative need to legalize party activity—proved stronger in this case than differences of background and temperament which played a part in later friction and conflict.

We did not succeed in forming the Workers Party without another split with die-hard undergrounders in the Communist Party. The two members of the Central Committee whom I remember as leaders of the secession were Dirba and Ballam. Wicks belonged to the Proletarian Party. He joined the seceding faction of the Communist Party—which became known as the United Toilers—only after the split, and was appointed editor of their paper.

Fraina—the founder

JUNE 15, 1954

Fraina: (Re: your letter of May 10.)

It is certainly correct to list Fraina as one of the most important personalities in the formative period of American communism. In my *History of American Trotskyism,*

I stated my opinion that he should be recognized as the founder of the movement.

I believe that John Reed and the *Liberator* did most to popularize the Russian Revolution and the Bolsheviks in the broad public of the American left wing. Fraina's influence was somewhat narrower; his *Revolutionary Age* was essentially an internal party paper. In that field he did more than anyone to shape the ideology of the young movement of American communism. At the same time he put the stamp of his own romanticism and sectarian rigidity upon it.

The official propaganda of later years, assigning the role of "founder" to Ruthenberg, always offended my sense of historical justice. Ruthenberg was a big man—in his way—and a strong man among the pioneers, but he was by no means the originator, the "founder."

I did not know Fraina personally. I first met him only casually at the National Left Wing Conference in New York in June, 1919. I met him a second time when he returned to this country as a member of the "Pan American Agency" of the Comintern with the mission to unify the two parties. This must have been late in 1920 or early in 1921. The other two members of this "Pan American Agency" were Charley Johnson ("Scott") and Katayama, the old Japanese socialist then living in New York, who later went to Moscow and remained there. I think this was a joint meeting of the negotiating committees of the two parties.

The only memory I have of the meeting is that Fraina spoke there impartially, on behalf of the Comintern, for unity and conciliation. As in all the joint meetings to negotiate "unity" in these days, the discussion must have been somewhat heated. I remember Charley Scott telling me afterward that Fraina had referred to my conduct at the joint meeting as "factional." This was probably not inaccurate, as I was decidedly hostile to the manifest ambition of the "Federationists" to "control" a united party. Scott's remark about Fraina's impression of me remained in my memory and enables me to peg the meeting.

Fraina left soon afterward on a mission for the Comintern in Latin America. Later we heard about his defection and the report that he had failed to account for some Comintern funds.

I recall a statement by Charley Scott in New York (it must have been late in 1921) to the effect that Fraina had misappropriated Comintern funds and that the matter was therefore out of the party's hands. Scott said: "For that he will have to account to the Comintern," or words to that effect. Somehow or other I remember that definitely. After that Fraina seemed to drop entirely out of the consciousness of the party leadership.

I cannot recall anything coming up about Fraina in Moscow in 1922. I have no recollection of any kind of official consideration of his case during my long stay there.

But here I can report an incident which may be of interest in piecing the Fraina story together. During one of my trips to New York (it must have been in 1924 or possibly in 1925) I was handed a letter from Fraina. I cannot remember who handed me the letter, but I am pretty sure it was addressed to me personally. In this letter Fraina stated that he was working and saving all he could from his wages; that he wanted to make arrangements to pay his debt in installments and to work his way back into the party, and asked me to help him. My recollection of this letter is sharp and clear.

On my return to Chicago I took the letter before the Political Committee and it was discussed there. The decision was made that since his affair concerned Comintern funds, it was outside the jurisdiction of the American party; and that Fraina would have to address himself to the Comintern and straighten out his relations there before the party could do anything about it. I conveyed this decision to Fraina through the comrade who had acted as intermediary—again for the life of me I can't recollect who it was—and that's the last report I had of Fraina until, years later, he began to write again under the name of Corey.

I never met him personally in those later days. But strangely enough, we came close to meeting. He appeared to be breaking with the political line of the official Communist Party, while remaining a communist, and there were some indications that he was becoming sympathetic to the Trotskyist position. It was soon after the Hitler victory, when a new party of anti-Stalinist communists was in the air. In a discussion I had with V.F. Calverton, Sidney Hook and a few others associated with Calverton's magazine at that time, we discussed the question of a new party. They asked what our attitude would be toward such people as Fraina, with whom they evidently had some contact and association.

I told them that I really didn't know what to say, because the old financial scandal would put a cloud over Fraina until it was cleared up in one way or another. Nevertheless, I was very much interested in Fraina, and hoped a way could be found to collaborate with him. When I visited Trotsky in France in the fall of 1934, I took up the question of Fraina and asked his opinion.

Trotsky also was interested and sympathetic and thought that we should by no means reject an overture from Fraina. He finally suggested the following policy: That the new party would be too weak to take upon itself the responsibility of an outstanding personality who had a financial scandal hanging over him. Our defense of him would not be effective enough to do any good, while involvement in the scandal would hurt the party. Fraina should go back to the Communist Party and straighten out his financial entanglements and get an official clearance from them. After that the new party we were forming could accept him as a member without any reservation.

That seemed to me to be the soundest position to take and I agreed to proceed along that line. Upon my return we became deeply involved in the final stage of negotiations with the Muste group, building up to our joint Convention in December. I think I relayed Trotsky's advice to Fraina through the Calverton group, but I am not absolutely sure of it. At any rate, we never had any direct contact with Fraina; and soon after that he began to move away from the communist movement altogether.

Fraina was truly a tragic figure. The deportation proceedings brought against him in the last year of his life, after he had fully renounced his youthful communism, added a final stroke of savage irony to a life which was offered to two opposing causes and was rejected by both.

In spite of all, the best part of Fraina—the young part—belongs to us. When one considers how primitive the American left-wing movement had been in matters of theory, and its desolating poverty of literary-political forces, the pioneer work of Fraina in this field stands out by contrast as truly remarkable.

I think it no more than just to say that Fraina was the first *writer* of pioneer American communism. He did more than anybody else to explain and popularize the basic program of the Russian Bolsheviks. American communism, which stems directly from the primitive American left-wing movement, owes its first serious interest in theoretical questions primarily to Fraina.

It is quite useless, however, to demand more from people than they can give. Fraina was too weak to be a leader. He could not stand up against the brutal bulldozing of the Russian Federation leaders who had the power of organizations and finances and wielded their power as a club. Fraina's capitulation to the Hourwich group, after the National Left Wing Conference in 1919 had decided to continue the legal fight within the SP, certainly did a lot of damage.

The premature split of the SP, and the monstrous absurdity of the split of the communist movement into two parties at the moment of its formal constitution; and then the hasty, ill-considered, and in my opinion, unnecessary plunge into total illegality—were calamitous mistakes, if not crimes, of leadership in which Fraina was more the intimidated accomplice than the author.

Nobody knows how many thousands of American radical socialists—potential communists—were lost and scattered as a result of these insane procedures, imposed upon the movement by the Russian Federation madmen. I have always believed that two people made it possible for this wrecking crew to work such havoc. They could not have done it alone. They needed both Fraina and Ruthenberg, and got them both for different reasons.

In my own mind I have always blamed Ruthenberg more than Fraina. Fraina was weak, and there is not much that can be done about that. Ruthenberg was far stronger, but he was swayed by an overreaching personal ambition. I ascribe more blame to him precisely because of that. The history of American communism would quite possibly have taken a different course, with far greater advantages in the long run, if Fraina in 1919 had been propped up and supported by people who knew what the movement needed and were strong enough to enforce their policy.

Instead of that, Fraina was brutally clubbed down by the strong bosses of the Russian Federation and left without support by Ruthenberg, who then, as always, thought too much of himself, his own position and his own role. Ruthenberg would probably have been greatly surprised if someone had told him, in those critical days, that the most important service he could render to the cause of American communism was to reinforce the position of Fraina; to create conditions for him to do his work as a political writer with a certain amount of latitude.

The sprawling left-wing movement, just emerging from the theoretical wasteland of its pre-history, needed time to study, to learn and to assimilate the great new ideas which had exploded in the Russian Revolution. The self-centered Ruthenberg could not possibly have understood that Fraina's work of exposition, at that time, was more important than his own, and that he should lend his strength to support it.

The early leadership

MAY 5, 1954

Your questions have aroused fresh recollections of events and incidents of the early days which have long been sleeping soundly in the bottom of my mind. I will go to work in earnest now and will answer all your questions, and any others you may wish to add, as fully and completely as possible.

Some of your questions made me painfully aware that you have been far more deeply immersed in this subject than I have been for many years. You probably know a great many things that I don't know, or can't remember at the moment. Nevertheless, my recollections and my slant on things may help you to get a more rounded picture.

In your questions regarding the period from 1922 on, I see no mention of John Pepper. This is a very big omission indeed. Is it possible that you have not run across any information about the extraordinary role played by this extraordinary figure?

The break up of the old factions and the assemblage of new ones destined to become "permanent"; the whole adventure of the "Federated Farmer-Labor Party" and the fantastic politics associated with it; and many other things in 1922–24—all these revolved mainly around Pepper.

I was his antagonist from first to last, but if his surviving friends of that time have not contributed any information about the decisive role he played in party affairs for quite a while, I would feel bound, in the interests of historical accuracy, to fill up this surprising gap in your information. If you will let me know what, if anything, you have learned about Pepper's activity, and how you have provisionally evaluated it, I will be in a better position to fill out the picture from my point of view.

In your letter of April 26 you ask two questions supplementary to your question about the leadership at the time of the formation of the Workers Party. You and I have to come to this early period by different paths. You are obviously far more familiar with the documentary record, such as it is, while I have to rely entirely on memory, my personal knowledge of the people and the events of that time, and the lasting impression they made on me.

The primitive character of our movement in that time is strikingly reflected in its inadequate documentation of the factional struggles. Far more was done and decided in action and personal conversation, committee meetings and unreported speeches, than was ever recorded and motivated in documents. That's not the best way, but that's the way it was done. I might say in our extenuation, however, that we were called to leadership and compelled to act before we had served a full apprenticeship and acquired the necessary schooling.

I am afraid that the documentary record of the entire first ten years of American communism—up to the formation of the Trotskyist faction and our expulsion in 1928—contains so many gaps that it can easily confront the historian with a puzzle or lead him astray if he relies on the documentation alone. I think you are wise to seek the personal recollections of various participants to supplement your reading, even though you will then probably run up against the additional problem of conflicting testimony.

The participants of the time, even those who want to tell the truth as they remember it, probably differ so much in their interpretations, and their recollections may be colored so much by their later evolution, that you will find few points of agreement in their reports. I can only promise, for my part, to adhere strictly to the truth in my report of any facts which I remember, without concealing my own conception of the real meaning of the first decade of American communism, and of how the various developments fit into and serve this larger theme. But then, I suppose you will recognize that the considered interpretations of the various participants, of events recollected in tranquillity long afterward, can also throw light on the period from different sides.

My statement (letter of April 21) that the Unity Convention in the spring of 1921 "brought a new leadership (Lovestone-Cannon, plus Weinstone and Bittelman) to the fore" requires a certain qualification. It certainly was "new," since not a single one of the decisive four had played a central part before; but it should also be described as an *interim* leadership.

It was decisive for that particular time, and it proved to be roughly adequate for the exigent historical task imposed upon it at the time—the task of breaking the fetish of underground organization and launching the Workers Party as the legal medium for the development of communist political activity.

In my opinion, this accomplishment can hardly be overestimated, for it, along with the adoption of a realistic trade-union program, which this leadership also sponsored and supported, marked the turning point, the beginning of the Americanization of American communism. The "Lovestone-Cannon combination" didn't last long, but while it lasted the results were positive in the highest degree.

This collaboration was a triumph of political necessity and political agreement over personal antagonisms. It would be hard to find two people with greater differences in background, character and temperament than Lovestone and me. In our relationship there was not a trace of personal congeniality, nor—on my part, at least—of personal regard, confidence and respect. Nevertheless, when confronted with an overriding political necessity, and a reasonable agreement on what had to be done about it, we worked together in an effective combination.

If one asks what part personal antagonisms and rivalries played in all the factional struggles of the first decade of American communism, it would have to be admitted that they played a big part. More than that, I would have to say, on the basis of more than 40 years of observation and experience, that such considerations seem to play a part in every factional struggle. But in this case, in the period of the struggle to break American communism out of its underground isolation and begin the Americanization of the movement, political considerations and political necessities proved to be stronger than personal antagonisms—to the benefit of the party.

As previously noted, Ruthenberg and Gitlow were in prison at that time; Foster, who only joined the party in the fall of 1921, on his return from Moscow, had not yet begun to play a significant role; and Pepper, who was later to play a big part, had not yet arrived or been heard from. With Ruthenberg's release from prison in the spring of 1922, and the entrance into party activity of Foster and Pepper, those three people began to assume the most prominent positions. The interim leadership, which had carried through the fight for the Workers Party, was thereafter assimilated into the larger leading staff, but they never again worked together as a unit.

There were others, of course, who played a part in the struggle of 1921. Bedacht was one of them, and there were a number of others; but it was my impression—then as now—that they played important supporting, rather than decisive, parts.

It is true that Lovestone had been rather prominent in the New York Local before that time; but among other things, he had been under a cloud which barred his participation in the central leadership until after the Unity Convention in the spring of 1921. I suppose you know the story of his testimony for the state in the Winitsky trial. If one is going to bear down very heavily, in a historical account, on the personalities involved, the Lovestone story, including the Winitsky trial episode and its aftermath, is certainly worth a chapter.

Bittelman previously had been prominent in the New York movement, and in the Jewish section of the party in particular, but his co-optation into the Central Committee in 1921 properly marked the beginning of his functioning in the national leadership. I personally didn't know him and had never heard of him until I came to New York in late 1920.

My designation of the 1921–22 leadership as "new" is certainly correct if one is speaking of the central and decisive core of the national leadership at that particular time. I got my first view of the original national leadership of the left wing at the National Left Wing Conference in New York in the spring of 1919. I was seeing them all with fresh eyes for the first time. I recognized four distinct groupings of leaders there, each representing substantial forces, with apparently very little cooperation between them. The conference impressed me, a delegate from the provinces, as a struggle of tendencies mixed up, as is so often the case, with personal rivalries.

First, there was the foreign-language federation group, dominated by Hourwich. They were demanding an immediate split with the Socialist Party and the constitution of the Communist Party right then and there. They were not living in this country, and I was dead set against the idea that they could lead the American movement.

Second, there were such personalities as Fraina, the outstanding "theoretician" and political figure at that time; and Ruthenberg, who represented the strong Cleveland organization and had already achieved national prominence and influence. They were opposed to the immediate split. Fraina was undoubtedly the most effective original popularizer of communist ideas, and I greatly appreciated the work he had done. I respected Ruthenberg for his fight against the war, and for his manifest ability, but his personality had no attraction for me, then or ever.

Third, there was the Michigan group headed by Batt and Keracher, who later formed the Proletarian Party. They seemed to me to be engaged in a hair-splitting debate with Fraina over his draft of the program, insisting that the phrase "mass action" be replaced by "action of the masses." I couldn't make head or tail of this argument and was not very sympathetic to these scholastics.

Fourth, there were Reed, Larkin, Gitlow, Wagenknecht, Katterfeld and others, who seemed to me to stand for a more American orientation. They were outspokenly opposed to the Hourwich foreign-language group domination and more interested in trade-union questions. I became associated with Reed, Larkin and Gitlow in the trade-union commission of the Conference, and felt them to be more my kind of people. I found myself in sympathy with this group which later became the leading nucleus of the Communist Labor Party.

The above is roughly a picture of what the national leadership of the left wing looked like to me in the spring of 1919 four months before the formal constitution of the two Communist Parties. Of course there were many other people who were active and prominent. Some of them I didn't know and others I have forgotten—but the people

I have mentioned were in the center of the stage in those early formative days. The impression they made on me, as a comparative newcomer to "politics" and a provincial stranger in New York for the first time, was definite and lasting.

Two years later, when the struggle for the legalization of the party's activity was put on the agenda, every single one of the most prominent original leaders was on the sidelines. Ruthenberg, Gitlow and Larkin were in prison. Batt and Keracher had a separate organization of their own, called the Proletarian Party. Reed was in Moscow, Wagenknecht and several others had failed of re-election at the 1921 election. Katterfeld had gone to Moscow.

In this situation, the main responsibility of leadership fell to, or was taken over by, the four people whom I have mentioned: Lovestone-Cannon, plus Weinstone and Bittelman. This team of four carried the party through the struggle for the fusion with the Workers Council group and the constitution of the Workers Party. The decisive role of this quartet lasted for about one year. It was never overthrown, but the individual members were integrated into larger groupings, as previously explained.

It would be difficult to prove that this new combination actually commanded the support of the majority of the party for any length of time. A number of those who had been eliminated from the Central Committee at the Unity Convention, such as Wagenknecht, Amter, Lindgren, etc., retained a strong influence in the party ranks. They soon began to put together an opposition faction, which later became known as the "Goose Caucus." Katterfeld joined them, and became probably the most influential leader. Gitlow, on his release from prison, also joined the "Goose Caucus." Minor was another member.

They gave a grudging support to the proposal to form the Workers Party; and, to that extent, they supported us against the die-hard leftists who split away on this issue. But they conceived of the new party as a mere shadow organization and were not willing to assign to it the broad political functions which we had in mind for it. Their hearts were in the underground. Thus two new factions came into being—the undergrounders-in-principle ("Goose Caucus"), and the faction driving for the complete legalization of the movement (the "liquidators"). Ruthenberg, on his release from prison in the spring of 1922, identified himself with the liquidators' faction. So did Foster, Browder, Dunne and the rest of the trade-union group who were only then beginning to become active in party affairs for the first time.

I left for Moscow in May 1922, as an advance delegate of the liquidators' faction, to seek the support of the Comintern for our policy. I remained in Moscow till January of the following year. What happened in the party at home in the meantime, I know only by hearsay. The factional struggle for control of the underground party raged furiously throughout that period, culminating in the famous Bridgeman Convention in the fall of 1922, which was raided by the police. I was not present at this Convention and never could get a clear account of just what happened there.

It is my impression that the forces were quite evenly divided, with the "Goose Caucus" having a slight advantage. But their prospects of gaining control of the leadership, and imposing their sterile policy on the party, were frustrated by two new factors in the situation. These turned out to be considerable factors indeed—namely, the decision of the Communist International and the personality of John Pepper.

Origin of the policy on the labor party

MAY 18, 1954

This replies to your inquiry of May 15 on the origins of the labor party policy.

I think this whole question of the party's activity in farmer-labor party politics in the first half of the Twenties ought to be separated into two parts. First, the original policy and how it came to be adopted by the party; second, the perversions of this policy in the experiments, more correctly the fantastic adventures in this field, under the tutelage of Pepper. Here I will confine myself entirely to the first part of the subject—the origins of the labor party policy—reserving the second part for a separate report.

There is not much documentation on this question and I find that my memory is not so sharp as to details as it is on the fight over legalization. That is probably because the real fight was over legalization. The labor party policy, the development of the trade-union work, and the whole process of Americanizing the movement, were subsumed under that overall issue of legalizing the party. Insofar as they took a position on the related questions, the factions divided along the same lines.

With considerable effort I have to reconstruct my memory of the evolution of the labor party question in the American movement. I may err on some details or miss some. My general recollection however is quite clear and is not far wrong. The approach to the question zigzagged along a number of high points in about this order:

(1) To start with, the left wing of American socialism had been traditionally rigid and doctrinaire on all questions—revolution *versus* reform, direct action *versus* parliamentary action, new unions *versus* the old craft unions, etc. The publication of Lenin's pamphlet on left communism marked the beginning of their comprehension that realistic tactics could flexibly combine activities in these fields without departing from basic revolutionary principle. We needed the Russians to teach us that.

(2) The first approach of the left wing to the question of the labor party was inflexibly sectarian and hostile. I recall an editorial by Fraina in the *Revolutionary Age* or in the *Communist* in 1919 or early 1920 against "laborism," i.e., the policy and practice of the British Labor Party and the advocates of a similar party in this country, who were fairly numerous and vocal at that time. In that period Fraina, who was the most authoritative and influential spokesman of the left wing, was an ultra-leftist. He seemed to be allied with this tendency in the Comintern, which was centered around the Dutch communists and some German leftists. This tendency, as you know, was vigorously combatted and defeated by Lenin and Trotsky at the Third Congress of the Comintern (1921).

(Incidentally, you will find Trotsky's two volumes on *The First Five Years of the Communist International,* published by Pioneer Publishers, informative reading on this period. It impinges on America at least to this extent: that Trotsky polemicized against Pepper (Pogany), who had been in Germany with a Comintern delegation, and at that time was himself an ultra-leftist.)

This article or editorial by Fraina expressed the general attitude of the party, which was ultra-leftist all along the line in those days. Perhaps I recall this particular article or editorial because I was a quite pronounced "right winger" in the early Communist Party, and I thought that people who were advocating a labor party were a hell of a long way out in front of the labor movement as I knew it in the Midwest. However, I must say that it never occurred to me at that time that we could be a part of the larger movement for a labor party and remain communists. Engels' perspicacious letters on this very theme were unknown to us in those days.

(3) The theoretical justification for such a complicated tactic—conditional support of a *reformist* labor party by *revolutionists*—came originally from Lenin. I think it is indisputable that Lenin's proposal to the British communists that they should "urge the electors to vote for the labor candidate against the bourgeois candidate," in his pamphlet on *Left-Wing Communism,* and his later recommendation that the British Communist Party should seek affiliation to the British Labor Party, gave the first encouragement to the sponsors of a similar policy in this country, and marks the real origin of the policy.

I don't think this contradicts the statement you quote, from the Foster-Cannon document of November 26, 1924—which was probably written by me and which I had long since forgotten—that the Comintern's approval of a labor party policy in 1922 was obtained "mainly on the strength of the information supplied by our delegates, that there was in existence a strong mass movement towards a farmer-labor party."

Lenin's intervention in England provided the original *justification* for revolutionists to support a labor party based on the unions. Our contention in Moscow in 1922 was simply that a realistic basis existed for the adaptation of this policy to America. There was considerable sentiment in the country for a farmer-labor party at that time. The

Chicago Federation of Labor was for it. The Farmer-Labor Party had had a presidential candidate in 1920, who polled about half a million votes.

It seemed to us—*after* we had assimilated Lenin's advice to the British—that this issue would make an excellent basis for a bloc with the more progressive wing of the trade-union movement, and open up new possibilities for the legitimization of the communists as a part of the American labor movement, the expansion of its contacts, etc. But I don't think we would have argued the point if we had not been previously encouraged by Lenin's explanation that revolutionists could critically support a reformist labor party, and even belong to it, without becoming reformists.

(4) I do not recall that the question of a labor party was concretely posed in the factional struggle between the liquidators and the undergrounders-in-principle. The real issue which divided the party into right and left wings, was the legalization of the movement. On all subsidiary questions—labor party, realistic trade-union program, predominance of native leadership, Americanization in general—the right wing naturally tended to be for and the left wing against.

As far as I can recall, all the liquidators readily accepted the labor party policy. After the leftists had been completely defeated on the central question of party legalization, any resistance they might have had to the labor party policy collapsed. I do not recall any specific factional struggle over the labor party by itself.

(5) Furthermore, it was the Comintern that picked up our information and our advocacy of a labor party policy at the time of the Fourth Congress, and formulated it most clearly and decisively. I am quite certain in my recollection that the Comintern letter to the Communist

Party of the U.S., announcing its decision in favor of the legalization of the movement, referred also to the labor party policy. The letter stated that the formation of a labor party in the U.S., based on the trade unions, would be "an event of world historical importance."

If you will check this letter, which it seems to me was printed either in the *Worker* or the *Communist* early in 1923, I think you will find the definitive answer to the question of the origin of the labor party policy.

(6) Pepper certainly had no part in initiating the policy in Moscow "before and during the Fourth Congress." He was in America at that time. In answer to your question: "Or did he pick up that ball and run with it after he came to the U.S.?"—I would simply say, Yes, but fast; in fact he ran away with it.

P.S.—I had never heard that Lenin raised the labor party question with Fraina in Moscow already in 1920. That is very interesting. I think it also supplies corroboration to my own conception, set forth above, that Lenin was the real originator of this policy. He must have turned over in his mausoleum, however, when he saw what was later done with his idea.

More on the labor party policy

MARCH 17, 1955

I think there is enough evidence to establish beyond dispute that the initiative for a positive attitude toward a prospective labor party in the United States came from

Moscow. Just when the decision was first made by the Comintern, and the specific steps taken by the American party in the process of putting the policy into effect, are not so easy to sort out.

My own recollections are far from clear. It had been my impression that the definitive decision of the Comintern on this question was made only at the time of the Fourth Congress at the end of 1922. I think the statement of the Foster-Cannon group, published in the *Daily Worker* of November 26, 1924, to the effect that the Comintern's approval was obtained "mainly on the strength of the information supplied to the Comintern by our delegates"—was intended to refer to the discussions in Moscow at the time of the Fourth Congress, and not to an earlier discussion.

It may be that the earlier 1922 American delegation—Bedacht and Katterfeld—discussed the question at the Plenum of the Executive Committee of the Comintern in February–March, 1922, and that some sort of directive issued from the discussion. But I have no recollection of it.

I don't remember the labor party statement issued by the American party in May 1922. Prior to my departure for Moscow about the middle of that month, I have remembered only general talk and general sympathy for the idea "in principle" but no concrete action to implement it. But now that you refresh my memory, I would say you are probably correct in your guess that the meeting of the Conference for Progressive Political Action in February 1922 stimulated the first *action* by the party. I recall a conversation on the subject with Lovestone, initiated by him. By party standards at that time, we were both "right wingers," looking for all possible openings for the party to break out of its isolation and become a factor in American life. That was probably his reason for approaching me first.

Lovestone said the party should try to get into this CPPA

movement some way or other. I was sympathetic to the idea, although it had not occurred to me until he brought it up. I don't recall anything concrete being done before I left for Moscow. But reconstructing the evolution of the question, it is probably safe to assume that Lovestone continued to press his idea after my departure and that his persistence contributed, first to the affirmative statement on the labor party question published in the *Worker,* June 24, 1922 and, later, to the decision to send Ruthenberg to the second conference of the CPPA in Cleveland, in December 1922.

In my memory, therefore, Lovestone stands out as the initiator of the first positive proposal to approach this CPPA movement, which led, in a chain of circumstances, to the Chicago Farmer-Labor convention of July 1923, arranged by a collaboration of the Workers Party with the Fitzpatrick leadership of the Chicago Federation of Labor.

It must be remembered, however, that in the meantime Pepper had become a factor in the affairs of the American CP—and what a factor!—and that he undoubtedly was the driving force in all the labor party experiments and adventures thereafter. When he entered the situation, the production of ideas and decisions was put on a whirling conveyor and things really moved. I recall now that toward the end of 1922, or early in the next year, before he had his feet wet in the country, he wrote a pamphlet on the problem of the labor party in America. This pamphlet was widely distributed in 1923 as an exposition of the party's position.

I was outside all these developments during my long stay in Moscow, and again for many months on my tour after my return. For that reason, I had no direct part in the decisions, but I was involved in them by a general sympathy with every move in an outward direction, even at the risk of opportunist errors to which, I must admit, I was not very sensitive at that time.

I do not recall that the question of the labor party was a specific issue between the liquidators and the leftists. But the liquidators had a more affirmative tendency to expand party activity and were undoubtedly the initiators of all the concrete moves, even if the leftists did not specifically oppose them. By the middle of 1923 the "Goose Caucus" of the leftists had been demolished and any opposition from its few recalcitrant members wouldn't have counted for much anyhow.

As far as I know, all the liquidators went along with the various decisions that led up to the organization of the July 3 convention at Chicago. The differences within their camp became serious, and took definite form, only after the catastrophe of the July 3 affair.

The 'American question' at the Fourth Congress of the Comintern

MAY 10, 1954

I arrived in Moscow on June 1, 1922 as the official delegate of the American Communist Party to the Plenum of the ECCI and to the pending Fourth Congress of the Comintern. I remained there until the following January. Besides attending to my duties in the ECCI and in the Congress, I had a good chance to look around and form some impressions of the country in the fifth year of the revolution.

After my return to the U.S., I covered the country on

a five-month tour, speaking on "The Fifth Year of the Russian Revolution." This lecture was published in pamphlet form at the time and has since been reprinted by Pioneer Publishers, together with another lecture, under the title *The Russian Revolution*.

I was seated as the American representative on the ECCI and was also made a member of its presidium, the smaller working body, which met frequently and handled all current political work of the Comintern in the same manner as the smaller political bureau of the national committee of a national organization.

This was my first view of the functioning of the Comintern, and my first chance to see the great political leaders at work in discussion and decision on questions of the world movement. I was well satisfied to sit quietly, to listen and try to learn. I really think I learned a lot in this priceless experience.

The problems of the various national parties, one after another, came up for review in the sessions of the presidium. The big questions of the time, as I recall, were the continuing crisis in the French party and the application of the tactics of the united front generally. All the important parties had permanent delegates in Moscow. They presented periodic reports on new developments in their respective countries and joined in the discussion.

The decisive lead was taken by the Russian delegation assigned to permanent work in the Comintern. These were Zinoviev as chairman, Radek and Bukharin. As a member of the presidium, I saw these leaders at work and heard them speak on an average of about once a week during the entire period of my stay in Moscow. There was no question whatever of the leading role played by the Russian representatives. This was taken as a matter of course and was never questioned. But the reasons for it were entirely just and natural.

They were the veterans who were schooled in the doctrine and knew the world movement, especially the European section of it, from study and first-hand experience in their years of exile. In addition, they had the commanding moral authority which accrues by right to the leaders of a victorious revolution. The delegates of the other parties, like myself, were mainly apprentices of a younger generation. I think all of us, or nearly all, felt that we were privileged to attend an incomparable school, and we tried to profit by the opportunity.

I also worked in the Executive Body of the Red International of Labor Unions (Profintern). There I became well acquainted with the leading figures in the trade-union work of different countries. I particularly remember Losovsky, Nin and Brandler. The Profintern Committee enjoyed a wide autonomy at that time in all the practical affairs of the international trade-union movement. Questions involving political policy, however, were coordinated with the presidium of the Comintern and eventually decided there.

In pursuit of my special objective—to gain Comintern support for our policy in the U.S.—I talked personally to Zinoviev, Radek, Bukharin and Kuusinen (the secretary of the ECCI). Bittelman came along to Moscow in the summer of 1922 on a special mission—to report on the Jewish movement in the U.S., I think. Bittelman and I worked closely together in Moscow. We cooperated in preparing written reports on the situation in the U.S. and attended the conversations with the various leaders together.

I noted that all the leaders, as though by a prior decision on their part, remained noncommittal in all these discussions of American policy at that time. They were extremely friendly and patient. They gave us freely of their time, which must indeed have been strictly limited, and asked numerous pointed questions which showed an intense interest in the question. None of them, however, expressed any opinion. The net result of the first round of conversations, which extended over a considerable period of time, was an informal decision to wait for the arrival of the delegates from the other faction, who would be coming to the World Congress, and to defer any decision until that time.

Nothing was said directly to indicate a definite position; but I did get the impression at that time that the Russian leaders were inclined to regard me as a "liquidator" of the type they had confronted in the Russian party in the period of reaction following the defeat of the 1905 revolution. These Russian "liquidators" had wanted to abandon the illegal party organization and to adapt Social Democratic activity to Czarist legality. The Bolsheviks had been traditionally opposed to such capitulatory liquidationism; and I felt that the reserved attitude of the Russian leaders in 1922 was at least partly conditioned by the memory of that old battle.

I noticed that one of the technical functionaries in the Comintern apparatus, a woman comrade who spoke English, told me that she had been assigned to help me study the experiences of the old Bolshevik struggle against the liquidators. She took me to a library and translated for me a number of Lenin's polemical articles of that time. I agreed with the articles, but I thought there was a difference between Czarist Russia and Harding's America. I had the uneasy feeling, throughout the summer of 1922, that I wasn't making a bit of headway in my effort to gain support for our policy.

Possibly the reserve of the Russian leaders was due to

the fact that previously the ECCI had sent a representative to America—Valetski, a Pole—and that they awaited his report.

Those were the good days of the Communist International, when its moral authority was the highest and the wisdom of its advice to the young parties from the various countries was recognized and appreciated by all. We knew nothing of any conflict or rivalry among the Russian leaders. We thought of the Russian leadership as a unit, with Lenin and Trotsky standing above and somewhat apart from all the rest.

Trotsky led the debate on the French question at the June Plenum of the ECCI of that year, and also at the Fourth Congress which followed some months later. Trotsky also appeared a few times at the meetings of the presidium, but only for a special purpose each time. I saw and heard Lenin only once, when he spoke for an hour at the Fourth Congress. We knew, of course, that he was ill; but there was confident optimism on every side that he would recover. As I said, all the daily work of the presidium of the ECCI was led by the special Russia delegation assigned to that function—Zinoviev, Radek and Bukharin. I can't recall that I either saw or heard of Stalin that time.

Meantime, at home the factional fight between the liquidators and the leftists was raging. Additional delegates to the Fourth Congress began to arrive from America. It was a big delegation, nearly a score all told, and all tendencies were represented. Max Bedacht and Arne Swabeck came for the liquidators; L. E. Katterfeld, Rose Pastor Stokes and others for the undergrounders. There was a youth delegation headed by Martin Abern. A number came as trade-union delegates; I remember Jack Johnstone, Rose Wortis and others. The youth and trade-union delegates both supported the liquidators. There was also a Negro delegate whose name has escaped me, who seemed to support the leftist faction. Trachtenberg represented the Workers Council group, which had not joined the CP. The seceding group of leftists (United Toilers) had two delegates who had been invited to come and present their appeal.

In addition, a number of individuals had come to Moscow on their own account. Among them were Max Eastman; the Negro poet, Claude McKay; and Albert Rhys Williams. In Claude McKay's autobiographical book, *A Long Way from Home,* he devotes a section to his Russian visit and the Congress. Zinoviev and the other Russian leaders made a great fuss over him. They included him in group pictures with them and other Congress leaders for propaganda purposes in the colonial world. In Chapter 16 of his book, McKay speaks about the Congress and the American Commission, which he attended. You might find this interesting as the independent impression of an artist.

After the full delegation had arrived and the Fourth Congress began to drag out its month-long course, the preliminary fight over the American question began in earnest. The first skirmishes took place in the special department of the Comintern for English speaking countries. Rakosi, the recently deposed Stalinist boss of Hungary, was in charge of this department. He spoke English fluently and I got to know him quite well. He was one of the younger members of the Hungarian leadership who had made their way to Moscow after the defeat of the Hungarian revolution.

Rakosi impressed me then as a rather rigid formalist and sectarian and he did not conceal his suspicion of us as "liquidators." We didn't mind that so much because we didn't take him too seriously. But the possibility that he might be reflecting the point of view of the official leaders made us rather uncomfortable. I must say that this was the general impression at that time, and it was reflected in the attitude of other technical functionaries in the Comintern apparatus.

They began to give me a bad time. On the eve of the Congress they shifted me from my privileged room in the Hotel Lux to a roughly improvised dormitory for overflow delegates. I really didn't mind that very much, being an old hobo, but political significance was attached to it, and my friends joked about my banishment from the Lux. This is what I meant when I referred in my *History* to my status during that period as a sort of "pariah." These "apparatchiks" were real weather vanes. I never liked this breed, then or ever.

Toward the end of the Congress we finally secured an interview with Trotsky. That changed everything overnight. We don't deserve a bit of credit for this decisive interview because, as far as I can remember, we never even thought of asking for it. The interview was arranged by Max Eastman on his own initiative.

Trotsky, the most businesslike of men, set the interview for a definite time. His fearsome insistence on punctuality, in contrast to the typical Russian nonchalance in matters of time, was a legend, and nobody dared to keep him waiting. Eastman only had about one hour to arrange it, and came within an inch of failing to round us up. He got hold of us at the last minute, as we were blithely returning from a visit to the Russian steam baths—my first and only experience with this formidable institution—and hustled us to Trotsky's office by auto just in the nick of time to keep the appointment.

Those who attended the interview, as I recall, were Max Bedacht, Max Eastman and myself. If any other American delegates were present, I don't remember them. Trotsky, bristling with businesslike precision, wasted no time on formalities. He asked us right away to state our case, and reminded us that we had only one hour.

I was struck by the difference between his manner and method and Zinoviev's. The latter had impressed me as informal and easygoing, even somewhat lackadaisical. He always seemed to have plenty of time, and could always be counted on to open a meeting two or three hours late. In spite of that he obviously did an enormous amount of work. It was just a difference in his way of working.

The greatness of Lenin and Trotsky was the greatness of genius. Zinoviev receded before them, but on a lesser scale he was a great man too. I had a soft spot for Zinoviev, and my affectionate regard for him never changed. I still hope, someday, to write something in justice to his memory.

The main exposition at the interview with Trotsky was made by me, supplemented by some remarks from Bedacht. My thesis, as I recall, had four points: (1) The lack of class consciousness of the American workers, and as a result, the elementary tasks of propaganda imposed on the Communist Party. (2) The actual political climate in the country which made possible and necessitated a legal party. (3) Our proposal to support the formation of a labor party based on the trade unions. (4) The necessity of Americanizing the party, of breaking the control of the foreign-language federations and assuring an indigenous national leadership.

Trotsky asked only a few questions about the actual political situation in the country, with respect to the laws, etc. He expressed astonishment, and even some amusement, over the theory that underground organization is a question of principle. He said the attempt of the foreign-language groups to "control" the American party was unrealistic and untenable. If they persisted, he said facetiously, the Russian party would invite them to return to Russia.

(It might be remarked, parenthetically, that the return to Russia of Hourwich, Stoklitzky, Ashkenudzie and other strong and fanatical leaders of the Russian Federation, did contribute to the eventual solution of the problem of party "control.")

I don't recall what, if anything, Trotsky said about the labor party question.

At the end of the discussion, which probably didn't last more than an hour as he had specified, Trotsky stated unambiguously that he would support us, and that he was sure Lenin and the other Russian leaders would do the same. He said that if Lenin didn't agree, he would try to arrange for us to see him directly. He said he would report the interview to the Russian Central Committee and that the American Commission would soon hear their opinion. At the end of the discussion he asked us to write our position concisely, on "one sheet of paper—no more," and send it to him for transmission to the Russian leadership.

It struck me at the moment, as a formidable task, after a solid year of unlimited debate, to be asked to say everything we had to say on one sheet of paper. Nevertheless, with the help of Eastman we did it that very day and sent it in. I would give a good deal today for the original of that document "on one sheet of paper."

That interview with Trotsky was the great turning point in the long struggle for the legalization of the American communist movement, which should never have accepted an illegal status in the first place. Soon afterward, the formal sessions of the American Commission of the Fourth Congress were started. The Russians showed their decided interest in the question by sending a full delegation—Zinoviev, Radek and Bukharin—to the Commission.

Nothing was hurried. There was a full and fair debate, in a calm and friendly atmosphere. Nobody got excited but the Americans. Katterfeld and I were given about an hour each to expound the conflicting positions of the contending factions. Rose Pastor Stokes, Bedacht and others were called upon to supplement the remarks of the main reporters on both sides. A representative of the seceding underground leftist group was also given the floor.

Then the big guns began to boom. First Zinoviev, then Radek and then Bukharin. The noncommittal attitude they had previously shown in our personal conversations with them, which had caused us such apprehension, was cast aside. They showed a familiarity with the question which indicated that they had discussed it thoroughly among themselves. They all spoke emphatically and unconditionally in support of the position of the liquidators.

Their speeches were truly brilliant expositions of the whole question of legal and illegal organization, richly illustrated from the experience of the Russian movement. They especially demonstrated that the central thesis of the underground leftists, namely, that the party had to retain its underground organization as a matter of principle, was false. It was, they explained, purely a practical question of facts and possibilities in a given political atmosphere.

They especially castigated the tendency to transplant mechanically the Russian experiences under the Czar, where all forms of political opposition were legally proscribed, to America which still retained its bourgeois democratic system intact and where the Workers Party was already conducting a satisfactory communist propaganda without legal interference. Illegal underground work, said Zinoviev, is a cruel necessity in certain conditions; but one must not make a fetish of it, and resort to costly and cumbersome underground activities, when legal possibilities are open. He told an amusing story of an old Bolshevik underground worker who insisted on carrying her old false passport even after the Bolsheviks had taken over the state power.

The result of the discussion in the American Commission was the unanimous decision: (1) to legalize the party; (2) to recommend that the party advocate and work for the construction of a labor party based on the trade unions; and (3) to appeal to the seceding leftists to return to the party, assuring them a welcome and rightful place in its ranks.

That was one time when a great problem of American communism, which it had not been able to solve by itself, was settled conclusively and definitely by the Comintern for the good of the movement.

All subsequent experience demonstrated the absolute correctness of this decision. It is appalling to think what would have been the fate of the American communist movement without the help of the Comintern in this instance. The two factions were so evenly matched in strength, and the leftists were so fanatically convinced that they were defending a sacred principle, that a definitive victory for the liquidators within a united movement could not be contemplated.

The main energies of the American communists would have been consumed in the internal struggle, at the expense of public propaganda and the recruitment of new forces. The prospect was one of unending factional struggles and disintegrating splits until the movement exhausted itself, while the great country rolled along and paid no attention to it. The intervention of Trotsky, and then of the Russian party and the Comintern, saved us from that.

This decision showed the Comintern at its best, in its best days, as the wise leader and coordinator of the world movement. Its role in this crucial struggle of the infant movement of American communism was completely realistic, in accord with the national political conditions and necessities of that time. Moreover, the Russian leaders, to whom American communism owed this great debt, showed themselves to be completely objective, fair and friendly to all, but very definite and positive on important political questions.

I always remembered their friendly help in this affair with the deepest gratitude. Perhaps that was one reason why I could never reconcile myself to the campaign against them and their eventual expulsion a few years later. I could never believe that they had become "enemies of the revolution," and I believe it even less today, 32 years afterward.

MAY 18, 1954

Valetski, the Comintern representative to the American party in 1922, was one of the leaders of the Polish Communist Party. I met him when he returned to Moscow after the Bridgeman Convention, and heard him speak in the American Commission several times. He did not fully support the liquidators and I had a number of clashes with him. His position after he returned to Moscow would indicate quite clearly that he had not been sent to America with a predetermined decision of the Comintern to support legalization. Rather the contrary.

The change of position and the eventual decision was made in Moscow as a result of our fight there and not on the recommendation of Valetski. He began to shift his position in the course of the debates, but he didn't go all the way. He tried to get us to agree to a compromise to blunt the edge of the decision, but we refused. I recall Zinoviev saying privately to us, when we complained to him about Valetski's position: "He is changing, but he is not fully on our line yet."

Valetski was obviously a learned and quite able man. I think he had originally been a professor, but he apparently had a long record in the Polish movement. They had had all kinds of faction fights in the Polish party. His experience would have qualified him to be sent as representative of the Comintern to a young and comparatively inexperienced party torn to pieces by factional struggle.

Factionalism and faction fights are frequently derided by sideline critics as aberrations of one kind or another, a disease peculiar to the radical movement. But I never knew a political leader of any consequence who had not gone through the school of factional struggles. To be sure, I have also known factional fighters—quite a few of them—who were no good for anything else; who became so consumed by factionalism that they forgot what they started out to fight for. But that's part of the overhead, I guess.

The reshaping of the leadership after the legalization of the party

MAY 19, 1954

QUESTION 3B—*The reshaping of the leadership after the legalization of the party.*

The police raid on the Communist Party Convention

at Bridgeman in August, 1922, seemed at the moment to justify the contention of the leftist faction (Goose Caucus) that political conditions made a legal Communist Party impossible and that the underground Communist Party would have to be maintained in all its functions. I was told later, although I did not hear it myself, that Ruthenberg's first reaction to the police raid on the Convention was a declaration that he had changed his position and would abandon the program to legalize the party at that time.

The raid on the Bridgeman Convention, however, turned out to be merely an episode, probably even an accident, or an attempt of Harding's Attorney General Daugherty to create a diversion. It contradicted the general sentiment in the country away from the fierce persecution of radicals which had marked the second Wilson administration. The elections in the fall of 1922 showed a trend toward liberalism. This was further confirmed by the circumstance that the Workers Party was permitted to expand its communist propaganda activities without any molestation by the authorities; and the Trade Union Educational League, under the leadership of Foster, developed wide-scale public activities.

These two factors—the expansion of the activities of both the Workers Party and the Trade Union Educational League—strengthened the trend of the party toward Americanization and the legalization of all its activities. The Communist Party itself (the underground "illegal" organization) had nothing to do but "control" this legal work, conducted by other organizations. It had no real functions of its own.

At the same time, the decision of the Comintern shortly after the Bridgeman Convention, in favor of the legalization of the party, rejected the "underground in principle" theory and demolished the leftist faction based on this erroneous theory. The leaders of this lost cause—Katterfeld, Wagenknecht, Minor, Amter, Gitlow, etc.—were badly discredited. Their authority as political leaders was shattered by their demonstrated misjudgment of the political situation in the country and by the Comintern's rejection of their erroneous theory.

On the other hand, the development and expansion of the legal work of the Workers Party and the TUEL, in which the "liquidators" were most prominent, plus the decision of the Comintern in their favor, raised the prestige of the leaders of the liquidators in the eyes of the party membership.

I don't think the history of the movement records another instance in which one group scored such a complete and unqualified victory in every respect, while its opponents suffered such an annihilating defeat, as happened in the settlement of this conflict.

Normally and logically, this outcome of the long struggle should have led to the consolidation of an expanded authoritative leadership, consisting of those who had played the most prominent parts in the victorious struggle and had worked generally together to bring about the victory. The necessary components of this new leadership combination were the following:

(1) The Lovestone-Cannon combination (plus Weinstone and Bittelman), which had played the decisive role in the internal fight to establish the Workers Party and develop it as the principal medium for communist activity and propaganda in the transition period when virtually the whole responsibility fell upon them.

(2) Ruthenberg, who had returned from prison in the spring of 1922 and became the national secretary of the Workers Party, with greatly enhanced prominence and prestige, as a result of his prison term, and his vigorous

development of the legal communist activity.

(3) Foster, who had joined the party in 1921 and had begun to develop the party trade-union activity on a broad scale for the first time.

That's the way it worked out in practice, by and large and in the long run. But those individuals mentioned, who had come into the decisive positions of national leadership in a genuine process of natural selection, were not destined to cooperate as a united body for very long. An *artificial* factor upset the equilibrium and played a decisive part in disrupting the new leadership combination before it had a good chance to coalesce.

This artificial factor was John Pepper. He first came to this country in the summer of 1922 and soon began to regulate party affairs with the arbitrary authority of a receiver appointed by the court to take over a bankrupt concern. His only trouble was that this particular concern was by no means bankrupt, and the receiver's operations met with challenge and opposition which limited his tenure to a rather short term. But while it lasted it was a real merry-go-round which left everybody dizzy.

In other writings I have seen various references to Pepper as a "representative of the Comintern." Was this really the case? What was Pepper's real status in the American movement and what, if any, authority did he have as a representative of the Comintern?

Strange as it may seem, that was never completely clear. I, at least, never knew for sure; and up till the present no one has ever explained it to me. I don't think anyone in the American party ever really knew. The officially accredited representative of the Comintern to the American party in the summer and fall of 1922 was the Pole, Valetski. Pepper came along at about the same time. We were told in Moscow that he had been shipped to America in one of the moves to break up the raging faction fight in the emigré leadership of the defeated Hungarian Communist Party, and that his assignment was to work with the Bureau of the Hungarian Federation of the party in the U.S.

As far as I know, that's all the official authorization he ever had. But Pepper, a manipulator deluxe, was never one to be stopped by the formal rules and regulations which act as restraints on ordinary mortals. That man worked fast. He was a European to his fingertips, dripping with the sophistication and facility of continental political journalism. But when it came to getting things done in a hurry and making his way around natural obstacles, he was more American than any hustler or corner-cutter I ever knew or heard about, and that covers a lot of territory.

I was absent from the country, as delegate to the Comintern, during the first six or seven months of Pepper's activities in the American party. He began his operations first in the Bureau and editorial board of the Hungarian Federation of the party and soon took over the whole works there. I was also told that he acted as some kind of assistant for Valetski, along with Boris Reinstein, without claiming any authority of his own. In these two positions he rapidly familiarized himself with the factional struggle and with all the leading people engaged in it. From that small toe-hold, he moved rapidly into the center of things; got himself elected or co-opted into the Central Committee of the Communist Party; and by the time I arrived back home, along about the first of February in 1923, he seemed to be in full charge of everything, deciding everything, including the positions and the fate of individuals who pleased or displeased him.

He was quick as a flash. His first stunt was to latch on to the Comintern decision and become its most energetic and vociferous interpreter—before the delegates, who had fought for the decision before the Comintern, had a chance to return and make their report. He proceeded to lead the fight for the liquidation of the underground party, and got it all over with in jig time. He became the reporter for the Central Committee before innumerable membership meetings and delegate bodies of the underground party, speaking at first, I was told, in German, with Ruthenberg as translator. (It wasn't long before he was making speeches in English, talking faster and more furiously in the newly acquired language than any of those who knew no other.)

I never heard that he claimed to be the official representative of the Comintern at those meetings where the bewildered and demoralized leftists were getting the bad news. But I don't doubt for a minute that he allowed that impression to be given out. It was not concealed that he was "from Moscow," and that was enough to clothe him with a counterfeit authority.

He was an orator of dazzling facility and effectiveness, and he used his remarkable talents in this field to the maximum. His method and design was to single out the more stubborn, more independent-minded leaders of the leftists for political annihilation, while offering rehabilitation and favor to the weaker capitulators. Katterfeld, for example, sectarian in his thinking, but a sincere communist of firm character and incorruptible integrity who had given a lot to the movement, was virtually destroyed by Pepper. There were other victims of his onslaughts too. The factional fights before that had been rough enough, but the game of "killing" opponents, or people who just seemed to be in the way, really began with Pepper.

Most of the leaders of the liquidators went along with this savage game of Pepper's, as it seemed to clear the field of all opposition to their monopoly of the leadership. But Pepper had other designs in his strategy. The most prominent liquidators were ensconced in the formal positions of leadership—with a string attached. The string was Pepper as an independent personal influence with a fanatical following of his own, and this string could more properly be called a rope.

Pepper rehabilitated all the defeated undergrounders who had capitulated, along with the seceding leftists who had returned to the party, and welded them together into a band of servitors who owed their political existence to him. In a very short time Pepper had an unavowed faction of his own. This gave him a power which all had to recognize.

With his faction of personal followers and dependents as a lever, he operated as an independent force in dealing with the stronger, independent leaders such as Ruthenberg, Foster and Lovestone.

The Pepper regime

MAY 27, 1954

QUESTION 3B (continued)—*The reshaping of the leadership after the legalization of the party.*

If, to borrow the terminology of the economic cycle, the years 1920–21 can be called American communism's period of depression, and 1922 the beginning of the upturn, then the year 1923 can be described as the year of the boom. This boom was partly real and largely speculative, short-lived and fatally headed for a bust. It was the Pepper era.

The party's ill-starred adventures of that period are a matter of published record, easily available to the interested student. So also are the policies which inspired the adventures. The fantastic view of American realities, as well as the fantastic theories of what to do about it, are permanently embalmed in the voluminous writings of Pepper published at that time. And let nobody make the mistake of thinking that Pepper's writings of that time can be passed off as the eccentric contributions of an individual not binding on the party.

Pepper ran the party with an iron hand in those hectic days, and what he wrote was party policy; what he said went. He "politicalized" the party to beat hell, and influenced his opponents almost as much as his supporters. Pepper was the chief fabricator of the policy which led to the resounding fiasco of the "Federated Farmer-Labor Party"—but the others went along.

This newcomer, who established himself as a combination czar and commissar over a somewhat bewildered party while he was still learning the language, in the brief span of a few months, did not confine himself to journalism and the formulation of the party's external policies. He operated on two fronts. His domination of the internal affairs of the party was no less total, and his policy in this field no less fantastic, than in the field of external policy.

However, Pepper's internal "regime," like his external politics, lacked a solid foundation in the realities of the situation, and was likewise destined for explosive disaster. His personal dictatorship—that's what it was, and it wasn't a benevolent dictatorship either—was bound to be a short-lived affair. But this nightmarish transition period of 1923, between the time when Pepper took over and "coordinated" everything and everybody (almost) under his bizarre regime, and the emergence of the Foster-Cannon opposition, was a humdinger while it lasted.

This period was another real turning point in the party's

development. And, as far I know, the real story has never been told, precisely because the role of Pepper has been slurred over. That is not true history. Pepper was the central and decisive influence in 1923.

The truth in this case is stranger than fiction. When one stops to consider his handicaps as a newly-arrived foreigner with a false passport, obliged to work under cover and to learn the language as he went along, Pepper's performance stands out as truly remarkable. In the limited space I can devote to my recollections, I at least feel obliged to give the devil his due. I use this figure of speech advisedly, for I think his work, on the whole, was evil. He was a phony, but by far the most brilliant phony I ever knew. He sparkled like an Arkansas diamond.

Beginning with 1923, party history began to enact itself in a different form, which cannot be adequately understood by a study of the records and documents alone. It was the real beginning of the "crisis of the leadership" which was never solved, and which was destined to culminate, after a long-drawn-out struggle, in a three-way split.

If, from the inception of the left-wing movement until the formation of the Workers Party at the end of 1921 and the legalization of the party a year later, the conflict of issues overshadowed the conflicts of personalities and subordinated them to its uses, the same hardly applies, at least not to the same extent, from 1923 to 1929.

By 1923, the transitory figures in the leadership, who had fared badly in the rough-and-tumble struggles of the earlier years, had been thrust aside or reduced to secondary rank. A definite, limited number of people had emerged and gained universal recognition as the authentic leaders of the movement of that time. There was no single leader among them recognized by the others, and able, by his personal authority, to act as coordinator. The official version, which later assigned this role to Ruthenberg, as the "founder" and "outstanding leader," is official claptrap. Ruthenberg was one of several.

They were all one-sided products of a primitive movement; they needed each other and complemented each other in various ways; but unfortunately they didn't fit together in a team very well. There was probably more conflict than cooperation between them. They would have had trouble getting along in any case, and Pepper's intervention aggravated and complicated the problem.

This was the line-up in the year 1923: Ruthenberg, returned from prison and widely recognized as the outstanding public figure of the party, was firmly established as National Secretary.

Foster, with his glittering prestige as the leader of the great steel strike, had come into the party with both feet, beginning as the unquestioned leader of the trade-union work.

Both men had turned forty. They were fully formed and at the height of their powers.

Pepper was in the situation; in fact, he was on top of it. He also was about forty, fully matured, and equipped with a rich European experience and political sophistication, plus a European culture—which distinguished him among the American shoemakers.

Lovestone, who had graduated from City College into party leadership without any detours, was no longer a boy and was developing his malevolent talents with an amazing precocity.

I, myself, had turned thirty and had assimilated a considerable experience in the mass movement as well as in the party. I didn't know much, but I was not in the least overawed by the others.

The relationship between those named people put its

stamp on everything that happened in the party in the next six years. This relationship—of mutual dependence and antagonism, of cooperation and conflict—propelled the party forward and pulled it back, held it together and ripped it apart, like an incongruous mechanism working for both good and evil.

There were many others who played important parts—the young party was loaded with eager talents and personalities in those days—but, in my opinion, the central figures I have mentioned were by far the most significant and decisive in the whole story. Three of them—Foster, Lovestone and Pepper—are each worth a book. Each of them was remarkable in his own way, and would unfailingly have made a big stir and commotion in any milieu. I, who had plenty to do with them, and have no favors to thank them for, would be the last to deprecate their exceptional qualities.

Despite all the trouble I had with them, I have always been disposed to look at them objectively. For that reason my impressions and opinions of them, my estimate of their strength and weaknesses, and my theory of their basic motivations, are probably different from those of others. I will undertake to formulate my impressions of these people in the shape of sketches as soon as I clear a few other questions out of the way.

In the new factional alignment and the factional struggle which began in the middle of 1923, and lasted for six solid years, the conflict of personalities in the leadership undoubtedly played a big part. That must be admitted. But it is not the whole story, for the quarrels of the leaders occurred under circumstances not of their making and outside their control. The tendentious accounts which represent party history of that time as a gang fight of unprecedented duration, with personal power and aggrandizement as the motivation common to all, and factional skullduggery as the accepted means to the end, contain perhaps a grain of truth. But no more than that.

The people involved did not operate independently of external conditions in the country. They were prisoners of an objective situation which conditioned and limited everything they did or tried to do. Personalities, it is true, played a big role; but only within this framework.

In 1923 American capitalism, fully recovered from the economic crisis of 1921, was striding into the first stage of the long boom of the Twenties. At that time the leaders of this pioneer movement of American communism—all of them without exception—were revolutionists. Their attempt to build a revolutionary party quickly—and that's what they were all aiming at—ran up against these unfavorable objective circumstances. The conservative influence of the ascending prosperity on the trade-union movement, and on the great mass of the American workers generally, doomed the party to virtual isolation in any case.

The basic thesis of the Comintern, that the First World War had signalized the beginning of the dissolution and collapse of capitalism as a world system, was the commonly accepted thesis of all the party leaders. But the extent to which capitalism could profit in the new world at the expense of the old, and furiously expand while the other was declining, was not fully comprehended at the time.

Later, when this conjunctural advantage of American capitalism was recognized, it was mistaken for permanence by the majority. This led to the conservatism of the leadership and the tacit abandonment of the revolutionary perspective in this country. This, in turn, set the stage for the conquest of the party by Stalinism, with its pie-in-the-sky theory of "Socialism in one country"—in Russia, that is, not in the United States.

But nothing of that kind was foreseen, or even dreamed of, by anybody in 1923.

The historian who considers the whole subject important, and wants to do a thorough, objective job, has indeed taken upon himself an enormous task. In addition to the mountainous labor of research, which is apparently already behind you, you have the even more difficult task of selection, of separating the important from the incidental; of distinguishing between the formally stated issues and the clash of personalities, and at the same time, relating them to each other—to say nothing of fixing the place of this tiny, but vital political organism in booming self-confident, capitalist America of the Twenties; and of estimating the significance of the party, and what happened inside it, for the future history of this country.

But that's your problem. I really sympathize with you, even if you did take it upon yourself without anybody forcing you. Your task is formidable, and in my opinion, important. I have no doubt that many historians to come will probe deeply into the records of the pioneer communist movement in this country, and trace many great events to their genesis in these first faltering attempts to construct the revolutionary party of the future.

Most of what has been written on the subject is false and tendentious. Your own researches will have convinced you of that. You, as the first to undertake the task of the historian seriously, have the opportunity and the responsibility, whatever your own point of view may be, to set a pattern of objectivity and truthfulness. The young party whose early history you are exploring deserves that and can stand it.

In spite of everything, it meant well for the workers, for the country and for the world. It can stand the truth, even when the truth hurts. It deserves and can bear the report of a historian who obeys the prescription of Othello: "Nothing extenuate, nor set down aught in malice."

I note from your numerous questions about Foster that you are reaching for the heart of the mystery in his case. I knew Foster—close up—precisely in that period when he decided to make the transformation from a trade-union leader to a party politician, and to pay whatever price it might entail in formal subservience to Moscow.

I thought I knew Foster in his bones thirty years ago, and still think so. His later evolution, sickening as it became to those who had known and respected him as a rebel, never surprised me at any stage. The basic decision he made at that time conditioned him for his step-by-step degeneration. He could not have made the decision, however, unless the tendency was inherent in his character.

Overthrow of the Pepper regime

MAY 28, 1954

QUESTION 3B (conclusion)—*The overthrow of the Pepper regime.*

With the formal liquidation of the underground Communist Party, and the transfer of all functions and powers to the National Committee of the Workers Party early in 1923, the old factional alignments fell apart. Outwardly the party was united. The National Committee, in which the former liquidators' faction heavily predominated, led the party as a united body. There was no formal falling out and break-up of the collaboration between the various elements who had composed the liquidators' faction as a whole. It was quite evident, however, that a shake-up and reshuffle in the central nucleus of the leadership was taking place, without anything being openly said about it or the reasons for it.

Under the façade of overall unity a new regime was shaping up, with Ruthenberg and Foster as the two outstanding public representatives of the movement and Pepper as the real boss of the party behind the scenes, and Lovestone as his first lieutenant. I agreed with the first part of the new arrangement but didn't care for the second part, and did not see exactly how I could fit into the new scheme of things. I wasn't very much worried about it at first, however, as my plans did not call for activity in the Center for the time being. I wanted to see the party and the country before settling down in one spot again.

I had returned to this country only about the first of February, 1923, after an absence of eight months. A few weeks after my return, I left New York on an extended speaking tour which covered the entire country and kept me on the road for nearly five months. The subject of my public lectures was "The Fifth Year of the Russian Revolution." I also spoke at party membership meetings on the Fourth Congress and on the trade-union question.

I was fully absorbed by the tour, reveling in the work which I have always loved most of all and which has always given me the greatest personal satisfaction—the work of propaganda. New York was out of my mind as I traveled the great country, giving out all I had in my speeches, and receiving in return the warm inspiration of new crowds and new acquaintances. Some friendships which began on that tour stuck for good.

I had little or nothing to do with the fateful decisions on party policy which were made and carried out in the first half of the year 1923, and recall them now as an observer rather than as a participant. This is not to say that I opposed the general line of the decisions. I was certainly in favor of the labor-party policy and considered that the practical alliance with the labor progressives, for the promotion of this movement, was correct and most advantageous to us. If I had no part in the decisions made in New York from week to week, I raised no objection to them and did not even suspect that they were driving inexorably to the catastrophic blow-up at the Chicago Convention of the Federated Farmer Labor Party in July.

I did not attend this Convention. I was speaking in the Pacific Northwest at the time; and if I remember correctly, I was in Portland, Oregon, when I read the news reports of the split with Fitzpatrick and the formal launching of the ill-fated Federated Farmer Labor Party. My first reaction, which never changed, was decidedly unfavorable. I could not agree with the optimistic assurances in our press to the effect that a great success had been scored at Chicago. The big "victory" looked like a big mistake to me.

I had been covering the country from one end to the other for months, and I knew very well that we were a small minority, with no more than a toehold in the labor movement. I knew how unrealistic it was to imagine that we could lead a mass labor party by ourselves, without the collaboration of a substantial wing of the trade-union bureaucracy. I can't speak for others, but my own attitude of abstention and watchful waiting in the internal party situation began to change to active opposition to the Pepper regime, specifically and definitely, right after the Chicago Convention, and over that issue.

What puzzled me, however, was Foster's support of the adventure. I could understand how the others, who had never had any connection with the labor movement and had no real knowledge of its tendency, could indulge in flights of fancy. But I respected Foster as a realist, and as a man who knew the labor movement through and through. I could not understand how he could deceive himself about the certain consequences of a break with the Fitzpatrick forces, and a decision of the Workers Party to create a labor party all by itself, with a few uninfluential non-party individuals as decorations.

A short time later I stopped at Duluth for a lecture on the last lap of my tour and met Foster, who was there for a trade-union conference and picnic at the same time. We spent the afternoon discussing party affairs under a shade tree in a corner of the picnic grounds. That conversation was the genesis of the Foster-Cannon Opposition. There were no formal commitments, but that's where the faction began.

Foster opened the conversation by giving me the official party line, and predicting that the trade-union delegates at the Chicago Convention, representing some hundreds of thousands of members, would affiliate their locals to the new party. I told him rather bluntly, right at the start, that I knew better; and that he, who knew the realities of the labor movement better than anybody, couldn't really deceive himself by such fantasies. He soon admitted that he was troubled by second thoughts and doubts about the prospects. I got the impression that he was glad to find someone to whom he could express his real sentiments and get some encouragement to resist the fatal course of the official policy.

He agreed that, without the support of the Chicago Federation of Labor, the trade-union delegates to the Chicago Convention would not be able to affiliate their locals and central bodies to the new "Farmer-Labor Party," and in most cases would not even try. I pressed him for an explanation of how he, of all people, could have sanctioned the precipitate break with Fitzpatrick over such a disadvantageous issue; and, if the break couldn't be avoided, why he agreed to plunge ahead anyway with the launching of the new so-called labor party.

His answer has always stuck in my memory as a bit of wisdom worth repeating, and I have often had occasion to repeat it. He said substantially as follows:

"You know, it's a funny thing. When people, who all want the same thing, get together in a closed room they tend to see what they want to see and they can talk themselves into almost anything. In the party caucus at the convention so many of our people, carried away by the enthusiasm of the moment, spoke so emphatically about our strength here, there and everywhere, including the Chicago Federation of Labor, that I got carried away myself and was convinced against my will and better judgment."

Then he added: "The trouble is, we've got the hangover, but the others in New York are still living in a fool's paradise. Something has to be done to change this course, or we will soon fritter away all the gains of our trade-union work up to now."

A short time later I was back in New York, making no secret of my disgruntlement. I wrote a few articles for the weekly *Worker* at that time (summer of 1923), in which I tried to give a different impression of the present realities in the American labor movement, the weakness of our forces and the tactical inadvisability of a definite split with the "progressives." I concluded one of the articles by stating that we should work in the direction of "a new rapprochement with the progressives." These articles were understood by everybody as an indirect criticism of the prevailing party policy, and they encouraged a lot of other people to express themselves along the same lines. I heard many declarations of approval and support for my stand in the party ranks.

At a meeting of the Political Committee shortly afterward, with Foster present, Pepper singled me out for the brass-knuckles treatment. He sought, by a combination of denunciation and ridicule, to put an end to my critical opposition forthwith. I didn't care for that treatment and said so. (We native American revolutionists had always been strongly individualistic and accustomed to free speech.) Ruthenberg, Lovestone and the others kept quiet during this skirmish. Foster, however, mildly indicated that he was beginning to re-evaluate the Chicago experience and the whole course of policy following from it.

Foster told me, after the meeting, that he was quite apprehensive about the whole situation, especially about Pepper's evident intention to bluff things through and make a bad situation worse. He saw the danger of all our trade-union positions crumbling. It was then that he began to relate the new turn of events to his own position in the party. I don't recall him saying so specifically, but I think it was at that time that Foster made his basic decision to throw his full energy into the party and to fight it out with Pepper for the leadership.

Prior to that time, he had devoted himself exclusively to the work of the Trade Union Educational League and was not publicly an avowed member of the party; he had taken no part in the internal fight for the legalization of the party, although he had let it be known where his sympathies lay; and the people most closely associated with him in the work of the TUEL, Browder in the first place, had taken an active part in the party fight.

Foster's original design, I think, had been to play the part of the outstanding mass leader, not publicly identified with the party, operating with a wide area of independence and getting the full support of the party on his own terms. He had once remarked to me: "Debs never wasted any time on caucuses. He built up his prestige among the masses. Then, after the party politicians had made their decisions in caucus, they first had to inquire what Debs thought about them before they could carry them out."

Things weren't working out that way in our party in 1923. Foster saw that when the showdown came, the party controlled everything; and that if he really wanted to control the trade-union work and keep it within the bounds of realism, he would have to have a big hand in the control of the party itself. I don't know whether he had already made up his mind, then, to shift the main axis of his activity from the TUEL work to the party; but that's what it came to in a very short time.

Before long the new factional alignments began to take shape, and the struggle for "control of the party," which was to last for six years, with many consequences unforeseen and undreamed of by the original initiators, was under way. I, for my part, was quite definite in my opinion that a real factional struggle was in the offing; and I went to work, seeking points of support in the party, without delay. I considered then, and still consider, that my course was completely consistent with that which I had taken at the National Left Wing Conference in 1919 and had persisted in ever since.

I thought it was not enough to legalize the party and

get it out of its self-imposed underground isolation. The party had to be Americanized and "trade-unionized" at the same time, if it was ever to become a factor in the labor movement and in American life generally. The party had to recognize realities, and adjust itself to them. It had to proletarianize itself, not merely in its membership, but in its leadership, too. A party regime dominated by "intellectuals," who knew nothing of the labor movement and had no roots in American reality, could only lead the party from one adventure to another until there was nothing left of the movement as a bona fide expression of American radicalism. Above all, the party needed an indigenous native leadership capable of surviving and maintaining its continuity in the harsh process of natural selection.

All that meant, in short: the dictatorial regime of Pepper had to be overthrown.

We began to fight along those lines, without bothering to formulate our program in theses or resolutions. The theses and resolutions came later—plenty of them, too many of them—but all of them put together never counted half so much as the informal program we started with. That was what the long war was really about.

Our first demand was that the party headquarters be moved from New York, which was an island to itself, to Chicago, the proletarian center of the United States. This demand was no mere eccentricity of residential preference. It symbolized the American-proletarian-trade-union orientation and was so understood in the party.

The Pepper Majority soon yielded to our demand to move the party headquarters to Chicago—why I never knew—and by the early fall of 1923 we were on our way. The national center of the party remained in Chicago for four years. Before leaving New York, however, I did all I could to fix some political fences there.

Disappointment over the Pyrrhic victory at the July Convention of the Federated Farmer Labor Party, and dissatisfaction with the Pepper regime which was extending its dictatorial operations in all directions, was much more extensive than the party majority knew. Their misjudgment of reality in the labor movement had its counterpart in their complacent assumption that all was well for them in the party ranks.

I knew from the beginning, from extensive conversations with innumerable people who were important in the party in various ways, that we would have substantial support if the fight should break out into the open. I must admit that I helped things along in this direction, for I was an indefatigable propagandist against the drift of party policy in general and the dictatorial internal regime in particular.

The most important success on this front at that time, and the one that I aimed at first, was the alliance with the leaders of the Jewish Federation. The leadership of this section of the party was itself divided into two factions. One was headed by Bittelman, who represented the original communists; the other by Olgin, who represented the considerable forces which had been brought into the party through the merger with the Workers Council group when the Workers Party was constituted in December, 1921. These two factions were at each other's throats in almost daily combat over control of the *Freiheit,* the Jewish daily paper.

I sought to enlist the support of both factions for a new party alignment, and succeeded without any difficulty whatever. In my first extensive talk with Bittelman he expressed full agreement with our aims, and thereafter he remained an influential participant in all the future developments of the struggle.

Olgin and his associates were particularly grateful to me for my fight, first to include their group in the fusion which brought about the formation of the Workers Party, and later, for the liquidation of the underground party, to which they had never belonged and whose secret "control" they had deeply resented.

There was a sound basis for our alliance with the Jewish leaders. It may seem incongruous that a new fight for "Americanization," with an outspoken proletarian, trade-union, Midwestern orientation, and a native American leadership, should begin with an alliance with the Jewish leaders who were all New Yorkers and intellectuals to boot. But it was not as contradictory in life as it looks in cold print.

The Jewish communists were, by far, more assimilated in American life than the other foreign language groups; they had a more realistic appreciation of the decisive significance of a party leadership which would appear to be a genuine American product. They wanted to be a part of a larger American movement, and not merely the leaders of a futile sect of New Yorkers and foreign-born communists. I think this was their main motivation in allying themselves with us, and it was a politically sound motivation on their part.

In addition, their speedy agreement on the alliance was probably facilitated, subjectively, by some burning grievances of their own against the regime of Pepper. The furious factional dogfight among themselves had been referred to the Political Committee several times. Pepper, seeking new worlds to conquer, came up with a solution for the factional struggle which infuriated both sides. Pepper sought to "take over" the Jewish Federation and the *Freiheit* by appointing a Political Committee "commissar" over the paper. His assignment was to create a third Pepper faction, incorporating a few capitulators from the other two warring factions, and thrusting the rest aside.

The unfortunate individual selected for this formidable task, which no realistic party politician would have touched with a ten-foot pole, was Gitlow. His lot was not a happy one. Besides having antagonized the main leaders of both sides by his ill-fated fight against the liquidation of the underground party, Gitlow was not at home in the Yiddish language and had no qualifications as a writer in this field. This latter circumstance was particularly galling to the *Freiheit* staff. They were first-class literary men and took a justifiable pride in their special qualifications in this respect.

The Bittelman and Olgin factions continued their own struggle for control. But after their alliance with us, they subordinated it to the larger struggle for a change of the party regime.

On the part of Foster and myself there was nothing really incongruous in the alliance either. We didn't have to make any concessions in regard to our basic aims, because the Jewish leaders fully supported them. On the other hand, our objections to a party leadership dominated by intellectuals did not extend to "anti-intellectualism" and the lunacy of imagining that intellectuals should not be included in the leading staff.

Foster, at that time, was very little acquainted with the various important personalities in the party outside its trade-union section. He left the business of dealing with them, in these preliminary stages of the fight, to me. He was well satisfied with the results; and this assurance of substantial support in the party cadres gave him more courage to take a stronger stand in the Political Committee after we set up shop in Chicago.

The fight did not break out into the open all at once. As is so often the case in the first stages of a factional struggle, friction and conflict in the Political Committee smoldered for a period of months, flared up and died down over one issue and another; attempts were made to patch things up; compromises were made with retreats on both sides. But every time the dead horse of the "Federated Farmer-Labor Party" was lugged into the room we would have a violent collision. Then, at the next meeting, other business would be dispatched with matter-of-fact objectivity and agreement. I remember Pepper, remarking at one meeting: "Isn't it strange that we always have a peaceful meeting when the 'Federated' is not on the agenda?"

At the Plenum, held a month or so before the scheduled Convention, the two groups in the Political Committee presented separate resolutions. But after a discussion at the Plenum, which was at times heated, we agreed on a compromise to present a common resolution to the Convention. Precisely what the differences were in the two resolutions, and what we finally agreed upon for a common resolution, is more than I can remember, and I haven't the interest to burrow through the old records and verify the point. It didn't make any real difference anyway.

The real conflict was over control of the party, between two groups who had different ideas about what to do with the party; not merely with respect to one issue or another, at one time or another, but over the whole course, the whole orientation, and the type of leadership that would be required over a long period. Separate resolutions, on some single political issues of the day, could not fully illuminate this basic conflict; nor could unanimous compromise resolutions obliterate it.

As the 1923 Convention approached, a muffled struggle broke out in the New York and Chicago membership meetings, and it was extended into the district conventions which selected the delegates to the National Convention. In that pre-convention period I saw Pepper give a demonstration of personal power and audacity, under the most adverse circumstances, which always commanded my admiration—even though we were on opposite sides of the party barricades, so to speak.

He was illegally in the country; it was dangerous for him to appear anywhere in public, or even to become personally known and identified by too many people; and he had had only about a year to study the English language. Despite that, at one tense general membership meeting in Chicago, where the fight broke out in real earnest and we were concentrating heavy fire on his regime, he appeared at the meeting, unannounced, to give us a fight. Facing a hostile crowd, which was excited to the brink of a free-for-all, he took the floor to debate with us—in English!—and his speech dominated the debate from his side of the meeting. It was a magnificent performance that failed.

He did the same thing at a closed session of the Convention, after it had been clearly established that the Foster-Cannon Opposition had better than a two-to-one majority. He came to a closed session of the Convention, especially arranged at his request, in a desperate attempt to turn the tide. He spoke powerfully and effectively. I recall Foster remarking to me, with admiration mixed with animosity—Foster really hated Pepper—"This room shakes when that man talks."

But Pepper's heroic efforts on this occasion were of no avail. The ranks of a new majority were solidified in the course of the Convention struggle, and a new leadership, giving the predominant majority in the Central Committee to the Foster-Cannon combination, was elected by the Convention.

That didn't end the fight, however, and we were not finished with Pepper. The Pepperites did not accept defeat. They seemed to feel that somehow or other they had been cheated out of their rightful control of the party by some kind of a fluke. The majority, on the other hand, were convinced that justice had been done and were resolved that it should not be undone.

The two factions in the leadership, which previously had been held together by informal understandings among key people on both sides, began to harden into solid, definitely organized and disciplined caucuses. These caucuses were gradually extended into the ranks, and eventually included almost every member in every branch, on one side or the other. We were lining up for a six-year war—but we didn't know it then.

Notes on the Third Party Convention

MARCH 22, 1955

The Third Convention (1923) took place before the extensive organization of caucuses of the factions in the party ranks. Probably a majority of the delegates came to the Convention uncommitted. As the delegates straggled into town on the eve of the Convention, both factions worked industriously to secure their allegiance. I suppose I was most active and effective on this front for our faction and Lovestone for the Pepperites.

The general disposition of the majority of the delegates in our favor, and their dissatisfaction with the Pepper regime, became fairly evident before the formal opening of the Convention. The election of Bittelman as Convention Chairman at the first session, by a decisive majority over the candidate of the Pepper faction, indicated a Convention line-up which was never changed during the subsequent debates.

We made no special efforts to win the support of Lore and the Finnish leaders and offered them no special inducements. That would not have been necessary in any case; they indicated their preference in the first discussions with them before the Convention was formally started.

I recall that they were pleased at the prospect of Foster graduating from his position as trade-union specialist and taking his place as a *party* leader, and that they strongly objected to Bittelman having a prominent position in the new leadership. In fact, they objected to Bittelman altogether. This was in deference to Olgin and his supporters in the Jewish Federation, who were closely associated with Lore, and who had had plenty of trouble with Bittelman.

Foster was impressed and worried by this opposition to Bittelman. Foster was always ready to dump anybody who was under fire, but I learned of his addiction to this annoying peccadillo only later. At the time, I attributed his concern in this matter to his unfamiliarity with party affairs and party people, and he yielded to my insistence on Bittelman. The Loreites finally accepted Bittelman as a "concession" on their part.

The pre-war Socialist Party

MAY 31, 1955

I am enclosing herewith an article on the IWW written on assignment for our magazine.* It turned out to be a pamphlet, but the whole thing is scheduled for publication in the Summer issue of *Fourth International*. It is quite lengthy, but if you have time to read it you may find some suggestions about the background of the early CP.

I have been wondering how you plan to lead up to the formation of the CP and to explain the preceding movements from which its component elements came.

Ira Kipnis' book, *The American Socialist Movement—1897–1912*, published in 1952, gives some interesting information about the evolution of the Socialist Party up to 1912. I assume you are familiar with it. Somehow or other this Kipnis book escaped my attention when it was first published. I just recently got hold of it and have not yet had a chance to read it thoroughly.

From what I have read I am inclined to be a bit suspicious of Kipnis' objectivity. There are some tell-tale expressions in the Stalinist lingo which should put one on guard. His book is overstuffed with references. They may all be accurate, but as you know, a history can be slanted

---

* Republished in this volume.

by selectivity of sources as well as by outright falsification.

In skimming through the book for the first time I was torn between my own unconcealed partisanship for the left wing and my concern for the whole truth in historical writing. I always thought the Hillquit-Berger wing was no good from a revolutionary point of view, and Kipnis' documentation seems to prove this beyond dispute. He proves it so completely and overwhelmingly in fact, that I got an uneasy feeling that he's proving too much.

I think the Socialist Party, on the whole, was considerably better than he makes it out. Otherwise, how explain its stand on the war and the fact that a majority of the members supported the left wing in the showdown and split of 1917–1919?

JANUARY 8, 1956

I received your letters of January 2, 3, and 4. I will answer them as best I can as soon as possible. Right now I am concentrating on a big article on the Debs Centennial.* I have to finish that first. A few other items on my agenda will also have to be taken care of before I can return to the questions dealing with the early CP days.

This business of shuttling back and forth between the first decade of American communism and the American movement before the First World War, and trying to keep up with current events, has been a devastating psychological experience for me. These are three worlds apart, and I feel somewhat as though I have been traveling through space in a compression chamber. I have really lived three different lives in the movement, and

---

* Republished in this volume.

it is exhausting to go back and live them over again in reminiscence.

❖

JANUARY 27, 1956

I finally got finished with the pamphlet on the Debs Centennial, which is to appear in the next issue of our magazine. I am enclosing a carbon copy; you may find some of it of interest as background material in your study of the origins of the American left wing.

My pamphlet is of necessity very condensed, and it puts particular emphasis on aspects of the old pre-war socialist movement which are of particular interest to us. In Chapter 4 I have paid tribute to the scholars who have been working in this field, and have recommended their books to students who want to pursue the subject further and get a more complete picture than I have given.

The pre-war anarchists

FEBRUARY 6, 1959

Your reference to Anton Johannsen in connection with the Farmer-Labor Convention of 1923, stirred up good memories of American radicalism in the years before the First World War. The anarchists were a recognized and respected part of the radical movement in those days. Johannsen was one of them, a "practical" anarchist more concerned with action than theory, who knew everybody from Gompers to Haywood and was accepted in all circles on his own terms. I remember Hutchins Hapgood's biography of Johannsen, *The Spirit of Labor,* as a very interesting evocation of the Chicago movement around the turn of the century.

Johannsen was a well-known and popular figure in radical circles in the old days. As a practical organizer, he was in good standing with the AFL officialdom and a paid representative of the International Carpenters Union, while retaining friendly and even intimate contacts with all kinds of radicals. He spent several months in Kansas City along about 1915, rounding up support and collecting funds for the defense of Schmidt and Kaplan, anarchists and personal friends of Johannsen who had finally been arrested and accused of complicity in the McNamara affair. (They were convicted and served long terms in San Quentin prison.)

With his official AFL credentials and his engaging manner, Johannsen had free access to the Kansas City Central Labor Union and all its affiliated unions, and collected a lot of money for the defense fund from them. In addition, he spent all his spare and social time with us radicals of various hues and affiliations. Browder and I got to know him well and cooperated with him in various activities in behalf of Schmidt and Kaplan.

Johannsen also attended the founding conference of the International Labor Defense in Chicago in 1925. He made a speech there, asking that Jim McNamara and Matt Schmidt (Kaplan had been released) be included in the list of class war prisoners worthy of support by the new organization, and his proposal was unanimously accepted. He wrote an article for us about Matt Schmidt, published in the July, 1926, *Labor Defender*, the monthly magazine of the ILD.

Somebody could write a mighty interesting book about these people. Matt Schmidt, whom I visited several times in San Quentin prison, was an unregenerate anarchist of pure nobility and courage. Jim McNamara was a man too, one of the best ever made—an anarchist-idealist without benefit of philosophy.

(Note: The following letter addressed to Myra Tanner Weiss seems to fit in here as further comment on the prewar anarchists.)

JULY 29, 1955

Dear Myra:

I received your letter of June 9. Sending you the manuscript of my IWW pamphlet was really a bit of sly calculation on my part. I knew my IWW pamphlet would stir up the old Wobbly in you.

Murry may be partly right in interpreting my sending the pamphlet to you as a recognition that you are an "anarchist." But he is dead wrong to deprecate that term as such. Anarchism is all right when it is under the control of organization. This may seem a contradiction in terms, but if it were not for the anarchism in us as individuals we wouldn't need the discipline of organization. The revolutionary party represents a dialectical unity of opposites. In one sense it is, in effect, the fusion of the rebel instincts of individuals with the intellectual recognition that their rebellion can be effective only when they are combined and united into a single striking force which only a disciplined organization can supply.

In my young days I was very friendly to the anarchists, and was an anarchist myself by nature. I dearly loved that word "freedom," which was the biggest word in the anarchist vocabulary. But my impulse to go all the way with them was blocked by recognition that the transformation of society, which alone can make real freedom possible, cannot be achieved without organization, and that organization signifies discipline and the subordination of the individual to the majority. I wanted to have my cake and eat it too—in fact, I still have the same idea—but I have never yet been able to figure out exactly how it could be done.

People who have grown up since the Russian Revolution and the First World War don't know and can't have a real feel of what the anarchist movement was before that time, before its theoretical assumptions had been put to the decisive test. Anarchism was then regarded as the most extreme form of radicalism. The anarchists had some wonderful people; they claimed the heritage of the Haymarket martyrs, and they were greatly respected in all radical circles. When Emma Goldman and Alexander Berkman came to Kansas City on lecture tours, we Wobblies used to pitch in and promote their meetings as a matter of course.

Emma Goldman was a great orator, one of the best I ever heard, and Berkman was a heroic figure of pure nobility. It was he who organized the first defense committee and movement for the defense of Tom Mooney, after he had been convicted and was on the way to the gallows, when everybody else was cowed and afraid to raise a voice. I remember his coming to Kansas City on a nationwide tour to arrange the first network of Mooney Defense Committees, and I recall fondly and proudly the fact that I was an active member of this first committee organized by Berkman. (Me and Browder!)

The impulses of the original anarchists were wonderful, but their theory was faulty, and it could not survive the test of war and revolution. It is shameful to recall that the Spanish anarchists became ministers in a bourgeois cabinet in the time of the Spanish Revolution; and that old-time

American anarchists in New York, or rather what was left of them, became social patriots in the Second World War. Nothing is so fatal as a false theory.

If I get wound up some day I will write something about the anarchist movement in America, as it was in the days before the First World War.

The pre-war left wing

JULY 22, 1954

RE: Bittelman's *History of the Communist Party of America* (Reprinted in "Special Committee on Communist Activities [Fish Committee] 1930, House of Representatives Hearings.")

I have studied this document, to which you called my attention, at the Los Angeles Public Library and found it very interesting indeed. It is obviously the synopsis of a series of lectures prepared by Bittelman for some classes either in New York or Chicago. I judge from internal evidence that it was written in the latter part of 1923 or early in 1924.

This "History" shows Bittelman at his best as a student and critic, and it explains why, at that time, he was appreciated by those of us who came to the party from syndicalism. Bittelman, as a student, knew a great deal more about the party-political side of the movement, its tradition and the theoretical differences within it, than we did.

The old pre-war division of the left-wing movement into a narrowly "political" party wing and an "anti-political" syndicalist wing was a very bad thing all the way around.

I have never seen this side of left-wing history adequately treated anywhere. Bittelman's exposition, despite its telescoped conciseness, is probably the best you will find.

I think there is no doubt that in the period before the Russian Revolution, the syndicalist wing of the American movement was the more revolutionary, had the best and most self-sacrificing militants and was most concerned with mass work and real action in the class struggle. But the syndicalist reaction against the futility of parliamentary socialism was a bad over-correction, which produced its own evil. By rejecting "politics" altogether, and the idea of a political party along with it, the syndicalists prepared the destruction of their own movement. The syndicalists made a cult of action, had little or no theoretical schooling or tradition and were rather disdainful of "theory" in general.

The difference between the two wings, as I recall it from that time, was often crudely formulated as "action versus theory." Being young then, and very fond of action, I was an ardent disciple of the Vincent St. John school of "direct action"—and to hell with the "philosophers" and "theorizers." I still believe in action, but the sad fate of the IWW in later years ought to convince anybody that action without the necessary theoretical direction is not enough to build an enduring revolutionary movement.

Bittelman's *History* is an instructive, succinct explanation of the defects of the pre-war left-wing movement in the SP, and a good factual account of its progressive evolution under the influence of the First World War and the Russian Revolution. His description and criticism of the left-wing conception of the party as "an auxiliary to the revolutionary union and a propaganda instrument of socialism" (Part IV, Section C) is quite pertinent. He might have added that the right-wing socialists had the same basic theory with a different twist. They simply interpreted the restricted role of the SP to mean in practice that it should not interfere with the affairs of the labor fakers *within the unions*, criticizing them only for their politics at election time.

Especially interesting is Bittelman's report about the role of Trotsky—during his sojourn in New York in 1917—in making *Novy Mir*, the Russian socialist daily, "a new ideological center of the left wing"; and his activity in promoting the publication of *The Class Struggle* as the first ideological spokesman "for the English-speaking elements" of the left wing. This corroborates Trotsky's own references to his work in America in his autobiography, *My Life*. Trotsky had a lot to do with the development of the communist movement in America from its beginning out of the left wing of the SP in 1917, through its big crisis over legalization in 1922, through the later period which culminated in our expulsion in 1928, and in the activity of our party ever since. Bittelman's truthful reference to the role of Trotsky in reorienting the left wing in 1917, even *before* the Bolshevik Revolution, shows me conclusively that his document was not written later than early 1924. After Trotsky was put in the minority in the first stages of the fight in the Russian party, Bittelman, who read the Russian press and took his lead from it automatically, could never have mentioned Trotsky favorably under any circumstances.

Bittelman's one-paragraph description of the "Michigan group" (later the Proletarian Party) is correct, to the point and complete. (Section XII.) One paragraph in the history of American communism is just about what those pompous wiseacres, who, as Bittelman says, "completely missed the everyday fighting nature of Leninism and communism," are worth.

Bittelman's account of the National Conference of the Left Wing in June, 1919 (Section XII), is well worth studying as the report of a strictly New York "political," alongside my own impressions as a provincial stranger in New York for the first time. (My letter of April 21, 1954.) Especially interesting is this quotation: "There was a third group at the conference, most of them English-speaking delegates from the western states, that favored going to the Socialist Party convention because they were totally unprepared for a break with the social reformists."

As I previously wrote you, we non-New Yorkers knew that the SP was not ready for a split in 1919. But Bittelman's statement is the first place I have seen it clearly written that the New Yorkers really understood the attitude of the "English-speaking delegates from the western states"—the "western states" being the whole country west of Manhattan Island. I may be a little out of focus, in view of everything that happened since June, 1919, but I still get burned up when I think about the ignorant arrogance of the New Yorkers who dragged the left wing into that premature and costly split.

Bittelman's account of the caucus of the Russian Federation at the first convention of the CP, and of how this caucus dominated the convention (Section XII, Subsection B), is the only inside report of this grisly business that I have ever seen. And despite its brevity, I believe it is completely accurate. Bittelman, himself a Russian, was obviously a member of the Hourwich (Russian) caucus and speaks with authority about its proceedings.

Bittelman's revelation is truly a priceless historical document. Just consider his report of the way the Russian bosses toyed with and chose between those leaders of the "English-speaking group" who broke the solidarity of the native movement to play the Russians' game:

"Leadership of federation caucus knew that it must have the services and support of an English-speaking group in order to form and lead the party. Two English-speaking groups to choose from. The Michigan group or the group of the *Revolutionary Age*. Each of the two groups presents its program to the federation caucus."

And this: "After long struggle, federation caucus adopts program of the group of *Revolutionary Age*."

And finally the conclusion of Bittelman's summary: "First meeting of central executive committee shows rift between federation group and English-speaking group."

Just to be reminded today by Bittelman's document of how this wrecking crew played with the native left-wing movement, at that critical turning point in its development, and the heavy costs of their mad adventure, makes me almost mad enough to want to go back and fight that battle all over again.

Bittelman's section on the "Role of Foster Group in the Labor Movement of the U.S." (Section XII, Subsection B), is grossly inflated and exaggerated. It shows Bittelman in his more accustomed role as factionalist, making a "case" for his own faction—the new Foster-Cannon-Bittelman combination—and forcing or inventing evidence to make it look good.

The facts are that the Foster group did not amount to a tinker's dam as a revolutionary factor in the AFL. They actually followed a policy of ingratiating adaptation to the Gompers bureaucracy, not of principled struggle against it. It is quite true that Foster himself, with a few assistants, did a truly great work of *organization* in the stockyards and later in the steel strike of 1919. But that was done by and with the consent of the Gompers bureaucracy, and at the cost of renouncing all principled criticism, including the principle of principles, the First World War.

(See the testimony of Gompers, Fitzpatrick and Foster himself in the U.S. Senate Committee report entitled: "Investigation of Strike in Steel Industries, (1919), Hearings Before the Committee on Education and Labor, United States Senate—Sixty-sixth Congress, first session"—quoted in *The Militant,* August 15, 1929.)*

I do not think it is historically correct to speak of the Foster group in the AFL as a serious current in the revolutionary left wing which was later to become the CP. It was pretty strictly a progressive trade-union group, and I never knew a half dozen of them who ever became communists.

Foster in World War I

(The material printed below, indicating the attitude of William Z. Foster toward American imperialism in World War I, consists of extracts from the public stenographic record of the Senate investigation of the steel strike in

---

* Extracts from this testimony follow this chapter.

1919. The published volume is entitled: "Investigation of Strike in Steel Industries. Hearings before the Committee on Education and Labor, United States Senate—Sixty-sixth Congress, first session. Pursuant to S. Res. 202 on the Resolution of the Senate to investigate the Strike in the Steel Industries.")

FOSTER AND GOMPERS

FITZPATRICK: He [Foster] is not preaching and is absolutely confining himself to the activities and scope of the American Federation of Labor, and has done so for the years that I have known him. This is not a new thing for me. I have known Foster for probably six or seven years. (Page 75.)

THE CHAIRMAN: Have you ever discussed this book (*Syndicalism*) with him at all?

FITZPATRICK: Oh, he joked about the views he had in his younger days, when he associated with men who were actuated with radical thoughts, and he was imbued by it, but when he got both his feet on the ground and knew how to weigh matters with better discretion and more conscience, he had forgot all of those things that he learned when he was a boy, and is now doing a man's thinking in the situation. (Page 76.)

GOMPERS: About a year after that meeting at Zurich—no, about two years after the Zurich meeting, (where Foster had appeared as an International delegate of the I.W.W.—Ed.) and about a year after that pamphlet (*Syndicalism*) had been printed, I was at a meeting of the Chicago Federation of Labor, conducted under the presidency of Mr. John Fitzpatrick. I was called upon to make and did make an address. One of the delegates arose after I had concluded and expressed himself that it would be wise for the men in the labor movement of Chicago and of the entire country to follow the thought and philosophy and so forth which President Gompers had enunciated in his address. I did not know who was the delegate. He was a new personality to me. I might say that I was rather flattered and pleased at the fact that there was general comment of approval of not only my utterances but of the delegate who had first spoken after I had concluded.

Much to my amazement, after the meeting was over I was informed that the delegate was W.Z. Foster, the man who had appeared in Zurich and the man who had written that pamphlet. I think I addressed a letter to him expressing my appreciation of his change of attitude, his change of mind, and pointing out to him that pursuing a constructive policy he could be of real service to the cause of labor. He was a man of ability, a man of good presence, gentle in expression, a commander of good English, and I encouraged him. I was willing to help build a golden bridge for mine enemy to pass over. I was willing to welcome an erring brother into the ranks of constructive labor. (Pages 111–112.)

FOSTER: I am one who changes his mind once in a while. I might say that other people do. I shook hands with Gustave Hervé in La Sante Prison. At that time he was in there for anti-militarism and for preaching sabotage, and today I think Gustave Hervé (Hervé had turned Socialist patriot.—Ed.) is one of the biggest men in France. (Page 396.)

THE CHAIRMAN (to Foster): But at that time, when you were advocating the doctrines of the I.W.W. through the country and abroad, you were running counter to the policies of the American Federation of Labor?

FOSTER: Yes, sir.

CHAIRMAN: Mr. Gompers, however, has not changed his views concerning the I.W.W., but your views have changed?

FOSTER: I don't think Mr. Gompers' views have changed—only to become more pronounced possibly.

CHAIRMAN: And you say now to the Committee that your views have so changed that you are in harmony with the views of Mr. Gompers?

FOSTER: Yes, sir, I don't know that it is 100 percent, but in the main they are. (Page 423.)

FOSTER AND THE WAR

SENATOR WALSH: What was his attitude toward this country during the war, if you know?

MR. FITZPATRICK: Absolutely loyal, and he did everything in his power to assist in every way. I worked with him. I worked with him during the whole of the war, and I know the service that he rendered to the country. I think that he rendered as great a service, not only to the United States Government, but to the Allies, as any man. (Pages 75–76.)

SENATOR WALSH (to Foster): What was your attitude toward this country during the war?

FOSTER: My attitude toward the war was that it must be won at all costs.

SENATOR WALSH: Some reference was made by Mr. Fitzpatrick about your purchasing bonds or your subscribing to some campaign fund. Do you mind telling the committee what you did personally in that direction?

FOSTER: I bought my share, what I figured I was able to afford, and in our union we did our best to help make the loans a success.

WALSH: Did you make speeches?

FOSTER: Yes, sir.

WALSH: How many?

FOSTER: Oh, dozens of them.

WALSH: I would like to have you, for the sake of the record, tell us how many speeches you made, what time you devoted, and what money you expended for bonds, for the Red Cross or for any other purposes.

FOSTER: Well, I think I bought either $450 or $500 worth of bonds during the war. I cannot say exactly.

WALSH: You made speeches for the sale of bonds?

FOSTER: We carried on a regular campaign in our organization in the stockyards.

WALSH: And your attitude was the same as the attitude of all the other members of your organization?

FOSTER: Absolutely. (Pages 398–399.)

Foster and Browder

AUGUST 4, 1954

My statement (letter of July 22) about the limited number of Foster's AFL group who became communists corresponds to the facts, and even probably gives this group a little the best of it. Only two of them, besides Foster—Joe Manley and Jack Johnstone—ever played a noticeable role in the party. I knew Jay Fox by reputation as an anarchist editor of pre–World War I days, but never encountered him anywhere in the CP. That meant pretty nearly for sure that he wasn't there, because I knew everybody who was in any way active or prominent from one end of the country to the other. The same applies to David Coutts whom Foster mentions (in his *History of the Communist Party of the United States*).

It is quite possible that these people and a few, but not "many," others of the Foster AFL group, formally joined the party and then dropped out without attracting anyone's attention. Sam Hammersmark played a minor role in the Chicago local organization during the time I was there in 1923–1927. But like most of those whose ideas and methods of work had been shaped in the narrow school of trade unionism, he was lost in the complexities of party politics.

Foster himself, in a big way, and Johnstone and Manley to a far lesser extent, made *personal* contributions to the CP. But it would be historically false to represent the Foster AFL *group* as a contributing current in the new movement. Even Browder, who had been a pre-war Fosterite syndicalist, did not come to the communist movement by way of Foster. He jumped over the head of the Foster group—if it is proper even to speak of such a formation as a definite ideological tendency—and came in as an individual three years ahead of Foster. It was Browder who was commissioned by the party to invite Foster to attend the Congress of the Profintern in 1921 and thus started him on the road to the party.

By one of those historical quirks, for which I ask neither praise nor blame, I was directly responsible for Browder's coming into the left wing of the SP in the first place in 1918; for his introduction to the national leadership of the CP and his coming to New York in 1921; and for his delegation to the Profintern in the same year. It was in Moscow at the Profintern Congress that Browder got together with Foster again and then became his first assistant, and a very efficient one, in the office of the TUEL.

Browder's background and my own were almost identical, as were the successive stages of our political evolution. We were both about the same age, both originated in Kansas, were both socialists from early youth, and both made the switch from the SP to syndicalism along about the same time. Thereafter, for a number of years our paths diverged a bit. Browder became a convert to the Fosterite version of syndicalism and I remained an IWW. However, partings of the ways organizationally never brought such a sharp break in cooperation and in personal relations as has been the case in later years after the war and the Russian Revolution.

In those days people in the various groups and tendencies used to maintain personal contact and cooperate with each other in causes of mutual concern, particularly in labor defense matters. Browder and I became well acquainted and worked together, along with radicals of other stripes in Kansas City, in defense committees for Tom Mooney, in the Schmidt-Kaplan case which grew out of the McNamara affair, and in similar activities of a "united front" character before we ever heard of that term.

We were drawn together more closely by America's entry into the First World War and our common opposition to it. Browder and his brothers were influenced by the anarchist propaganda of Berkman and Goldman and attempted to organize an open fight against conscription, refusing on principle to register for the draft. I took a somewhat different tactical line—favored by most of the IWW's and left socialists—of registering for the draft as a "conscientious objector."

Shortly before his first imprisonment for a year in 1917, for refusing to register for the draft, Browder had made a trip to New York. There he contacted the people connected with the Cooperative League of America and began to lean very strongly in the direction of work in the cooperative movement, both as an occupation and as a means of political expression. While he was in jail I was completely revising my syndicalist views under the influence of the Russian Revolution and the popularization of its leading ideas in *The Liberator* and *The Revolutionary Age*.

To put my newly acquired political conceptions into practice I decided to rejoin the Socialist Party and connect myself with the national left wing, then being promoted by *The Revolutionary Age*. I got together with A.A. ("Shorty") Beuhler and a number of other militants in Kansas City, who were favorable to the idea of a new political alignment, and we decided to start a weekly paper in Kansas City to express our views. At an early stage in the promotion of this project Browder and his brothers were released from jail and I immediately took up the new program with them.

I am quite sure that such a drastic reorientation had not occurred to Browder before this meeting. But he, like myself, was a pronounced anti-capitalist revolutionist to start with, and I found him receptive and sympathetic to the new idea. We soon came to agreement and then went to work in earnest to launch our paper, the *Workers World*. We joined the Socialist Party Local at the same time, along with a number of other live-wire militants in Kansas City—former IWW's, AFL syndicalists, socialists, and quite a few independent radicals who had previously dropped out of the SP, finding it an inadequate expression of their radical views.

Browder was the first editor of the paper, but a short time later he had to go to Leavenworth to begin serving a second two-year term for conspiracy to obstruct the draft, and I took over the editorship. We ran the paper for about six months, until I was arrested in December, 1919, and indicted under the war-time Lever Act, because of my agitation in the Kansas coal fields against the anti-strike injunction of the federal government.

When Browder finished his second prison term, along about January, 1921, I was already in New York, a member of the Central Committee and in the thick of party politics. Browder was unknown to the other party leaders, but on my motion was brought to New York and placed in charge of organizing the delegation to the Profintern Congress. It was in that function that he resumed his contact with Foster and arranged for Foster also to attend.

This is a rather long and involved explanation of the original point—that the Foster AFL group was not the medium through which Browder came into the CP, although he had been previously connected with Foster.

In his *History of the Communist Party of the United States* Foster makes an elaborate attempt to back-write history by blowing up the minuscule Foster group of practical trade unionists in the AFL, and representing it as a serious ideological tendency and a contributing current to the movement of American communism. Here Foster really outwits himself. He actually does himself an injustice, although I would not accuse him of such an intention. If no more were involved than that, one could well afford to let the matter rest. But since history is no good, and is even worse than useless, if it is not true, I feel obliged to defend him against himself in order to set the record straight.

Foster's astounding success in organizing the packinghouse workers (1917–1918) in an AFL craft union set-up almost designed and guaranteed to make such a thing impossible, and his repeat performance in the steel strike (1919) under still more difficult conditions, were extraordinary *personal* accomplishments.

In the late Thirties the unionization of the steel industry was a pushover; the official leaders simply rode the tide of a universal labor upsurge generated by the long depression, and Lewis got U.S. Steel's signature to a contract without a strike. But in the year 1919—before the depression and before the rise of the CIO—no one but Foster, with his executive and organizing skill, his craftiness, his patience and his driving energy, could have organized the steel workers on such a scale and led them in a great strike, through the road-blocks and booby-traps of craft unionism, under the official sponsorship of the Gompers AFL.

Foster's steel campaign was unique. It was all the more remarkable precisely because he did it all by himself against all kinds of official sabotage, and with the assistance of only a small handful of people of secondary talents who were personally attached to him and worked under his direction. His ex post facto attempt to represent himself in this grandiose action as the instrument of an ideological tendency tributary to the communist movement, not only falsifies the historical facts, but by indirection, detracts from the magnitude of his personal achievement.

The Foster group in the AFL began with a revolutionary program outlined in a pamphlet based on French syndicalism (1913). But this first programmatic declaration was soon withdrawn, rewritten and watered down to nothing but a tongue-in-cheek affirmation that mere trade-union organization would automatically solve all problems of workers' emancipation. Thereafter, Fosterism was simply a method of working in the AFL by adaptation to the official leadership.

By adaptation individuals can get a chance to work. Foster demonstrated that to the hilt in practice. But adaptation is not a movement and cannot create a movement, for the question of who is serving whom always arises. Gompers, who knew Foster's past and was no fool, thought that Foster's work and adaptation could serve Gompers' aims. He permitted Foster to work under AFL auspices for that reason, as he testified with brutal frankness before the Senate Committee Hearings on the Steel Trust Strike. Fitzpatrick was evidently of the same opinion. Both he and Gompers proved to be correct. Foster's later adaptation to the Communist Party worked out the same way.

Foster's work and achievements in the early days of the Trade Union Educational League (TUEL) under the Communist Party, were no less remarkable than his stockyard and steel campaigns. His rapid-fire organization of a network of effective left-progressive groups in a dozen or more different unions demonstrated most convincingly that his previous successes in the AFL were no fluke. It proved, for the second time, under different auspices, that given the forces and the machinery to work with, Foster was a trade-union organizer without a peer. In each case, however, his work was permitted and controlled by other forces which Foster had to serve. For that reason there never was and never could be such a thing as a Foster "movement" or, strictly speaking, even a Foster group. Foster has been condemned throughout his career, ever since he left the IWW, to serve the aims of others whom he sought to outwit by adaptation.

Foster was the leader of his own faction in the CP only within this framework. In the very first showdown in the original Foster group in 1925, when political issues of party interest were posed point-blank, he found himself in the minority and discovered that the policy of the Foster group was not his to determine at will.

In the second showdown of the group, by then reduced to a smaller composition of ostensibly pure Fosterites—in 1928, at the Sixth Congress caucus meeting of the opposition delegates in Moscow—the leader found himself completely isolated. Bittelman, seconded by Browder and Johnstone, attacked him most brutally and disdainfully on that occasion and took complete charge of the "Foster group." He was left without a single friend or support in the caucus. (The rest of us, members of the opposition bloc but not Fosterites, simply stood aside and let the Fosterites fight it out.)

All Foster had left at the time of the Sixth Congress in 1928, was his name and the manifest intention of Stalin to use it for his own purposes. His name represented not a political tendency, however small, which had to be recognized. It was the symbol, rather, of his personal achievements as an organizer, of his public renown which was not yet seriously tarnished by his internal party defeats.

But, ironically, even his name and fame, which had been well earned by real performance, and which gave him a scrap of a special position in the party, was an obstacle to the realization of his ambition to be the official leader of the party, be it only by the grace of Stalin. For his own purposes Stalin needed in the U.S., as elsewhere, leaders without independent strength, leaders made by him and completely dependent on his favor. Browder filled the bill. He was the perfect example of the candidate distinguished not by the defect of his qualities, but by the quality of his defects.

Browder was an intelligent, industrious and dependable chief clerk by nature, but in no case an executive leader of independent capacity and resource. He was capable of filling the office of formal leader of the party by the permission of Stalin for 15 years without having, in his wildest imagination, previously entertained such an ambition and without having the slightest idea of how it came about or how his regime was brought to an end so precipitately and so easily. I don't doubt that Browder began to think he was ten feet tall in the long period where he walked on stilts above the party multitude. But I doubt very much whether he could explain to himself or others how he got up so high in the first place, or why the stilts so suddenly gave way under him.

The original relationship between Foster and Browder, and the proper one, considering the personal qualities of each, had been the relation between executive and first assistant. The appointment of Browder to the first position in the party, with Foster subordinated to the role of honorary public figure without authority, really rubbed Foster's nose in the dirt. It was not pleasant to see how he accepted the gross humiliation and pretended to submit to it.

When Browder was finally deposed 15 years later, Foster was permitted to officiate at the ceremonies. It was pitiful to see how he gratified his long-standing grudge and gloated over the victim in celebration of his hollow victory. In reality the great organizer, who accepted the office of formal leadership without the power, was celebrating his own utter defeat as an independent political figure.

Lovestone and Bittelman

AUGUST 4, 1954

Lovestone was indubitably a central figure in the enigmatic drama. Wolfe and Bedacht were also important, but in a secondary way. With all their talents and abilities they were supporting figures in the Lovestone circle, not prime movers.

Wolfe was a more serious student, he was better educated and more effective both as speaker and writer than Lovestone himself. And Bedacht, a product of the old prewar German school, knew far more about formal Marxist doctrine and took it more seriously. But both of them lacked Lovestone's will, his ruthless and driving ambition, to say nothing of his truly diabolical passion for intrigue, and his indefatigable energy in setting men against each other and fouling things up generally.

Bittelman was a student and critic; hardly more than that. But taking the movement as it was at the time, that was a lot. It also explains the contradictory nature of his contributions. Bittelman had assimilated the formal doctrines of Marxism. When he wrote about the early history with no factional axe to grind, and criticized the errors and defects of different sections of the movement, he did, on the whole, a good job, and his productions are well worth attention. As a politician, however, he was sterile and lacking in originality.

His politics consisted of a quick assimilation of the latest Russian pronouncements and their translation into English for mechanical application. His facility in this regard was quite impressive at first to those who read no Russian at all and hadn't read Marxism very much in any language, but there was never anything creative in Bittelman's work from beginning to end. Even his early *History* stands up only as a work of criticism and lacks any distinctive contribution of his own.

I have, in my files, two issues of Bittelman's *Communist Unity* published early in 1921. It is more tainted with factionalism than his later work in 1923–1924. But in the main, in his criticism—of others—he is substantially correct. He leaves out his own big mistake in going along with the Hourwich (Russian Federation) faction in the original split of the left wing and, still worse, in sticking to the Hourwich group even after Ruthenberg broke with it to unite with the CLP in 1920.

By 1921, with the formation of his "Unity Committee," Bittelman was beginning to correct his original mistake, but in a roundabout manner without recognizing or acknowledging it, and covering it up with his criticism—most of it accurate and pertinent—of the mistakes of others.

I have to break away from CP history for a while to take care of some other assignments in connection with our forthcoming party Convention and to prepare some lectures for the party Summer School here.

I must admit that I leave the subject of early CP history regretfully after having been drawn into it so deeply more or less by accident, and certainly without any prior design on my part. I am now playing with the idea of a speculative article, outlined briefly in my letter to you of July 20, on what might have happened in the Thirties if the CP hadn't been derailed in the last half of the Twenties. But this has to be postponed for the time being.

The interviews you have had with various people, and other aspects of your research work, are evidence of the seriousness of your approach to your task, and of your intention to do a thorough job which will be recognized as the standard work of reference on the history of early American communism.

You need only to recall the lively youth movement of the Thirties to assure yourself that your exposition will find a continuing audience in times to come. With the approach of the next social crisis in this country, shoals of eager students will be going to the libraries in search of authentic information about the origins and early days of American communism. A conscientious man must feel an obligation to them, to put some factual truth and rational interpretation in their way, alongside the malicious gossip, the fantasies, the fairy tales and the official lies. I feel a great interest and sympathy for your enterprise from this point of view.

The Foster-Cannon group

MARCH 17, 1955

The Foster-Cannon group, as a definite faction in the party, originated as a direct result of the labor party convention in Chicago, on July 3, 1923, which culminated in the split with the Fitzpatrick group and the formation of the stillborn "Federated Farmer-Labor Party" under CP leadership and control. It would be a big mistake, however, to isolate this single "political issue" from its context and to judge the ensuing struggle purely in terms of differences on the labor party question. The sources of conflict were far deeper and more complicated than that. The launching of the ill-fated "Federated Farmer-Labor Party" simply triggered the explosion, which had been building up out of the general situation in the party.

Behind the unfortunate action at Chicago stood Pepper, and "Pepperism" was the real issue in the first stages of the long fight. The author of the policy which produced the Chicago fiasco was Pepper, and the fire of the new opposition was at first directed against his adventuristic policy, and his dictatorial domination of the party. The new opposition came into conflict with Ruthenberg only after he definitely aligned himself with Pepper, and after efforts, repeatedly made by Foster, to come to an agreement with him had failed. There were profound reasons for Ruthenberg's alignment, as well as for ours, and these reasons transcended the political dispute of the moment.

The labor party question—more specifically, the question of the "Federated Farmer-Labor Party"—was the immediate and central question of policy at issue in the first stages of the faction fight. But at the bottom of the conflict there were other causes. Each of the contending factions had deep roots in different past experiences and traditions, and the alignments on each side in the "power struggle" took place very quickly, and all the more "naturally," because of that.

It should be recalled that prior to the Russian Revolution the revolutionary movement in this country, as in some other countries, notably France, had been split into a party-political wing, conceiving "political action" in the narrow sense of electoral and parliamentary action, and a syndicalist wing, rejecting "politics" altogether. For the greater part, the two tendencies had been separated from each other organizationally. Therewith there had been a rather sharp division in their activities and fields of work. The "politicals" devoted themselves primarily to socialist propaganda and election campaigns, while the syndicalists concentrated on "direct action" in the economic struggle—union organization campaigns and strikes.

The attempt of the Comintern to fuse these two tendencies together in the new communist parties had more success in the United States than elsewhere. Prominent activists from both sides of the old movement came into the CP, and they brought a part of their old baggage with them. The "politicals" had come to recognize the importance of trade-union work, but—at that time—it was still a strange field for them; they had no real understanding of it, no "feel" for it. The ex-syndicalists and practicing trade unionists had come to recognize the necessity of a party and the importance of "political action," but—again at that time—their first interest was trade-union work.

There were exceptions, of course, but by and large, the old predilections determined the tendency of the party activists to align themselves with one faction or another; they felt more at home with people of their own kind. These differences of background and temperament, which were also reflected in different social habits and associations and different ways of working, made for an uneasiness in personal relations among the leaders. This was evident even in the period prior to the blow-up in July 1923, when they were collaborating most effectively on the main projects of the time—to legalize the party and to expand its public activities, and to swing the party support behind the Trade Union Educational League.

We were all beginning-learners in the field of Marxist theory and politics; and, in the best case, further study, time and experience in working together would have been required to fuse the two tendencies together into a harmonious working combination. I believe there was a general will to effect such a fusion, and things might have worked out this way in a normal course of development. But the high-powered intervention of Pepper, with policies, methods and designs of his own, cut the process short, disrupted the collaboration and deepened the division.

I was quite well aware of Pepper's general operations and machinations in the party—far more perceptively, I venture to say, than Foster and the other Chicagoans—and I didn't like the way things were going. I thought at first that my objections were restricted to internal party affairs. It took the shock of the July 3 Convention to convince me that Pepper's politics was all of one piece; that the fantastic unrealism of his internal party policy had its counterpart in external adventurism.

For that reason, perhaps, when the conflict over the catastrophic policy at the July 3 Convention broke into the open, I was not content to rest on that single issue. From the beginning of the fight I conceived of it as a general struggle to overthrow the Pepper regime. It didn't take Foster long to come to the same conclusion, and that's the way the issue was posed. The alignments, on both sides, in the ensuing struggle took place on that basis. Pepper's labor policy was only one item in the catalogue.

Within this context, it would be completely correct to say that the formation of the Foster-Cannon faction took place as a reaction to the July 3 Convention at Chicago. The unavowed faction of Pepper, however, existed long before that. The presentation of the Ruthenberg-Pepper "thesis," attempting to justify the "Federated Farmer-Labor Party," and the vote of Foster, Bittelman and Cannon against it, at the Political Committee meeting of August 24, 1923, could perhaps be taken as the formal starting point of the internal struggle.

Prior to that, and leading up to it, were my conversation with Foster at Duluth, as related in my letter of May 28, 1954, and my articles in the *Worker* in the summer of 1923, which indirectly criticized the official party policy. Other background material, and my account of the struggle up to and at the December 1923 Convention of the party, are contained in my letters of May 19, 27 and 28, 1954. I have checked these letters again and find nothing to change. That's the way it was; at least that's the way it looked to me.

You ask how I look at my own role in the formation of the Foster-Cannon group. I think that is indicated in the account I have written in those letters. I had the highest regard for Foster's ability in general, and for his feel and skill as a mass worker in particular—a most essential quality which the leaders of the other faction seemed to lack—but I never belonged to Foster's staff of personal assistants and was never in any sense a personal follower. Relations between me and Foster, from start to finish, always had the same basis. Cooperation in internal party affairs depended on agreement on policy, arrived at beforehand. That was no trouble in 1923; our thinking ran along the same lines.

Foster was the party's outstanding mass leader and most popular figure, and he carried himself well in that role. But he was not a political infant as he has often been represented; he knew what he was driving at. He symbolized the proletarian-American orientation, which the party needed and wanted, and I thought he was justly entitled to first place as party leader and public spokesman.

He was rather new to the party at that time, however,

and was still feeling his way carefully. As one of the original communists, I knew the party better. I had closer connections with many of the decisive cadres and probably had more influence with some of them. Our combination—while it lasted—was an effective division of labor, without rivalry, at least as far as I was concerned. Each made independent contributions to the combination and each carried his own weight.

Browder's belated claim that it was he, not Foster, who conducted the labor party negotiations with the Fitzpatrick leadership in Chicago could be true only in a technical sense. Behind Browder stood Foster; Browder was the agent and, as always, an intelligent and capable agent, but in no case the "principal." Foster's influence in the Chicago Federation of Labor, and his authority, solidly established by his great work in the campaigns to organize the packinghouse workers and steel workers, in which he had secured the effective collaboration of Fitzpatrick and won his confidence, determined and governed Fitzpatrick's relations with the Workers Party forces, from the first liaison to the break at the July 3 Convention.

Further, Browder's report of his activities in the internal party situation of that time may be factually correct, but they certainly did not have the significance which he attributes to them. His attempt to depict himself as playing an independent role in the internal struggle of 1923–1924 strikes me as historical "back-writing"—as an adjustment of the facts of that period to fit the role he later came to play in the party, by grace of Stalin, after Foster had lost his original influence, and after such inconvenient obstacles as Pepper, Ruthenberg, Lovestone and Cannon were out of the way.

If Browder played any independent part whatever in

1923 I didn't know anything about it; and I surely should have known it because I was in the center of things where the decisions were made and was in a position to know how and by whom they were made. There is no doubt that he, like many others, was bitterly dissatisfied with the Pepper policy and its results. This widespread sentiment, which could probably be classified under the head of disgruntlement, provided the material, ready-made, for an effective, and eventually victorious, opposition. But this opposition first had to be organized by people with the necessary influence and authority to carry the party; and they had to know where to begin and whom to begin with.

As I have previously related, the opposition of 1923, as a definite movement in the party aiming at party control, began with the agreement between Foster and me. That was decisive step number one. The next was the agreement with Bittelman. The leading people of the Chicago District—Browder, Johnstone, Swabeck and Krumbein—and the better half of the leadership of the youth organization—Abern, Shachtman and Williamson—along with numerous other influential party militants such as William F. Dunne, were important supporters of the new opposition from the start. But the *initiative* came from the three people mentioned above, and the main influence in the leadership, from the beginning until the break-up of the faction in 1925, was exerted by them. This was so well established, and so widely recognized, that Browder's present report is the first I have heard to give a different interpretation.

I don't know what went on in Browder's head at the time, or what he imagined he was doing, but I do know that his latter-day recollections of furious activity as an independent force have very little relation to reality. Browder's report and interpretation of his conversation and agreement with Ruthenberg in August 1923 impress me as an unwitting revelation of his own naivete. He may very well have had such a conversation with Ruthenberg, but his impression that Ruthenberg agreed to a combination with him, regardless of Pepper and Foster, not to speak of Lovestone and Cannon, was most certainly a misunderstanding on Browder's part.

Ruthenberg knew the relation of forces in the party too well for that. Ruthenberg was pretty cagey, he knew what he wanted, he had a high opinion of himself and was concerned with problems of self, and I don't think he rated Browder very highly as a party leader. Moreover, Ruthenberg had shown no disposition to oppose Pepper's policy. Just the contrary—witness the Ruthenberg-Pepper "thesis," presented at the very time Browder imagined he had secured Ruthenberg's agreement to separate himself from Pepper—*August 24, 1923!*

What probably happened was that Browder talked and Ruthenberg simply listened, and Browder came away with the impression of an "understanding" that did not exist. I do remember Browder telling me, along about that time, that Ruthenberg had expressed antagonism to Lovestone on the ground that he exacerbated the factional situation and poisoned the atmosphere generally. This was quite true about Lovestone, and the objection to his ugly quarrelsomeness would have been in character for Ruthenberg, who was himself invariably polite, courteous and "correct"—I used to think he was too "correct"—in all discussions and relations with colleagues in the Committee. Browder may have taken Ruthenberg's remark about Lovestone for an "understanding" in the internal party situation.

However, as is usually the case, as the internal struggle unfolded, the deep-going political differences cut across and cancelled out minor irritations in both camps. Ruthenberg, as events had shown and were to continue to show, was in essential agreement with Pepper's political line, and it was foolish to think he could be influenced by Browder to determine his course in the party on secondary issues. I don't think Ruthenberg "broke faith" with Browder. More likely, Browder's "understanding" with him was a misunderstanding on Browder's part.

Ruthenberg was a proud man, with a high-and-mighty haughtiness. Unlike Foster, he appeared to stand above the dirty little vices, such as outright lying, double-dealing, betrayal of confidence. He would have considered such things, if he thought about them at all, as not simply wrong but, more important, beneath his dignity.

Foster's knowledge and feel of the trade-union movement surpassed that of all the other party leaders in the early days, but his experience in that field was not all profit. He had learned too much in the school of the labor fakers, who got what they wanted one way or another, without regard to any governing theory or principle, and he mistakenly thought such methods could be efficacious in the communist political movement. Crude American pragmatism, which "gets things done" in simple situations, is a poor tool in the complexities of revolutionary politics.

Foster was somewhat mechanical and eclectic in his thinking, and this frequently led him to summary judgments in complex questions which called for qualified answers. His one-sided, almost fetishistic concentration on "boring from within" the AFL, as the sole means of radicalizing and expanding the labor movement—a concept which had to be thrown overboard in 1928, and which was brutally refuted in life by the rise of the CIO—is an outstanding example of his limitations as a thinker.

But in the frame of comparison with the other leading figures of the pioneer communist movement in this country, which in my opinion is the proper way to judge him historically, Foster was outstanding in many ways. Attempts to represent him as some kind of babe in the woods, led astray by craftier men, which have been recurrently made throughout the history of the party, beginning with his alliance with me in the formation of the Foster-Cannon group, never had any foundation in fact.

Foster was a shrewd and competent man, far more conscious and deliberate in all his actions than he appeared and pretended to be. Everything that Foster did, from first to last, was done deliberately. In fact, he was too shrewd, too deliberate in his decisions, and too free from the restraint of scruple; and by that he wrought his own catastrophe. The actions which, in a tragic progression, made such a disgraceful shambles of his career, derived not from faulty intelligence or weakness of will but from defects of character.

Foster was a slave to ambition, to his career. That was his infirmity. But this judgment, which in my book is definitive, must be qualified by the recognition that he sought to serve his ambition and to advance his career in the labor movement and not elsewhere. Within that field he worshipped the bitch goddess of Success as much as any business man, careerist on the make, or politician in the bourgeois world.

Foster was a man of such outstanding talent, energy

and driving will that—in the conditions of the country in his time—he could easily have made his way in any number of other occupations. But the labor movement was his own milieu, deliberately chosen in his youth and doggedly maintained to the exclusion of virtually all other interests. Within that limit—that he had no life outside the labor movement—Foster subordinated everything to his mad ambition and his almost pathological love of fame, of his career. To that, with a consistency that was truly appalling, he sacrificed his pride and self-respect, and all considerations of loyalty to persons and to principles and, eventually, to the interests of the movement which he had originally set out to serve.

Shakespeare's Gratiano said they lose the world "that do buy it with much care." Foster's too-great consistency in his single-minded pursuit of fame and career at any price became a self-defeating game. His willingness to humiliate himself and surrender his opinions to gain favor with the Stalinist "power" only disarmed him before repeated exactions in this respect, until he was stripped of the last shred of independence. His disloyalty to people robbed him of any claim on the loyalty of others and left him without support at the most critical turning points. His readiness to profess opinions he didn't hold, for the sake of expediency, to lie and cheat to gain a point, lost him the respect of his colleagues and eventually destroyed his moral authority in the party cadres. He ended up friendless and alone as early as 1928, incapable of contending for leadership in his own name, and fit only for the role of figurehead leader.

But even for that shabby substitute for fame and career Foster has had to grovel in the dust, and to contribute his bit systematically, year after year for more than a quarter of a century, to the gross betrayal of the workers' cause which he had proclaimed as his own. "Success" in the world of Stalinism is dearly bought indeed—if by some horrible misunderstanding one should call Foster's pursuit of fame and career successful!

Browder's role

MARCH 22, 1955

BROWDER. I dealt with Browder at considerable length in my letter of March 17, and also in an earlier letter (August 4, 1954). Here are a few smaller points. I never heard, and haven't the slightest recollection, of Browder and the other Chicago leaders making a special demand that Ruthenberg be re-elected as secretary after the 1923 Convention of the party. As far as Foster and I were concerned, probably also Bittelman, we had no intention whatever of displacing Ruthenberg. In fact, our maximum program at the time was simply to end Pepper's domination and to change the majority of the Committee enough to shift the balance of power and control of policy. We still hoped at that time to come to an eventual accommodation with Ruthenberg, and in general to share party responsibilities with the others, within that frame-work. Along the same line, we did not remove Engdahl who had previously been designated as editor of the newly-founded *Daily Worker*, but merely put Dunne in as co-editor. We also made a few changes of District Organizers, but not many.

Browder's revelation that he and Johnstone "put the bug in Foster's ear to become chairman replacing Cannon," is likewise news to me. Foster never told me anything about it. The proposal to make the change came from me. I simply thought it corresponded to the realities. I had been elected chairman of the Workers Party at its foundation, a time when the list of appropriate candidates was more limited. Ruthenberg was in prison; Foster had just joined the party a few months previously and was not yet openly known as a member.

When Ruthenberg was released from prison in the spring of 1923 I made the first proposal that he should take over the office of Executive Secretary. I had spoken to him previously about it and he said that he personally was willing to take either that post or the post of editor of the paper. Ruthenberg, with his great prestige and special aptitude for executive work, was the indicated man for Executive Secretary. This was undoubtedly the general opinion of the party ranks.

Once Foster had become fully identified with the party, it was perfectly obvious to me that he, with his greater prominence and public prestige, should succeed to the office of Chairman. The only question was whether Foster was ready to identify himself publicly with the party. I believe the change met with general approval, but I am equally certain that it would not have taken place at that time and under the conditions of the time if I had not myself proposed it. Browder had nothing to do with the decision—except to vote for it when it came up for formal action in our caucus, after Foster and I had come to a prior agreement to make the shift.

Browder and Johnstone may have thought of themselves as "constituting a sort of sub-group by themselves." But I am sure that very few people in the party knew anything about it. I didn't. In party work they were direct assistants to Foster—Browder as managing editor of the *Labor Herald* and Johnstone as organizer of the TUEL. It would probably be more correct to describe them as restless and somewhat disgruntled subordinates, because Foster was a hard taskmaster and paid little regard to their wishes and opinions. As far as the party knew, and as far as I knew, Browder was a one-hundred-percent member of the Foster-Cannon faction, holding a place of influence within it about equal to that of Swabeck, Chicago party organizer, Krumbein, Abern and a number of others, somewhat less than that of William F. Dunne, and considerably below that of Bittelman. Johnstone's influence in the faction was even less.

Browder's indication that there was some antagonism between himself and me at that time is also a new revelation. From the time that he and I first got together in Kansas City in 1918, on the platform of the Russian Revolution and the decision to rejoin the Socialist Party and line up with the left wing, up until the split of the Foster-Cannon group in 1925, Browder and I worked together hand in hand. His relations with me were probably closer and more confidential than with anyone else. I do not recall a shadow of conflict between us until the blow-up of the faction at the 1925 Convention over the issue of the Comintern cable. Our personal friendship, as well as our political collaboration, ended abruptly there and was never reconstituted.

Fourth Plenum of the Comintern—1924

MARCH 31, 1955

I did not attend the Fourth Plenum of the Comintern in the spring of 1924. We had no report of it except that given by Foster. This was not so much a report on the

Plenum as on the decisions on the "American Question." At least, that's what we were primarily interested in and that's all I remember. We had been prepared for the decision against the "Third Party Alliance" by previous letters from Foster as well as by a telegram directly from the Executive Committee of the Communist International.

I don't recall that anybody in either faction raised any objections to the decision. We were pronounced "Cominternists" at that time and Comintern decisions, especially those on political questions, were accepted as coming from the highest authority and as binding on all. Both sides were far more interested in the question of party control, and what bearing the Moscow decisions might have on that, than in the La Follette question.

I believe it would be risky to say flatly that "the beginnings of anti-Trotskyism coincided with the beginnings of pro-Stalinism" in the American party—or for that matter, in the Russian party and in the Comintern. That's the way it worked out, but the process by which Stalin came to complete domination was gradual and insidious, and all the more effective because of that.

I do not recall that we identified Stalin as the leader of the Russian majority in 1924 as much as Zinoviev, who was the Chairman of the Comintern with whom the party had had the most direct dealings.

The opposition of Trotsky had been represented to us as the revolt of a single individual against the "Old Guard" of Lenin who constituted the Central Committee of the Russian party, the official leadership. We knew nothing of any differences within the ruling group at that time. Stalin came fully into prominence in our understanding only after the split between him and Zinoviev, and even then Stalin appeared in alliance with Bukharin, with the latter as Chairman of the Comintern.

It may be that the conflict between Zinoviev and Stalin within the camp of the Russian majority was already being prepared in 1924 and that the Ruthenberg faction, which had Pepper in Moscow as a representative and source of information, knew what was pending better than we did, and were better prepared to jump on the new bandwagon before it started rolling. But even at that, they were not sharp enough to break with Bukharin in time, and this hesitancy cost Lovestone his head in 1929.

After the 1924 elections

MARCH 22, 1955

Here are some brief comments on matter-of-fact questions in your letters of December 21 and February 28, not specifically dealt with in my long letter of March 17. After the 1924 presidential election, as I recall it, the Ruthenberg faction (still master-minded to a considerable extent by Pepper from Moscow) wanted to continue the old labor party policy as if nothing had happened. We considered the labor party a dead issue for the time being and were opposed to any policy that would lead to the creation of a caricature of a labor party under communist control without any mass base in the trade unions.

In one of my articles in the *Daily Worker,* in the public party discussion after the November 1924 election, I stated that we were not opposed to the labor party in principle but conditioned our support of the labor party slogan on the existence of a mass sentiment for it in the trade unions. There's no doubt, however, that we did bend the stick backward in the course of the conflict and that we began to show a decided sectarian trend. I think it fair to say that Bittelman's influence came into play in this situation more than at any other time.

Foster himself was the initiator of the proposal to drop the labor party slogan, on the ground that the movement lacked vitality and that it would be a waste of time and effort to try to build a shadow labor party which in essence would be a mere duplicate of the Communist Party. I repeat, Foster was the initiator of this change of policy; but we all readily agreed with him. The change was accomplished without difficulty in all the leading circles of our faction. As I recall it, there were some objections from the Loreites such as Zimmerman (now a vice-president of the ILGWU).

It was also Foster who initiated the proposal to drop the candidates of the "Farmer-Labor Party" nominated at the St. Paul Convention in June 1924 and to nominate our own party candidates instead. On this we also followed Foster's lead, and the Ruthenberg group went along without opposition.

In general, the main initiative in determining the policy of our faction, from the time of Foster's return from the Comintern Plenum of April–May 1924 until the conflict within the faction over the Comintern cable at the 1925 Convention, came from him. I went along in general agreement. But I did not share the sectarian twist which Bittelman and Browder tended to give to the policy, and was careful to emphasize in my writings during the discussion that our opposition to the labor party at the given time was based on the lack of mass sentiment for it and was not put as a question of principle.

I believe Foster tended to go overboard a little bit in

the direction of Bittelman's slant, but this was probably due more to overzealousness in the faction struggle than to real conviction. Foster was no sectarian. While Foster and I were in Moscow in the early part of 1925, Bittelman and Browder were running things in the party, and I remember that we were both quite dissatisfied with the sectarian trend they were manifesting.

I probably had less difficulty in accepting the Comintern decision in favor of a continuation of the labor party policy than Foster did. In retrospect it appears to me now that this decision of the Comintern was dead wrong, as were virtually all of its decisions on the American question thereafter. After the internal struggle broke out in the Russian party, the American party, like all other sections of the Comintern, became a pawn in the Moscow game and Comintern decisions on national questions were no longer made objectively. But that is the wisdom of hindsight. I was a thoroughgoing "Cominternist" in those days and it took me three more years to get the picture straight.

I didn't know what was really going on in the Comintern, and I can't recall that I even knew of any differences between Trotsky and Zinoviev on the American question. It may be true that Pepper was in reality Zinoviev's agent, and that Zinoviev yielded to Trotsky on the La Follette question to avoid a showdown on an inconvenient issue. Trotsky's polemics against the Zinovievist policy on the so-called "Peasants' International," and the whole business of seeking to build a communist party by maneuvers with petty-bourgeois leaders of peasant movements, later revealed a big controversy around this point.

I did not get a grasp of this dispute until I first saw Trotsky's "Criticism of the Draft Program" (published later in America under the title *The Third International After Lenin*) at the Sixth Congress of the Comintern in 1928. As

I have related in my *History of American Trotskyism,* I was preoccupied with "our own" American questions at that time and did not know, or even suspect, that the fate of our party was so directly involved in the Russian party struggle.

1925: The 'Parity Commission' and the 'cable from Moscow'

MARCH 31, 1955

FIFTH PLENUM OF THE COMINTERN

I attended the Fifth Plenum of the CI in 1925 together with Foster. Both factions had their delegates in Moscow weeks in advance of the Plenum. Our work there before the Plenum consisted chiefly of an endless round of interviews with various leading people in the Comintern, particularly with the Russian leaders, in an attempt to obtain their support.

The eventual decision was pretty clearly intimated beforehand. I soon got the chilling impression, and I think Foster did too, that the position of our faction was far weaker in Moscow than at home, and that we couldn't do anything about it. The other faction had the advantage there. With Pepper as an active representative, busy in the apparatus of the Comintern, the Ruthenberg faction seemed to have the inside track.

Bukharin was particularly outspoken in favor of the Ruthenberg faction and acted like a factional partisan. So also did the leftists then representing the German party, particularly Heinz Neumann. Zinoviev appeared to be more friendly and impartial.

I had the definite impression that he wanted to correct our position on the labor party question without upsetting our majority, to restrain the majority from any suppression of the minority, and in general to slow down the factional struggle. I remember him saying to Foster at the end of one of our talks, in a friendly, persuading tone: "Frieden ist besser." ("Peace is better.") If I remember correctly, we did not see Stalin and did not know that he was becoming the real power behind the scenes.

My memory is not too sharp about the details of the negotiations and proceedings that led up to Zinoviev's original proposal that "the new Central Committee [of the American party] is to be so elected at the Party Conference that the Foster group obtains a majority and the Ruthenberg group is represented proportionately at least by one-third."

Foster was jubilant about the proposal, but I wasn't. The idea that the composition of the American party leadership should be arbitrarily fixed in Moscow did not sit well with me, even if we were to be the beneficiaries of the decision at the moment. In arguing with me Foster emphasized the point that it would guarantee our majority control of the party. He was more interested in the bare question of party control than I was at that time, and this difference between us—at first apparently a nuance—grew wider later on.

I was disturbed because I had become convinced in our discussions with the Russians, that we had made a political error in our estimate of the prospects of a labor party in the United States, and I was most concerned that we make a real correction. With inadequate theoretical schooling

I was already groping my way to the conception, which later became a governing principle, that a correct political line is more important than any organizational question, including the question of party control.

Looking back on it now, in the light of later developments in the United States, I think the evaluation we had made of labor party prospects in this country, and our proposals for party policy on the question, were far more correct and closer to American reality than those of the Ruthenberg faction. Even the 1925 Comintern decision on the question, which was more restrained and qualified, was way off the beam. But at the time I was convinced by the arguments of the Russians, and perhaps also by the weight of their authority.

There was hardly a trace of a genuine labor party movement in the United States in the ensuing years, and the feverish agitation of the party around the question, based on the Comintern decision, came to nothing. This was tacitly recognized in 1928 when the party again nominated its own independent candidates for President and Vice President and relegated the labor party to a mere slogan of propaganda.

THE 'PARITY COMMISSION' OF 1925

The decision of the Comintern in 1925 to set up a Parity Commission to arrange the Fourth Convention of our party, with Gusev, a Russian, as chairman, was manifestly a decision against us, for in effect it robbed us of our rights as an elected majority. I do not think Zinoviev was the author of this decision; it was far different from his original proposal. His acceptance of the parity commission formula manifestly represented a change on his part, and probably a compromise with others who wanted to give open support to the Ruthenberg faction.

After the arrival of Gusev in Chicago and the setting up of the Parity Commission—Foster, Bittelman and Cannon for our faction, Ruthenberg, Lovestone and Bedacht for the other side—the elected Central Committee and its Political Committee, as such, virtually ceased to exist. All questions of party policy, organization matters, convention preparations and everything else were decided by the Parity Commission, with Gusev casting the deciding vote in case of any disagreements.

Within that strict framework the struggle for Convention delegates proceeded furiously. Gusev proclaimed a strict neutrality, but he gave us the worst of it whenever he could do so neatly and plausibly. The fact that under such conditions we gained a majority of 40 to 21 at the Convention, is the most convincing evidence, I think, of the real will of the party members to support our majority and to reject the Ruthenberg group, which should more properly be called the Ruthenberg-Lovestone group, with the latter playing an increasingly important role in the struggle.

I think the beginning of the degeneration of the internal life of the party, from conflicts of clearly defined political tendencies, which had characterized all the previous factional fights since the beginning of the movement in 1918, into an increasingly unprincipled struggle of factional gangs, can be traced to the year 1925.

As far as political issues were concerned, the situation in the party, in the period of preparation for the Fourth Convention, could be approximately described as follows: Both sides had accepted the Comintern decision on the labor party, which had favored the Ruthenberg position with some important modifications. The trade-union policy of Foster had been accepted by the Ruthenbergites. From a political point of view there really wasn't much to fight about.

This was shown most convincingly by the circumstance that the Parity Commission agreed unanimously on both the political and trade-union resolutions, the former written for the greater part by Bittelman and the latter by Foster.

The party members had only one set of resolutions before them, and they accepted them unanimously all up and down the party. Normally, such unanimity should have called for a moderation of the factional atmosphere, a trend toward the unification of the contending groups in the leadership, and toward the liquidation of the factions. But that's not the way things went. The factional struggle raged more fiercely than ever before in the history of the party—over the issue of party control.

The debate over political issues, insofar as there was such a debate, could deal only with nuances and factional exaggerations. There was not much for the party members to learn in that kind of a fight, and not much satisfaction in it for conscientious communists who hadn't forgotten the great ideal they had started out to serve. I believe I already began to feel at that time that we were all caught in a trap; and that the only sensible thing to do was to look forward to a liquidation of the factional gangs and an agreement of the leading people to work together in a united leadership.

But the task in hand at the time was to secure a majority for our faction in the Convention, and I worked at that as earnestly as anyone else. We won a two to one majority in the fight for delegates on a strict basis of proportional representation. But it didn't do us any good.

THE 'CABLE FROM MOSCOW'

As the drawn-out Fourth Convention in the summer of 1925 was nearing its end, Gusev called us to a meeting of the

Parity Commission to hand us the famous "cable from Moscow." This cable stated that "the Ruthenberg group is more loyal to the Communist International and stands closer to its views," and prescribed that the Ruthenberg group should be allotted not less than 40 per cent of the representatives in the new Central Committee. That was a sudden blow for which we were in no way prepared, a blow calculated to put one's confidence in the Comintern to a rather severe test.

My immediate reaction was to wait, to say nothing there at the session of the Parity Commission. As I recall, Bittelman also kept silent. But Foster exploded with a statement that he would not accept the majority under such conditions, that the Ruthenberg group should take over the majority of the new Central Committee, and that he personally would not accept membership. I decided immediately to oppose such an attitude but did not say it there. I think it was on my proposal that we adjourned the meeting to report the cable to the majority caucus of the Convention delegates who were assembled and waiting for us.

This was the one time that Foster, Bittelman and I went straight into a caucus meeting without prior consultation and agreement among ourselves as to what we would recommend. I don't know why we skipped this customary procedure, but that's the way it happened. Foster seemed bent on taking his defiance directly to the caucus and I was no less determined to oppose it.

He had no sooner reported the cable to the caucus and announced his decision to let the Ruthenbergites have the majority in the Central Committee, to which he would not belong, than I took the floor with a counter-proposal that we lock up the new Central Committee on a 50-50 basis, with each faction sharing equally in the responsibility in the leadership.

Dunne and Swabeck supported my position, Bittelman

and Browder supported Foster. Abern and Shachtman spoke for my proposal. Johnstone and Krumbein spoke for Foster's. One by one, as the ominous debate proceeded, the leading people from all parts of the country took positions, and the split of our faction right down the middle began.

It is an effort to describe this stormy conflict in tranquillity thirty years afterward, without the embellishment of hindsight wisdom; to report it as it really happened, what we did with what we knew and didn't know and with the sentiments which actuated us at the time.

As I have remarked previously, I was then a convinced "Cominternist." I had faith in the wisdom and also in the fairness of the Russian leaders. I thought they had made a mistake through false information and that the mistake could later be rectified. I did not even suspect that this monstrous violation of the democratic rights of our party was one of the moves in the Moscow chess game, in which our party, like all the other parties in the Comintern, was to be a mere pawn.

I thought Foster's attitude was *disloyal;* that his ostensible willingness to hand over the majority to the Ruthenbergites, and to withdraw from the Central Committee himself, was in reality designed to provoke a revolt of our faction against the Comintern. Foster made the dispute between us a question of confidence in himself personally, as the leader of the faction. This hurt him more than it helped him, for the communist militants in those days were not the regimented lackeys of a later day. There was outspoken resentment at Foster's attempt to invoke the "follow the leader" principle.

I felt that I was fighting for the allegiance of the party to the Comintern, and I think the majority of the delegates who supported my motion, were actuated by the same sentiment. The final vote in favor of my motion, after an all-night-and-next-day debate, not only ended Foster's revolt against the Comintern—and I repeat my conviction that that was the real meaning of his proposal to "step aside." It also ended all prospects of his ever realizing his aspiration to rule the American party with a group of subordinates who would support him out of personal loyalty and serve in an advisory capacity, something like a presidential "cabinet," but leave final decisions to him.

I had thought that the adoption of my motion for a 50-50 Central Committee would stalemate the factional struggle, make each faction equally responsible for the leadership, and compel them to work together until the situation could be worked out with the Comintern. I was not permitted to nurse that childish illusion very long.

When we went to the first meeting of the new 50-50 Central Committee, the Machiavellian Gusev made another contribution to what might be called "The Education of a Young Man" who had a lot to learn about the ways of the Comintern in the post-Lenin era. Gusev blandly announced that while the agreement was for a parity Central Committee he, as Chairman, would feel obliged to follow the spirit of the Comintern decision and support the Ruthenberg group.

That meant, he said, that the Ruthenberg faction should have a majority in the Political Committee and in other party bodies and institutions. So it turned out that Foster's caucus proposal to hand over the majority to the Ruthenbergites was actually carried out in practice, and my proposal to freeze the committee on a parity basis was deftly frustrated by Gusev.

If I admit that I went along with this treacherous double-play and still refused to have any part in any revolt against the Comintern, it is not to claim any credit for myself. I write down this distasteful recollection now simply to show that devotion to the Comintern, which had originally been one of the greatest merits of the pioneer communists, was being turned into a sickness which called for a radical cure.

That sickness, on my part, hung on for three more years and affected everything I did in the party. It was not until 1928 that I took the cure. But with the help of Trotsky, I took it then for good and all.

APRIL 1, 1955

Writing about the dark period from 1925 on is tough, but it was tougher to live through without sliding into cynicism as did so many others—good companions in earlier endeavors. Despite all that happened afterward to separate us irreconcilably, and eventually to draw a line of blood between us, I cannot write about them—*as they were then*—without a certain sympathy. I suppose that is Irish sentimentalism. But there is also the compulsion of conscience to play fair with the young rebels to come, who will be no less ardent, no less eager for the truth, than we were in our time.

'Party life' in the Twenties

FEBRUARY 4, 1959

From the abundance of material you have dug up about the internal "Party Life" in the middle Twenties you could easily draw a picture in great detail of organizational chaos and futility during the vain attempt to "bolshevize"—in reality Russianize—the organizational structure. But too much should not be made of that. The party rolled along just the same in spite of all, and was ten or a hundred times more active in all fields than the other radical organizations of the same period.

Also, too much should not be made of the reports about dull branch meetings, poor attendance, etc., as revealed in quotations from internal documents. Allowance should be made for the fact that this was typical "self-criticism," purposely picking out extreme cases to drive home the point that branch meetings should be livelier and better attended, etc.

The defects cited in the quotations are common to all voluntary organizations in normal times. The real difference between the CP and other organizations of the Twenties in this respect—if the subject is worth more than mere passing notice—was that the Communist Party branch meetings, as a rule, were better attended and had more on the agenda than the others, simply because the communists were more serious than the others and had more tasks assigned to the branches to carry out.

It is common knowledge that the ordinary meeting of a local union these days often doesn't attract one-tenth of one percent of the membership. But that doesn't mean that the unions are dead, or dying. When a new contract is up for discussion or a strike is in prospect, the members turn out. The Retail Clerks here in Los Angeles have membership meetings only four times a year, I am told. But when a conflict with the employers came to a head New Year's Day, they went out to a man and a woman and stayed solid for nearly a month until they got a pretty good settlement.

If I don't pull up short, I'll find myself writing a scholarly essay, based on long experience and observation, on the subject: "How to Make Branch Business Meetings Interesting and Well-Attended in Normal Times—and Why It Can't Be Done." In my youth, among my derelictions, I was a member of the Fraternal Order of Eagles, a lodge to which all the "regular fellows" from the saloons and pool halls in Rosedale, as distinguished from the YMCA and church social crowd, belonged. Like all other lodges of that time, the Eagles had insurance features, but the real attraction was the club room where a deserving brother could get a glass of beer and play a game of pinochle in prohibition territory without fear of interference by the constables who respected the political influence of our noble order.

But even so, the regular semi-monthly business meetings of the local lodge were dull and dreary affairs which only a corporal's guard ever attended—in normal times. The problem of "How to Make the Business Meetings Interesting and Get Out the Crowd"—which incidentally is up for discussion right now in the local branch of the Socialist Workers Party in Los Angeles, and probably in every other branch of every other party—was solved by a simple device. About every three months our worthy officials would decide that the state of the treasury could stand the expense of a beer bust. On such occasions, the negligent brothers would show up en masse for a lively meeting, with beer and sandwiches and good fellowship for all. But the next meeting would be back to the same old dull routine.

In the political movement, we are limited to less effective inducements such as "educational lectures" or "special reports" on something or other, which help a little, but not as much as the free beer and sandwiches at the Rosedale "Aerie" of the Fraternal Order of Eagles.

The Passaic strike

JUNE 9, 1955

I remember the December 1925 Plenum of the CP of the U.S. I was allied with the Ruthenberg faction at this particular Plenum and took a very active part in the debate on the trade-union question. It probably marked the tentative beginning of resistance to AFL fetishism, although the details of the specific issues in dispute at the Plenum have not remained in my memory.

According to my recollection, the Passaic issue came up at the Plenum, but it did not originate there. It was rather thrust upon the party by the cyclonic activities of Weisbord, who had gone into the field and actually begun to organize the unorganized textile workers. Looking back on it now, we deserve censure, not for giving conditional support to the organizing work of Weisbord, but for failing to go all-out in such support and to make the issue of AFL fetishism clear-cut.

The "United Front Committee" under which the organizing campaign in Passaic proceeded, instead of under the auspices of a new union, which the situation really called for, was a concession to the party's prevailing policy of AFL-ism. To be sure, the recruitment of *individual members* to the "United Front Committee" twisted the conception of the united front, as *an alliance of organizations,* out of shape. But the real problem at Passaic was to organize the unorganized, unskilled and low-paid workers neglected by the AFL.

The Fosterite opposition to the recruitment of individual members to this "United Front Committee" showed up the bankruptcy of the ultra-AFL policy in a clear light for the first time. It could have had no other effect than to paralyze the organization of the textile workers in Passaic for fear of committing the sin of "dual unionism"—for which the Fosterites had a real phobia.

The Passaic strike started in the spring of 1926 while we were still in Moscow attending the Sixth Plenum of the Comintern. I don't know or remember any of the immediate circumstances attending it. It is my definite impression, however, that the strike was not precipitated by the party leadership. Rather it was dumped in its lap as a result of Weisbord's successes in organizing the textile workers there.

Gitlow's pretensions about masterminding the Passaic situation, as related in his compendium of distortions and fabrications entitled *I Confess,* should be taken with a grain of salt. All his stories which are not outright inventions are slanted to enlarge his own role in party affairs and to denigrate others—in this case, Weisbord.

The organization of the workers in Passaic and the effective leadership of the strike itself, were pre-eminently Weisbord's work. I had a chance to see that on the ground after we returned from Moscow. I, myself, had nothing to do with the Passaic strike, but I spent a little time there and had a good chance to see Weisbord in action. As a strike leader he was first class, no mistake about it.

It is true that he worked under the close supervision and direction of a party committee in New York appointed by the national party leadership in Chicago. But it's a long way from committee meetings in a closed room, off the scene, to the actual leadership of a strike on the ground.

The full credit for that belongs to Weisbord.

There was an apparent contradiction between the decision of the Sixth Plenum of the CI to confirm Foster's faction—with its pro-AFL policy—in its hegemony over party trade-union work and the concurrent conduct of the Passaic strike under the auspices of a "United Front Committee" outside the AFL. That was not due to factional manipulation. It happened that way because life intruded into the internal affairs of the party.

It happened because Weisbord—a brash young egocentric fresh out of college, and in general an unattractive specimen at close range, but a powerful mass orator and a human dynamo if there ever was one—stirred up a lot of workers and organized them into the "United Front Committee." The sense of strength that came from their organization emboldened them to call a strike without waiting for the sanction of the AFL union. The strike soon exploded into violent clashes with the police which were splashed all over the front pages of the metropolitan press. The Passaic strike was the Number One labor news story for a long time.

This action at Passaic did indeed violate both the letter and the spirit of Fosterite trade-union policy, which the party had followed for years and which had been implicitly supported once again in Moscow. But that didn't change the fact that the party had a big strike on its hands. And the party certainly made the most of its opportunity.

The Passaic strike really put the party on the labor map. In my opinion it deserves a chapter in party history all by itself. It revealed the Communists as the dynamic force in the radical labor movement and the organizing center of the unorganized workers disregarded by the AFL unions—displacing the IWW in this field.

The Passaic strike was well organized and expertly led,

and under all ordinary circumstances should have resulted in a resounding victory. The only trouble was that the bosses were too strong, had too many financial resources and were too determined to prevent the consolidation of a radical union organization. The strikers, isolated in one locality, were simply worn out and starved out and there was nothing to be done about it.

A poor settlement was the best that could be squeezed out of the deadlock. Such experiences were to be repeated many times before the unionization drive in the Thirties gained sufficient scope and power to break the employers' resistance.

The Passaic strike was destined to have an influence on party trade-union policy which in the long run was far more important than the strike itself. The genesis of the drastic change in trade-union policy a few years later can probably be traced to it. There was a belated reaction to the party's attempt to outwit the textile bosses and the AFL fakers by yielding to their principal demands—the elimination of the strike leader, Weisbord.

When it became clear that the strike was sagging, and that the bosses would not make a settlement with the "United Front Committee," negotiations were opened up with the AFL Textile Union. The AFL was invited to take over the organization and try to negotiate a settlement. These accommodating fakers agreed—on one small condition, which turned out to be the same as that of the bosses, namely, that Weisbord, the communist strike leader, should walk the plank.

I do not know who first proposed the acceptance of this monstrous condition. What stands out in my memory most distinctly is the fact that both factions in the party leadership agreed with it, and that there was no conflict on the issue whatever. The fateful decision to sacrifice the strike leader was made unanimously by the party leadership and eventually carried out by the strike committee.

Such questions cannot be viewed abstractly. Perhaps those who, in their experience, have been faced with the agonizing problem of trying to save something from the wreckage of a defeated strike have a right to pass judgment on this decision. Others are hardly qualified. The main consideration in the Passaic situation was the fact that the strike had passed its peak. Real victory was already out of the question and the general feeling was that a poor settlement would be better than none. Other strikes have been settled under even more humiliating conditions. Workers have been compelled time and time again to "agree" to the victimization and blacklisting of the best militants in their ranks as a condition for getting back to work with a scrap of an agreement.

But what stands out in retrospect in the Passaic settlement—and what is painful even now to recall—was the alacrity with which the party leadership agreed to it, the general feeling that it was a clever "maneuver," and its falsely grounded motivations.

The decision to sacrifice the strike leader and to disband the "United Front Committee," implied recognition that the moth-eaten, reactionary, good-for-nothing AFL set-up in the textile industry at that time was the "legitimate" union in that field; and that the "United Front Committee" was only a holding operation and recruiting agency for the AFL union.

All that was wrong from start to finish. The "United Front Committee" should have been regarded as the starting point for an independent union of textile workers. For that it would have been far better to "lose" the strike than to end it with a disgraceful settlement. Independent unionism was the only prescription for the textile industry, and had been ever since the great days of the IWW. "Boring from within" the AFL union in that field, as an exclusive policy, never had a realistic basis.

The Passaic settlement and the motivations for it carried the AFL fetishism of Foster, with which all the others in the party leadership had gone along more or less uneasily, to the point of absurdity. It brought a kickback which was to result, a couple of years later, in a complete reversal of party policy on the trade-union question.

When the Comintern got ready for its wild "left turn" toward "red trade unions" in 1928, Losovsky singled out the Passaic capitulation as the horrible example of the party's policy of "dancing quadrilles around the AFL." The party then embarked on an adventurous course, going to the other extreme of building independent communist unions all up and down the line.

The disastrous results of this experiment with the Trade Union Unity League, as the organizing center of a separate communist labor movement, were in part a punishment for the sin of the Passaic settlement.

The overriding issue in the factional struggle of 1925–1928

JUNE 27, 1955

Gitlow's book *(I Confess)* is very unreliable and it would be risky to take anything he says on trust without corroboration from some other source. He was obviously writing stuff that Hearst would buy—I think it was serialized before book publication in Hearst's magazine—and felt constrained to spice it up and tell more than he knew. He pads out his tendentious report of some facts known to him personally with a lot of hearsay, supposition and invention which he also passes off as facts.

In general, Gitlow didn't know nearly as much of what was really going on in the party as he thinks or pretends he did. The course of events in the internal struggle was decided by others, not by him. Gitlow's role as an independent figure ended with the catastrophic defeat of the "Goose Caucus" in 1923. After that he was first Pepper's tool and then Lovestone's tool. He was there all right, but he didn't see very well, and he doesn't even give an honest report of what he saw.

My article, "The Degeneration of the Communist Party and the New Beginning,"* published in *Fourth International*, Fall, 1954, along with what I said in my *History of American Trotskyism*, states the essential meaning of party developments in the 1925–1928 period, as I saw it. I had intended to let these contributions stand as my report, and say no more about it. Your letters, however, have prodded me to attempt a more detailed exposition of what really went on in those years and I am working on it now.

The second point deals with your reference to the Fifth National Convention of the party, August, 1927. You express interest in the scanty material indicating the first evidence of Lovestone's theory of "American exceptionalism" at this Convention. Fortunately, documentation exists to trace the origin of Lovestone's ideas on this important question even farther back.

---

* Republished as the introduction to this volume.

On page 19 of his *Pages from Party History,* Lovestone quotes the opposition comrades as saying, "Ruthenberg was a leftist. But now that Ruthenberg is gone, the party has gone to the right." That happened to be one of Lovestone's correct statements, not only as to what was said by the "opposition comrades," but also as to what had actually happened.

Very soon after Ruthenberg's death in March, 1927, Lovestone and Wolfe began to give freer expression to their own specific ideology, which was decidedly more to the right than that of Ruthenberg. Some evidence is easily available on this point. At the Sixth Congress of the Comintern in 1928 the delegates of the Foster-Cannon bloc presented a lengthy indictment of the Lovestone administration in a document entitled "The Right Danger in the American Party." I think it is well worth while reading even today.

This statement of the opposition begins with the thesis that *"the present economic depression must inevitably become the forerunner of a deep-going crisis,* even though American capitalism may succeed in postponing its coming with the help of the reserve powers which it still enjoys. This depression cannot be viewed merely as a 'normal' cyclical depression having only slight and passing effects. On the contrary . . . every such cyclical depression intensifies to the highest degree the contradictions of capitalism, undermines deeper the entire structure, eventually leading to deep-going crises." (Emphasis added.)

Considering the fact that the 1929 stock market crash was only 15 months away, this prognostication, drawn up in July, 1928, came pretty close to hitting the nail on the head.

The Foster-Cannon document on the "Right Danger" went on to indict the Lovestoneites as having a different conception of the perspectives of American capitalism on

11 points. It accused them of "following the lead of bourgeois economists in evaluating the present depression only as a 'recession,'" etc. Then it cited the documentary source of this contention: "This tendency of the Lovestone group finds its expression in the original draft of the February [1928] theses, the C.E.C. Plenum resolution of *May, 1927* and in the writings and speeches of comrades Lovestone, Pepper, Wolfe, Nearing, etc., etc." (Emphasis added.)

"The Right Danger in the American Party" was published in *The Militant,* Volume 1, No. 1, November 15, 1928 and in succeeding issues.

The conservative perspective of Lovestone-Wolfe—attuned to the pre-1928 right swing of the Comintern under Bukharin—did contribute to a sharpening of our opposition struggle in 1928. This is manifested by the document cited above. But if the truth of the party history of that time is to be told, it must be said that the right-wing orientation of the Lovestoneites was not the sole, or even the principal issue. The Lovestoneites were perfectly willing to become leftists if the Comintern's change of line required it. This is evidenced in Lovestone's *Pages from Party History* and in their resolution at the 1929 Convention denouncing Bukharin and demanding his removal from the chairmanship of the Comintern.

The one big overriding issue in the factional struggle of 1925–1928 was the question of the party regime, and the maintenance of hard and fast factions in the party after the issues which had brought them into being had been largely outlived.

It was not until we adopted the platform of Trotskyism after the Sixth Congress in 1928, and the Lovestoneites' hands were freed by their own expulsion six months later, that the inherent tendencies of the factions took clearly distinguishable political form. The blind factional struggles in the three years before that were merely *anticipations* of the principled struggles to come.

After 1925: Permanent factionalism

JULY 14, 1955

The three-year period following the 1925 Convention of the Communist Party must present far more difficulties for the inquiring student than all the preceding years put together. The Party entered into a uniquely different situation, without parallel in all the previous history of American radicalism, and the seeds of all the future troubles were sown then. It was a time when factionalism without principle in the internal party conflict prepared and conditioned many people for the eventual abandonment and betrayal of all principle in the broader class struggle of the workers, which the party had been organized to express.

The printed record alone obscures more than it explains about the real causes of the party troubles in these bleak years. The important thing, as I see it, is not the specific disputes and squabbles over party policy, as they are recorded in print, but the general situation in which all the factions were caught—and which none of them fully understood—and their blind, or half-blind, attempts to find a way out.

Prior to that time the factional struggles, with all their excesses and occasional absurdities, had revolved around basic issues which remain fully comprehensible; and settlement of the disputes had been followed by the dissolution of the factions. From the 1925 Convention onward, the evolution of party life took a radically different turn. The old differences had become largely outlived or narrowed down to nuances, but the factions remained and became hardened into permanent formations.

After 1925 the factional gang-fights for power predominated over whatever the rival factions wanted—or thought they wanted—the power for. That, and not the differences over party policy, real or ostensible, was the dominating feature of this period. The details of the various skirmishes are important mainly as they relate to that.

The factional struggle became bankrupt for lack of real political justification for the existence of the factions. For that reason nothing could be solved by the victory of one faction, giving it the opportunity to execute its policy, since the policies of the others were basically the same. There were differences of implicit tendency, to be sure, but further experience was required to show where they might lead. The factions lived on exaggerations and distortions of each others' positions and the anticipation of future differences.

At any rate, the real differences on questions of national policy, in and of themselves, insofar as they were clearly manifested at the time, were not serious enough to justify hard and fast factions. The factions in that period were simply fighting to keep in trim, holding on and waiting, without knowing it, for their futile struggle to fill itself with a serious political content.

The factions were driving blindly toward the two explosions of 1928–1929, when the latent tendencies of each faction were to find expression and formulation in real political issues of international scope, issues destined to bring about a three-way split beyond the possibility of any further reconciliation. But that outcome was not foreseen by any of the participants in the futile struggles of those days. These struggles, for all their intensity and fury, were merely anticipations of a future conflict over far more serious questions.

I began to recognize the bankruptcy of factional struggle without a clearly defined principled basis as early as 1925, and began to look for a way out of it. That still did not go to the root of the problem—the basic causes out of which the unprincipled factionalism had flourished—but it was a step forward. It set me somewhat apart from the central leaders of both factions, and was a handicap in the immediate conflict. Blind factionalists have more zeal than those who reflect too much. But the reflections of 1925 eventually helped me to find my way to higher ground.

The experiences of the conflict in the Foster-Cannon caucus at the 1925 Convention had revealed the Fosterites' basic conception of the faction as that of a permanent gang, claiming prior loyalty of its members in a fight for supremacy and the extermination of the opposing faction. I couldn't go along with that, and the disagreement brought us to a parting of the ways.

The definitive split of the Foster-Cannon faction took place, not at the 1925 Convention, where the first big conflict over the "Comintern cable" arose, but some weeks later, after numerous attempts to patch up the rift. When Foster and Bittelman insisted on their conception of the faction, and tried to press me into line for the sake of factional loyalty, I, and others of the same mind, had no choice but to break with them.

It was a deep split; the cadres of the faction divided right down the middle along the same lines as the division in the caucus at the Convention. Prominent in support of my position were the following: William F. Dunne, and with him the whole local leadership of the Minnesota movement; Arne Swabeck and Martin Abern in Chicago; the principal leaders of the youth organization—Shachtman, Williamson, Schneiderman and several others who later became prominent in the party: Hathaway, Tom O'Flaherty, Gomez; Fisher and his group in the South Slavic Federation; Bud Reynolds of Detroit; Gebert, the Pole, later to become District Organizer in Detroit before his departure for Poland; and several District Organizers of the party.

The conception of the central leaders of the Ruthenberg-Lovestone faction was basically the same as Foster's, as was soon demonstrated in a brief and futile experiment in cooperation with them. I didn't agree with the claim of either group to party domination and could see no solution of the party conflict along that line. This left no room for me in either faction as a full-time, all-out participant, which is the only way I can function anywhere.

The simple fact of the matter, as I came to see it in 1925, was that the party crisis could not be solved by the victory of one faction over the other. Each was weak where the other was strong. The two groups supplemented each other and were necessary to each other and to the party.

While I considered that the Foster group as a whole was more proletarian, nearer to the workers and for that reason the "better" group, I had begun to recognize all too clearly its trade-union one-sidedness. In this respect I was nearer to the Ruthenberg-Lovestone group. But the latter, although more "political" than the Fosterite trade unionists, was too intellectualistic to suit me. I thought that the Ruthenberg-Lovestone group by itself could not lead the party and build it as a genuine workers' organization, and nothing ever happened in the ensuing years to change that opinion.

The cadres of both groups were too strong numerically, and had too many talented people, to be eliminated from the party leadership. The two groups, united and working together, would have been many times stronger and more effective than either one alone. We thought the time had come to move toward the liquidation of the factions and the unification of the party under a collective leadership.

In relating this I do not mean to intimate that I had suddenly become a pacifist in internal party affairs. I was as much a factionalist as the others, when factional struggle was the order of the day, and I have never seen any reason to deny it or apologize for it. Those pious souls who were not factionalists didn't count in the days when the party life was dominated by internal struggle, and have nothing to report. It is true that factionalism can be carried to extremes and become a disease—as was the case in the CP after 1925. But professional abstainers, as is always the case, only made the game easier for the others who were not restrained by qualms and scruples.

I was not against factions when there was something serious to fight about. But I was already then dead set against the idea of *permanent* factions, after the issues which had brought them about had been decided or outlived. I never got so deeply involved in any factional struggle as to permit it to become an end in itself. In this I was perhaps different from most of the other factional leaders, and it eventually led me on a far different path.

This was a deliberate policy on my part; the result of much reflection on the whole problem of the party and the revolution. I was determined above all not to forget what I had started out to fight for, and this basic motivation sustained me in that dark, unhappy time. I felt that I had not committed myself in early youth to the struggle for the socialist reorganization of society in order to settle for membership in a permanent faction, to say nothing of a factional gang. I tried always to keep an over-all party point of view and to see the party always as a part of the working class.

And by and large I succeeded, although it was not easy in the atmosphere of that time. Many good militants succumbed to factionalism and lost their bearings altogether. It is only a short step from cynicism to renegacy. Betrayal of principle in little things easily leads to betrayal in bigger things. I have lived to see many who were first-class revolutionists in the early days turn into traitors to the working class. Some even became professional informers against former comrades. Cynical factionalism was the starting point of this moral and political degeneration.

We could see that the factional struggle was degenerating into a gang fight, and we set out to resist it. Being serious about it, we did not disperse our forces and hope for luck. On the contrary, we promptly organized a "third group" to fight for unity and the liquidation of all factions. This may appear as a quixotic enterprise—and so it turned out to be—but it took a long struggle for us to prove it to ourselves.

The international factor, which had frustrated all our efforts, eventually came to our aid and showed us a new road. When I got access to the enlightening documents of Trotsky in 1928, I began to fit the American troubles into their international framework. But that came only after three years of fighting in the dark, on purely national grounds.

No one can fight in the dark without stumbling now and then. We did our share of that, and I am far from contending that every move we made was correct. No political course can be correct when its basic premise is wrong. Our premise was that our party troubles were a purely American affair and that they could somehow be straightened out with the help of the Comintern, particularly of the Russian leaders, as had been done in earlier difficulties.

That was wrong on both counts. The objective situation in the country was against us, and we all contributed our own faults of ignorance and inadequacy to the bedevilment of the party situation. But the chief source of our difficulties this time was the degeneration of the Russian Communist Party and the Comintern; and the chief mischief-makers in our party, as in every other party of the Comintern, were these same people whom we trustingly looked to for help and guidance.

It took me a long time to get that straight in my head. In the meantime I fumbled and stumbled in the dark like all the others. My basic approach to the problem was different, however, and it eventually led me to an understanding of the puzzle and a drastic new orientation.

In the objective circumstances of the time, with the booming prosperity of the late Twenties sapping the foundations of radicalism, with the trade-union movement stagnating and declining, feverish activity in the factional struggle in the party became for many a substitute for participation in the class struggle of the workers against the bourgeoisie. This sickness particularly infected those who were most isolated from the daily life of the workers. They did not take kindly to our formula for party peace and party unity through the liquidation of the factions. They didn't understand it, and above all they didn't believe in it.

In the underworld of present-day society, with which I

have had contact at various times in jail and prison, there is a widespread sentiment that there is no such thing as an honest man who is also intelligent. The human race is made up of honest suckers and smart crooks, and that's all there is to it; the smartest crooks are those who pretend to be honest, the confidence men. Professional factionalism, unrelated to the living issues of the class struggle of the workers, is also a sort of underworld, and the psychology of its practitioners approaches that of the other underworld.

In the eyes of such people, for whom the internal struggle of the Communist Party had become the breath of life, an end in itself, anyone who proposed peace and unity was either a well-meaning fool or a hypocrite with an axe to grind. In our case the first possibility was rejected out of hand by the esteemed colleagues with whom we had been associated in numerous struggles, and that left only the second. A third possible reason or motivation for our position was excluded.

Our formula for party unity and party peace was not taken at face value by the leaders of the Foster-Bittelman and Ruthenberg-Lovestone groups. We were regarded as trouble-making anarchists, violating the rules of the game by forming a "third group" when the rules called for two and only two.

The Fosterites waged an especially vicious campaign against me as a "traitor," as if I had been born into this world as a member of a family and clan and was required by blood relationship to have no truck with the feuding opponents on the other side of the mountain. That was a complete misunderstanding on their part; they had my birth certificate all mixed up.

As for the Lovestoneites, they even introduced motions in the party branches specifically condemning the formation of a "third group." For them, two groups belonged to the accepted order of things; a third group was unnatural. This dictum, however, was not binding on us for the simple reason that we did not accept it.

It was evident from the start that our program could not be achieved by persuasion. Some force and pressure would be required, and this could be effectively asserted only by an organized independent group. We set out to build such a group as a balance of power, and thus to prevent either of the major factions from monopolizing party control.

Despite the all-consuming factionalism of the top and secondary leaders, our stand for unity undoubtedly reflected a wide sentiment in the ranks of both factions. Many of the rank and file comrades were sick of the senseless internal struggle and eager for unity and all-around cooperation in constructive party work. This was strikingly demonstrated when Weinstone, secretary of the New York District, and a group around him, came out for the same position in 1926.

That broke up the Ruthenberg "majority," as our earlier revolt had broken up Foster's. Weinstone soon came to an agreement with us, and the new combination constituted a balance of power grouping in the leadership. It didn't stop the factional struggle—far from it—but it did prevent the monopolistic domination of the party by one faction and the exclusion of the other, and created conditions in the party for the leading activists in all factions to function freely in party work.

I had been closely associated with Weinstone in the old struggle for the legalization of the party—1921–1923—and knew him fairly well. We always got along well together and had remained friendly to each other, even though we were in opposing camps in the new factional line-up and struggle which began in 1923. He had gone along with the Ruthenberg-Pepper-Lovestone faction and was its outstanding representative in New York while the national center was located in Chicago.

In the course of the new developments I came to know Weinstone better and to form a more definitive judgment of him. He was one of that outstanding trio—Lovestone, Weinstone and Wolfe—who were known among us as the "City College boys." They were still in school when they were attracted to the left-wing movement in the upsurge following the Russian Revolution, but they were thrust forward in the movement by their exceptional qualities and their educational advantages.

They came into prominent positions of leadership without having had any previous experience with the workers in the daily class struggle. All three of them bore the mark of this gap in their education, and Lovestone and Wolfe never showed any disposition to overcome it. They always impressed me as aliens, with a purely intellectualistic interest in the workers' movement. Weinstone had at least a feeling for the workers, although in the time that I knew him, he never seemed to be really at home with them.

All three were articulate, Wolfe being the best and most prolific writer and Weinstone the most gifted speaker among them. Lovestone, who had indifferent talents both as writer and speaker, was the strongest personality of the three, the one who made by far the deepest impression on the movement at all times, and most times to its detriment.

It was everybody's opinion that Lovestone was unscrupulous in his ceaseless machinations and intrigues; and in my opinion everybody was right on that point, although the word "unscrupulous" somehow or other seems to be too mild a word to describe his operations. Lovestone was downright crooked, like Foster—but in a different way. Foster was in and of the workers' movement and had a sense of responsibility to it; and he could be moderately honest when there was no need to cheat or lie. Foster's crookedness was purposeful and utilitarian, nonchalantly resorted to in a pinch to serve an end. Lovestone, the sinister stranger in our midst, seemed to practice skulduggery maliciously, for its own sake.

It was a queer twist of fate that brought such a perverse character into a movement dedicated to the service of the noblest ideal of human relationships. Never was a man more destructively alien to the cause in which he sought a career; he was like an anarchistic cancer cell running wild in the party organism. The party has meaning and justification only as the conscious expression of the austere process of history in which the working class strives for emancipation, with all the strict moral obligations such a mission imposes on its members. But Lovestone seemed to see the party as an object of manipulation in a personal game he was playing, with an unnatural instinct to foul things up.

In this game, which he played with an almost pathological frenzy, he was not restrained by any recognized norms of conduct in human relations, to say nothing of the effects his methods might have on the morale and solidarity of the workers' movement. For him the class struggle of the workers, with its awesome significance for the future of the human race, was at best an intellectual concept; the factional struggle for "control" of the party was the real thing, the real stuff of life. His chief enemy was always the factional opponent in the party rather than the capitalist class and the system of exploitation they represent.

Lovestone's factional method and practice were systematic miseducation of the party; whispered gossip to set comrades against each other; misrepresentation and distortion of opponents' positions; unrestrained demagogy and incitement of factional supporters until they didn't know whether they were coming or going. He had other tricks, but they were all on the same order.

The party leaders' opinions of each other in those days varied widely and were not always complimentary; but at bottom, despite the bitterness of the conflicts, I think they respected each other as comrades in a common cause, in spite of all. Lovestone, however, was *distrusted* and his devotion to the cause was widely doubted. In intimate circles Foster remarked more than once that if Lovestone were not a Jew, he would be the most likely candidate for leadership of a fascist movement. That was a fairly common opinion.

Wolfe, better educated and probably more intelligent than Lovestone, but weaker, was Lovestone's first assistant and supporter in all his devious maneuvers. He was different from Lovestone mainly in his less passionate concentration on the intrigues of the moment and less desperate concern about the outcome.

A prime example of Lovestone's factional method is his 1929 pamphlet, *Pages from Party History*. He makes an impressive "case" against his factional opponents by quoting, with a liberal admixture of falsification, only that which is compromising to them and leaving out entirely a still more impressive documentation which he could have cited against himself. Wolfe's factional writing was on the same order, crooked all the way through. His 1929 pamphlet against "Trotskyism" shows Wolfe for what he is worth. These two people in particular had little or nothing to learn from Stalin. In their practices in the factional struggles they were Stalinists before Stalin's own method was fully disclosed to the Americans.

Weinstone was different in many ways. He was not as shrewd and cunning, and he lacked Lovestone's driving will. But he was more honest than Lovestone and Wolfe, more party-minded, and in those days he was undoubtedly devoted to the cause of communism. Also, in my opinion, Weinstone was more broadly intelligent, more flexible and objective in his thinking, than any of the other leaders of the Ruthenberg-Lovestone group.

Weinstone never got completely swamped in the factional struggle. That was the starting point for his independent course in 1926–1927. He recognized the merits of the comrades in the other camp. More clearly than others in his group, he saw the blind alley into which the factional struggle had entered at that time, and was honestly seeking to find a way out in the higher interest of the party.

Weinstone was perhaps dazzled for a time by the phony brilliance of Pepper, but he was never a personal follower of either Ruthenberg or Lovestone. His criticisms of both, in numerous conversations with me, were penetrating and objective; at least so they seemed to me. He was revolted by the Ruthenbergian claim to party "hegemony"—they actually proposed the formula of "unity of the party under the hegemony of the Ruthenberg group"! That sounded something like the unity of colonies in an imperialist empire, and that is really the way it was meant. Weinstone feared, with good reason, that encouragement of such an unrealistic and untenable pretension would lead to a party stalemate which could only culminate in a split.

Already in 1926, before the death of Ruthenberg, Weinstone began to take a stand within the faction for unity, through the dissolution of the factions and the establishment of a "collective leadership" of the most capable and influential people, without factional barriers to their free collaboration. This naturally brought him into consultation and eventually into close collaboration with us, since we had evolved the same position out of our own experiences in the Foster faction.

The Lovestoneites, who proceeded from the *a priori* judgment that everything that happens is the result of a conspiracy, and that nothing is ever done through good will and the exercise of independent intelligence, were dead sure that I had cooked up Weinstone's defection and talked him into his factional heresy. That's the way Gitlow tells it in his sorry memoirs; but that's not the way I remember it.

When Weinstone became secretary of the New York District, as a result of the overturn manipulated by the Comintern in 1925, the bigger half of the effective militants in the New York District, who only yesterday had been the duly elected majority, became an artificially created minority. Weinstone recognized their value as party workers and deliberately instituted a policy in the New York District, on his own account, of conciliation and cooperation.

Most of the New York Fosterites, after a period of suspicious reservation, responded to Weinstone's conciliatory policy, and a considerable measure of cooperation with them in party work was effected. This favorable result of local experience induced Weinstone to extend his thoughts to the party problem on a national scale. That soon brought him to virtually the same position that we had worked out in Chicago.

I doubt whether I personally had much to do with shaping his thoughts along this line—at least in the early stage. The fact that he came to substantially the same position that we had already worked out gave us a certain reassurance that we had sized things up correctly; and it naturally followed that we came into closer and closer relations with Weinstone.

We came to a definite agreement to work together already before the sudden and unexpected death of Ruthenberg in March 1927. We often speculated how things might have worked out if Ruthenberg had lived. Ruthenberg was a factionalist like the rest, but he was not so insane about it as Lovestone was. He was far more constructive and responsible, more concerned for the general welfare of the party and for his own position as a leader of a party rather than of a fragmented assembly of factions. Moreover, he was far more popular and influential, more respected in the party ranks, and strong enough to veto Lovestone's factional excesses if he wanted to.

It is quite possible that an uneasy peace, gradually leading to the dissolution of factions, might have been worked out with him. His sudden death in March 1927 put a stop to all such possibilities. The Ruthenberg faction then became the Lovestone faction, and the internal party situation changed for the worse accordingly.

International Labor Defense

APRIL 17, 1958

I received your letters about the ILD.

The subject is indeed close to my heart. It is one of the purest and cleanest memories of my time in the Communist Party of the Twenties, a memory of honest work and solid achievement for solidarity in the old IWW spirit.

It is really an interesting and, I think, important story of the projection of Bill Haywood's influence—through me and my associates, Rose Karsner, Tom O'Flaherty, Max Shachtman and Martin Abern—into the movement from which he was exiled, an influence for simple honesty and good will and genuine non-partisan solidarity toward all the prisoners of the class war in American prisons. You uncovered the starting point of the ILD when you noticed Bill's reference in the *Labor Defender,* June, 1926, to his talks with me in Moscow in 1925. I will explain how that came about in another letter.

I am somewhat disturbed that the bulk of your questions refer to possible factional implications and maneuvers in setting up and operating the ILD. All that was secondary. The real story of the ILD is the story of the work it did, the campaigns it organized, the scrupulous handling and public accounting of its funds, and the broad, out-going non-partisan spirit in which all its activities were conducted. Strange as it may seem, not the least reason why this was possible was that I was identified with a party faction! Our faction served the ILD as a border guard to keep factional disruption out of the ILD, or, in any case, to reduce it to a minimum. Factionalism, which was devouring the party in those years, affected the ILD less than any other field.

FEBRUARY 6, 1959

Professional anti-communists always proceed from the premise of that man in the Bible who did not believe that any good thing could come out of Nazareth. Or, to paraphrase the modern expression of confidence men, they never give a communist an even break. For example, one of them once described my motives in helping the

IWW prisoners through the ILD as "not altogether philanthropic," because, as a communist, I was serving the interests of the party.

The description is inaccurate. My motives were not "philanthropic" at all. I really believed in the principle of solidarity with all class war prisoners—the tradition in which I had been brought up in the radical movement of the earlier days. To be sure, I was an undisguised communist, and I thought and said that the honest work of solidarity practiced by the ILD would bring, at least indirectly, some credit to the Communist Party. But don't people who represent all kinds of causes and organizations do what they consider their good works with this double motivation?

The IWW in the old days supported strikes of the rival AFL and supported other labor defense cases. They were completely honest about it, but at the same time they expected that the IWW would gain credit among radical workers for this consistent policy of solidarity. And that is what really happened. Catholic nuns who dedicate their entire lives to the service of sick people in hospitals, undoubtedly feel that they are doing the Lord's work. But they also hope and expect that the church will gain credit from their dedicated work. And that's the way it works out too. When a Rockefeller or a Dubinsky provides funds for some community service, don't they think at the same time—just a little bit—that it may help "public relations" of the Standard Oil Company or the Dubinsky union?

I don't like the implication of a double standard for communists and others. But that hypocritical moralism runs like a greasy thread through all anti-communist writings.

The ILD, under my administration, strictly limited its expenditures to labor defense work. I never at any time permitted any encroachments on this principle. I was quite conscious in the strict enforcement of this policy and had a double reason for it. In the first place, I believed in scrupulous honesty in the handling of labor defense funds. In the second place, I was deliberately concerned about my reputation in radical circles generally. That is why, during my administration, the ILD published in the *Labor Defender* a monthly accounting of all contributions by the serial numbers of the receipts, so that they could be subjected to a public check. In addition, the *Labor Defender* published an annual report of receipts and expenditures by a Certified Public Accountant.

When the Sacco-Vanzetti Committee in Boston raised a question about funds for the Sacco-Vanzetti case being collected by the ILD, I promptly published in the January 1927 *Labor Defender* a statement of funds received, with the sources indicated, which had been earmarked for this purpose, together with a photostat of checks showing that the full amount had been forwarded to the Sacco-Vanzetti Defense Committee. At the same time, I invited the Sacco-Vanzetti Defense Committee to appoint a representative and an accountant to examine our books to check my report.

The work of the ILD, and its general reputation, greatly benefited from the fact that I was not only a true believer in labor solidarity and financial responsibility in labor defense matters, but also a politician and a factionalist able to defend the autonomy of the ILD in these respects.

FEBRUARY 10, 1959

As I have told you before, it has long been on my conscience to do justice to the memory of Bill Haywood in connection with the origination of the ILD and the general pattern of its work of solidarity in the early days. In assembling material for a collection of my speeches to be published in book form, we found that I had spoken about this very subject in a published speech ten years ago, which I had forgotten all about. In a speech advocating solidarity in the defense of the Communist Party leaders, despite all political differences with them, I referred to the tradition of the ILD in this respect and told about Bill Haywood's part in inspiring it. The speech, titled *Trial of the Stalinist Leaders,* was given in New York on February 6, 1949 and was published in *The Militant* on February 14, 1949, where it can be checked.* After reciting the tradition of labor solidarity in defense cases from the Moyer-Haywood case onward, I said:

"The Communist Party itself was once the exponent of this proud tradition of solidarity. The International Labor Defense, which was formed in 1925 under the direct inspiration of the Communist Party, was specifically dedicated to the principle of nonpartisan labor defense, to the defense of any member of the working class movement, regardless of his views, who suffered persecution by the capitalist courts because of his activities or his opinions.

"I can speak with authority about that because I participated in the planning of the ILD, and was the National Secretary from its inception until we were thrown out of the Communist Party in 1928. The International Labor Defense was really 'born in Moscow'; that I must admit, although it was strictly an American institution in its methods and practices. The ILD was born in Moscow in discussion with Bill Haywood. The old fighter, who was exiled from America with a 20-year sentence hanging over him,

---

* See: Cannon, *Speeches for Socialism* (Pathfinder Press, 1971), pp. 139–49 [2008 printing].

was deeply concerned about the persecution of workers in America. He wanted to have something done for the almost forgotten men lying in jail all over the country.

"There were over 100 men—labor organizers, strike leaders and radicals in prisons at that time in the United States—IWW's, anarchists, Mooney and Billings, Sacco and Vanzetti, McNamara and Schmidt, the Centralia prisoners, etc. In discussions there in Moscow in 1925 we worked out the plan and conception of the International Labor Defense as a non-partisan body which would defend any member of the working class movement, regardless of his opinion or affiliation, if he came under persecution by capitalist law.

"I never will forget those meetings with Bill Haywood. When we completed the plans which were later to become reality in the formation of the ILD; and when I promised him that I would come back to America and see to it that the plans did not remain on paper; that we would really go to work in earnest and come to the aid of the men forgotten in prisons—the old lion's eyes—his one eye, rather—flashed with the old fire. He said, 'I wish I could go back to give a hand in that job.' He couldn't come back because he was an outlaw in the United States, not for any crime he had committed but for all the good things he had done for the American working class. Up to the end of his life he continued to be an active participant in the work of the ILD by correspondence.

"The plans for the International Labor Defense as a non-partisan defense organization, made there in Bill Haywood's room in Moscow, were carried out in practice during its first years. There were 106 class war prisoners in the United States—scores of IWW members railroaded in California, Kansas, Utah and other states under the criminal syndicalist laws. We located a couple of obscure anarchists in prison in Rhode Island; a group of AFL coal miners in West Virginia; two labor organizers in Thomaston, Maine—besides the more prominent and better known prisoners mentioned before. They added up to 106 people in prison in this land of the free at that time for activities in the labor movement. They were not criminals at all, but strike leaders, organizers, agitators, dissenters—our own kind of people. Not one of these 106 prisoners was a member of the Communist Party! But the ILD defended and helped them all.

"The ILD adopted as its policy to remember them all and raise money for them. We created a fund so that $5 was sent every month to each of the 106 class war prisoners. Every Christmas time we raised a special fund for their families. The Centralia IWW group, almost forgotten for years, were remembered, publicity was given their case and efforts made to help them. The same with all the old half-forgotten cases. The ILD was the organizing center of the great world-wide movement of protest for the two anarchists, Sacco and Vanzetti. All this work of solidarity had the backing and support of the Communist Party, but that was before it became completely Stalinized and expelled the honest revolutionaries.

"The principle of the International Labor Defense, which made it so popular and so dear to the militants, was nonpartisan defense without political discrimination. The principle was solidarity. When you consider all this and compare it with the later practices of the Stalinists; when you recall what has happened in the last 20-odd years, you must say that the Stalinists have done more than any others to dishonor this tradition of solidarity. They have done more than any others to disrupt unity for defense against the class enemy.

"That terrible corruption of disunity in the face of the class enemy has penetrated other sections of the labor movement too. The Social Democrats do a great deal of pious moralizing about the Stalinists, but their conduct isn't much better, if any. For the greater part, they make no protest against the persecution of the Stalinists. The labor officials, both of the CIO and AFL, stand aside, and many even support the prosecution.

"They think there is no need to worry about the Smith Act; that it is only for Stalinists. That is what the Stalinists thought when we were on trial seven years ago—that this evil and unconstitutional law is only for Trotskyists. I heard in San Francisco that a Stalinist party speaker, harassed by an interrogator as to the relation between their trial and ours, said, 'This whole trial is a mistake and a misunderstanding. The Smith Act was meant for the Trotskyists.' But the Smith Act chickens came home to roost for the Stalinists, and the same thing can happen to others too.

"If the Stalinists are convicted, establishing another precedent to buttress the precedent of our case, the same law can be invoked against other political organizations, against college professors, and even preachers who happen to have opinions contrary to those of the ruling powers, and have the courage to express them. It is a great error, a terrible error, to neglect this trial and refuse to protest; an error for which we will all have to pay—they and we, and all of us, all who aspire by whatever means, or by whatever program or doctrine, toward a better and freer world through the unity and solidarity of the workers. We will all have to pay if the federal prosecutor wins this case and makes it stick with the support of public opinion. That is why we would like to see every effort made, even now while the trial is going on, to reverse the present trend, to overcome the passivity and indifference.

"It is, of course, utopian to hope or expect that a great united movement, cooperating loyally as in the old days, can be formed with the Stalinists. The Stalinists cannot cooperate loyally with anyone. We offered them a united front. They refused it. Even now, when the witch-hunt and loyalty purges are directed against them, they refuse to say one word in defense of James Kutcher, the legless veteran who was removed from his Veterans Administration job in New Jersey because of his political opinions as a member of the Socialist Workers Party.*

"Because of the attitude of the Stalinists, as well as for other considerations, it would be utopian to hope for an all-inclusive united front. But the trade unions and anti-Stalinist political organizations should join together, for their own reasons, and in their own interest, to protest this prosecution. We would join and give our support to such an effort. But in any case, whether it can be done cooperatively or separately, all should raise their voices in protest against the political trial going on in Foley Square. Not for the sake of the Stalinist gang, but for the sake of free speech, for those democratic rights which the labor movement has dearly won and badly needs for its informed and conscious struggle to reach higher ground."

1927: From Ruthenberg to Lovestone

JULY 22, 1955

The sudden death of Ruthenberg in March 1927 upset the shaky equilibrium in the party, and called forth the second direct intervention of the Comintern to thwart the

---

* See: James Kutcher, *The Case of the Legless Veteran* (Pathfinder Press, 1973).

will of the party majority and to determine the composition of the party leadership over its head.

Ruthenberg had always played a big role in the party, and he had seemed to be perennially established in the office of General Secretary. His death in the prime of his life really shook things up.

The two "big names" in the party at that time were those of Foster and Ruthenberg, and the prestige of both had been well earned by their previous record of constructive activity.

Foster was renowned for his work as organizer and leader of the great steel strike of 1919 and his subsequent achievements as organizer of the TUEL; Ruthenberg for his heroic fight against the war and his outstanding activity as a pioneer communist, and also for his prison terms, bravely borne. The party members were well aware of the value of their public reputations and, by common consent, the two men held positions of special eminence as party leaders and public spokesmen for that reason. Factional activity had added nothing to the prestige of the two most popular leaders; if anything, it had somewhat tarnished it.

Of all the leading people in his faction, Ruthenberg had by far the greatest respect and personal influence in the party ranks. The faction was demonstratively called the "Ruthenberg Group" in order to capitalize on his prestige. But the Ruthenberg group, *with* Ruthenberg, was a minority in the party, as the hard-fought elections to the 1925 Convention had clearly demonstrated.

At the time of the 1925 Convention the "cable from Moscow," as interpreted by the Comintern representative on the ground, had abruptly turned this minority into a majority and left the party members, who had innocently voted for their choice of delegates to the party convention, looking like fools who had mistakenly thought they had some rights and prerogatives in the matter of electing the party leadership.

Another "cable from Moscow" worked the same miracle of turning a minority into a majority in 1927. Supplementary decisions along the same line gradually bludgeoned the party members into acquiescence and reduced their democratic powers to a fiction. The role of the Comintern in the affairs of the American Communist Party was transformed from that of a friendly influence in matters of policy into that of a direct, brutal arbiter in organizational questions, including the most important question, the selection of the leadership.

Thereafter, the party retained only the dubious right to go through the motions; the decisions were made in Moscow. The process of transforming the party from a self-governing, democratic organization into a puppet of the Kremlin, which had been started in 1925, was advanced another big stage toward completion in 1927. That is the essential meaning of this year in party history. Everything else is secondary and incidental.

The shaky formal "majority" of the Ruthenberg group had been upset even before Ruthenberg died by the defection of committee members Weinstone and Ballam. Then came the sudden death of Ruthenberg, to deprive the faction of its most influential personality and its strongest claim to the confidence of the party ranks. How then could such an attenuated minority faction, *without* Ruthenberg, hope to "control" the party and avoid coming to agreement for cooperation with the other groups who constituted the majority in the Central Executive Committee?

We took it for granted that it couldn't be done, and proceeded on the assumption that a rearrangement of the leading staff had to follow as a matter of course. But it didn't work out that way. The cards were stacked for a different outcome, and we were defeated before we started. All we had on our side were the rules of arithmetic, the constitutional rights of the majority of the Central Executive Committee, the logic of the situation, and the undoubted support of the majority of the party at the time. All that was not enough.

On his side, Lovestone had his own driving frenzy to seize control of the party, regardless of the will of the majority, and—the support of Moscow. These proved to be the ace cards in the game that was drawn out over a period of six months to its foreordained conclusion. Lovestone came out of the skirmish of 1927 with the "majority"—given to him by the Comintern—and held it until the same supreme authority decided to take it away from him two years later.

Lovestone took the first trick by having himself appointed by the Political Committee to the post of General Secretary, vacated by Ruthenberg's death. Constitutionally, this was out of order. The right to appoint party officers belonged to the full Plenum of the Central Executive Committee, the Political Committee being merely a subcommittee of that body.

We demanded the immediate calling of a full Plenum to deal with all the problems arising from Ruthenberg's death, including the appointment of his successor in the post of party secretary. Weinstone and I had come to agreement with Foster that Weinstone should become the new party secretary; and since we represented a majority of the Plenum, we expected to execute the decision.

Then came trick number two for Lovestone. The Comintern cabled its decision that the Plenum could meet all right, but it could not make any binding decisions on organizational questions pending a consideration of the whole matter in Moscow. All the leading representatives of the factions were to come to Moscow for that purpose. Since the chief "organizational questions" were the reorganization of the Political Committee along the lines of the Plenum majority, and the appointment of a new party secretary, this cable of the Comintern, ostensibly withholding judgment, actually left Lovestone in control at both points—*de facto* if not *de jure*.

The meeting of the sovereign Plenum of the Communist Party of the United States, forbidden in advance to make any binding decisions, was made even more farcical by the failure of Lovestone to show up for the second session. He and Gitlow had abruptly departed for Moscow, where the decisions were to be made, without so much as a by-your-leave or goodbye to the elected leading body of the party to which they, like all other party members, were presumably—or so it said in the constitution—subordinate.

In a moderately healthy, self-governing party, involved in the class struggle in its own country and functioning under its own power, such reckless contempt for its own leading body would no doubt be sufficient to discredit its author and bring prompt condemnation from the party ranks. Nothing like that happened in reaction to the hooligan conduct of Lovestone on this occasion. The majority of the Plenum blew up in anger. Foster fussed and fumed and gave vent to his indignation in unparliamentary language. But there was nothing that we, the duly elected majority, could do about it; we could not make any "binding decisions" on any question—the Comintern cable had forbidden that.

Since 1925 the party had gradually been acquiescing

in the blotting out of its normal rights as a self-governing organization until it had already lost sight of these rights. Lovestone's scandalous action on this occasion only underscored the real status of the party in relation to the Moscow overlords.

There was nothing to do but head for Moscow once again in order to try to straighten out another supposed "misunderstanding." Viewed retrospectively, our credulity in those days passeth all understanding, and it gives me a sticky feeling to recall it. I feel a bit shy about admitting it even now, after the lapse of so many years and the occurrence of so many more important things, but Weinstone and I went to Moscow together full of confidence that our program for the rearrangement of the leadership on a collective basis, and the liquidation of the old factions, would receive the support of the Comintern.

Since neither of the other factions claiming the right to control and "hegemony" in the leadership could muster a majority in the Central Executive Committee, while we constituted a definite balance of power, we believed that the other factions would be compelled to acquiesce in our program, at least for the next period.

We ourselves did not aim at organizational control of the party, either as a separate faction or in combination with one of the others. Our aim was to loosen up all the factional alignments and create conditions in the leading committee where each individual would be free to take a position objectively, on the merits of any political question which might come up, without regard to previous factional alignments.

In discussion among ourselves, and in our general propaganda in the party, we were beginning to emphasize the idea that political questions should take precedence over organizational considerations, including even party "control." There were no irreconcilable political differences between the factions at the moment. That seemed to favor our program for the assimilation of the leading elements of each faction in a collective leading body. We believed that the subordination of political questions to organizational considerations of faction control—a state of affairs already prevailing to a considerable extent—could only miseducate and corrupt the party membership as well as the leadership.

For my part, I was just then beginning to assimilate with full understanding, and to take in dead earnest, the Leninist principle that important political considerations should always come first. That marked the beginning of a reorientation which was eventually to lead me out of the factional jungle of that time onto the high road of principled politics. I did not see how the Comintern, which I still regarded as the embodied representative of the principles of Lenin, could fail to support our stand.

Sharp practices in many factional struggles have given rise to the skeptical saying: "When one accepts a position 'in principle' it means that he rejects it in practice." That is not always true, but that is what we got in Moscow in 1927—an acceptance of our program "in principle," with supplementary statements to vitiate it. We found agreement on all sides that the factions should be liquidated and the leadership unified. But this was followed by the intimation in the written decision that the Lovestoneites should have "hegemony" in the unification—which was the surest way to guarantee that the "unification" would be a farcical cover for factional domination.

The official decision condemned "the sharpening of the factional struggle"—which the Lovestoneites had caused by their conduct at the party Plenum—but blamed the "National Committee of the Opposition Bloc" for this "sharpening." The decision incorporated our formula that "the previous political and trade union differences have almost disappeared." Then it went on to condemn "factionalism without political differences as the worst offense against the party"—which was precisely what the Lovestoneites' attempt to seize party control consisted of—but blamed this "offense" on the "Opposition Bloc." The Comintern decision on the "American Question" in 1927 is a real study in casuistry—for those who may be interested in that black art.

There was nothing clear-cut and straightforward in the Comintern decision this time, as had been the case in earlier times over disputed political questions. The moderation of factional struggle, party peace, unity and cooperation were emphasized. But the official decision was slanted to imply—without anywhere clearly stating—that the Lovestone faction was favored in the coming election of delegates to the party convention. That made certain that there would be no unity and cooperation, but a factional gang-fight for control of the convention, and a factional regime in the party afterward if the Lovestoneites gained a majority.

We knew that we had won no victory at Moscow in 1927. But the acceptance of our "general principles" encouraged us to continue the fight; we knew that these general principles did not have a dog's chance in the party if the Lovestone faction established itself in control with a formal majority at the Convention.

It was only then, in the course of the discussion in Moscow and after the formal decision, that the bloc of Weinstone-Cannon with Foster was formally cemented to put up a joint slate in the pre-convention struggle for delegates to the pending party convention. Previously there had been only an agreement at the Plenum to vote for Weinstone as party secretary. Now we agreed to unite our forces in the pre-convention fight to prevent the Lovestoneites from gaining factional control.

That six-months period, from the death of Ruthenberg to the party convention at the end of August, was an eye-opener to me in two respects. First, clearly apparent changes had taken place in the party which already then aroused in me the gravest misgivings for the future. The party had started out as a body of independent-minded rebels, regulating its internal affairs and selecting its own leaders in an honest, free-and-easy democracy. That had been one of its strongest attractions.

But by 1927 the Communist Party was no longer its original self. Its membership was visibly changing into a passive crowd, subservient to authority and subject to manipulation by the crudest demagogy. This period showed, more clearly than I had realized before, the extent to which the independent influence of the national party leaders, as such, had been whittled down and subordinated to the overriding authority of Moscow. Many party members had begun to look to Moscow, not only for decisions on policy, but even for suggestions as to which national leader or set of leaders they should vote for.

Secondly, in 1927 Lovestone became Lovestone. That, in itself, was an event boding no good for the party.

Previously Lovestone had worked under cover of Ruthenberg, adapting himself accordingly and buying the favor, or at least the toleration, of the party on Ruthenberg's credit. In those days, even the central leaders of the factions, who encountered Lovestone at close quarters and learned to have a healthy awareness of his malign talents, never saw the whole man.

We now saw Lovestone for the first time on his own, with all his demonic energy and capacity for reckless demagogy let loose, without the restraining influence of Ruthenberg. It was a spectacle to make one wonder whether he was living in a workers' organization, aiming at the rational reorganization of society, or had wandered into a madhouse by mistake.

The death of Ruthenberg was taken by everyone else as a heavy blow to the faction he formally headed. But Lovestone bounded forward from the event as though he had been freed from a straitjacket. Beginning with the announcement, before Ruthenberg's body was cold, that he had expressed the dying wish for Lovestone to become his successor in office, and a simultaneous appeal to Moscow to prevent the holding of a Plenum to act on the question, Lovestone was off to a running start in the race for control of the party; and he set a pace and a pattern in party factionalism, the like of which the faction-ridden party had never seen before.

Many critical observers were amazed and depressed by the cynical efficiency with which Eisenhower and Nixon were packaged and sold to a befuddled electorate in the last presidential election. I was perhaps less astonished by this slick and massively effective manipulation because I had seen the same kind of thing done before—in the Communist Party of the United States. Allowing for the necessary differences of scale and resources involved, Lovestone's job of selling himself as the chosen heir of Ruthenberg and the favorite son of Moscow, in the 1927 party elections, was no less impressive than the professional operation of the Madison Avenue hucksters in 1952.

The sky was the limit this time, and all restraints were thrown aside. The internal party campaign of 1927 was a masterpiece of brazen demagogy calculated to provoke an emotional response in the party ranks. The pitch was to sell the body of Ruthenberg and the decision of the Comintern, with Lovestone wrapped up in the package. Even the funeral of Ruthenberg, and the attendant memorial ceremonies, were obscenely manipulated to start off the factional campaign on the appropriate note.

Lovestone, seconded by Wolfe, campaigned "For the Comintern" and created the atmosphere for a yes or no vote on that question, as though the elections for convention delegates simply posed the question of loyalty or disloyalty to the highest principle of international communism. The Comintern decision was brandished as a club to stampede the rank and file, and fears of possible reprisals for hesitation or doubt were cynically played upon.

These techniques of agitation, which, properly speaking, belong to the arsenal of fascism, paid off in the Communist Party of the United States in 1927. None of the seasoned cadres of the opposition were visibly affected by this unbridled incitement, but all along the fringes the forces of the opposition bloc gave way to the massive campaign. New members and weaker elements played safe by voting "for the Comintern"; furtive careerist elements, with an eye to the main chance, came out of their hiding places and climbed on the bandwagon.

The Lovestone faction, now headed by Lovestone, perhaps the least popular and certainly the most distrusted man in the party leadership, this time accomplished what the same faction, formerly headed by the popular and influential Ruthenberg, had never been able to do. Lovestone won a majority in the elections to the party convention and established the faction for the first time in real, as well as formal, control of the party apparatus.

Lovestone sold himself to the party as the choice of Moscow. He couldn't know at that time, and neither could we, that he had really oversold himself. The invocation of the authority of Moscow in the internal party elections, and the conditioning of the party members to "vote for the Comintern," rebounded against Lovestone himself two years later, when the same supreme authority decided that it was his time to walk the plank. Then it was easily demonstrated that what the Lord had given the Lord could take away.

The "majority" he had gained in the party was not his own. The same party members whom Lovestone had incited and conditioned to "vote for the Comintern" responded with the same reflex when they were commanded by the Comintern to vote against him. By his too-successful campaign "for the Comintern" in 1927, Lovestone had simply helped to create the conditions in the party for his own disaster.

Notes and sidelights on the year 1927

JULY 26, 1955

In his sorry memoir called *I Confess*, Gitlow reports that my original discussions with Weinstone in 1926–1927 concerned a division of party offices—with me as Chairman, Weinstone as General Secretary and Foster as head of the trade-union department (page 405). This is merely a sample of Gitlow's method of reporting his own suspicions for facts. Weinstone and I never discussed party offices at all before the death of Ruthenberg, and then only the post of General Secretary, which had become suddenly vacant. Our dealings with Foster then concerned only the single question of the secretaryship, which we assumed had to be decided right away. The office of Chairman had been abolished, if I remember correctly, when the Ruthenberg faction was installed as a majority by the Comintern cable and the vote of P. Green (Gusev), Comintern representative, after the 1925 Convention.

Gitlow was conditioned by his association with Lovestone to assume, as a matter of course, that whenever two or more people got their heads together something was being cooked up for their personal advantage. His whole account is studded with such reports of his suppositions as facts.

Gitlow's report that, after Ruthenberg's death, Weinstone wobbled over to Lovestone's side, on the promise of the secretaryship, does not correspond to my recollection. I was in close communication with Weinstone during all that period. He reported to me all his discussions with the Lovestoneites. As far as I know, he never wavered at all on the basic position we had agreed upon—to oppose the domination of the party by either of the other factions—until after the 1927 Convention. I do not believe that he was primarily interested in office at that time; or that it was ever his principal motivation, as Gitlow surmises.

Weinstone's importance in the situation in that period

derived from his personal popularity in New York, his strategic position as Secretary of the New York District, and the unquestionable sincerity of the non-factional position he had arrived at. The fact that Stachel also went along with Weinstone at first, was particularly disturbing to the Lovestoneites. Weinstone also had some support among the youth; Sam Don, who later became an editor of the *Daily Worker,* was with him all the way in that period. Weinstone also had the support of a group in the South Slavic Federation.

I suppose this is the only place in the whole printed record you have examined, where you will find a good word by anybody, however qualified, for Stachel. But the truth is that in 1926–1927, Stachel, who was Organizational Secretary of the New York District in Weinstone's administration, was actually won over to Weinstone's non-factional policy and carried it out in practice until some time after the death of Ruthenberg. I recall Krumbein, New York leader of the Fosterites, telling me that he had "never seen such a change come over a man," and that his changed demeanor had greatly moderated the factional situation in the New York District.

Stachel participated in many of the early discussions that I had with Weinstone and expressed full agreement with our program. At one time he proposed that I come to New York as District Secretary, to carry through the program in New York if Weinstone went into the National Office. After several months of persistent effort Lovestone finally got Stachel back into line. But there was one brief period in the life of this man, which seemed to be otherwise devoted exclusively to vicious factionalism, when he responded to higher considerations of party interests.

As for Wolfe, neither Weinstone nor I had any confidence in him nor in his professions of sympathy for Weinstone's program. I remember Weinstone telling me that Wolfe was Lovestone's agent all the time; that he had come along in pretended sympathy for a short time only to keep hold of Stachel and hold him back and to use Stachel to hold Weinstone back. Such a complicated Machiavellian maneuver would be right in character for Lovestone. But I still do not believe that Stachel was a conscious party to it, although Wolfe almost certainly was.

Ballam came along with Weinstone at that time and remained with us in the opposition bloc all the way through the 1927 Convention. That was a twist in the situation that I will admit I never understood. Ballam was one of a number of people in the party at that time who just lacked something of the qualities of leadership, and who made a political living, so to speak, by factionalism—not as leaders, but rather as henchmen of one faction or another. Since away back I had regarded him as a cynic, and I think everybody else did too.

He had been the "English" mouthpiece of the Russian Federation faction, after they split with Ruthenberg in 1920 and lost all their more capable and influential "English-speakers." He held that position with the Federation leftists all through the fight over party legalization, up until their debacle in 1922–1923. Then he was rehabilitated and legitimatized by Pepper and became his factional henchman, continuing with the Pepper-Ruthenberg-Lovestone line-up for four years until he broke loose and took his stand with Weinstone in 1927.

Ballam had a bad reputation in the party, and very little, if any, personal influence. Our people felt a bit uneasy when they heard that he was coming along with Weinstone in the new grouping. But he seemed to accept our whole program and we had no ground to exclude him. I was frankly puzzled by Ballam's stand at that time. I could easily imagine him in any kind of a faction except a faction to end factionalism. But in intimate discussions at that time he expressed the same sentiments as ours, to the effect that the factional fight had brought us all into a blind alley and that we would have to find a new way for a while.

I remember asking him at one time how he thought things would turn out, and he said: "I have absolute faith in the Communist International." Nevertheless, he went along with us after the Comintern decision—up to the Convention. After that he seized the first opportunity to slip back into the Lovestone caucus.

Weinstone did the same thing, but the motivations of the two should by no means be equated. I think Weinstone came to the conclusion that the Comintern decision and the Lovestone victory based on it, had destroyed the possibility of unifying the party along the lines we had projected and that the "hegemony" of the Lovestone group would have to be accepted. But he never became a "Lovestoneite" in the sense that most of the others in the faction did. As soon as Lovestone got into trouble with the Comintern in 1929 Weinstone was one of the first to break with him and support the new line of the Comintern.

The United Opposition Bloc. As I recall, the bloc was formed when we were in Moscow in 1927, not before. Previously there had been merely a touch-me-not agreement on the support of Weinstone as General Secretary. The new combination was demonstratively called a "bloc" to signify that there was no fusion into a single faction, as Foster would have preferred. Neither Weinstone nor I had any sympathy for the idea of Foster dominating the party, nor of getting into a single faction with him where we might possibly be controlled by a majority vote. Everything that was decided in the course of our relations during that period had to be done by agreement each time, rather than by majority vote.

The essence of the situation, as we saw it, was that none of the factions had a recognizable difference of political position on questions of capital importance at that time. That was the "political basis" for our contention that the old factions should be dissolved. But the other factions demanded of us what they did not demand of themselves. Since we did not bring forward a new political platform we were accused of having "no political program." When we formed the bloc with Foster, the Lovestoneites raised the same hue and cry against the bloc. This throws an interesting sidelight on the prevailing psychology of the old factions in those days. The two old factions, the Fosterites and the Lovestoneites, were taken for granted, having a right to separate existence as established institutions. But a third group, or a new "bloc," was required to have a new "political basis." Factionalism carried out too long after the original "political basis" has been outlived can produce some queer thinking.

The bloc was formed to try to prevent the Lovestoneites from dominating the party with a clear majority. We didn't doubt that Foster had ideas of dominating the party himself, but also we knew he couldn't do it without our support. That we never intended to give him. Foster had more rank-and-file backing than we had. But we had the majority of the more capable cadres, and Foster was compelled to agree to a 50-50 basis in all agreements we made regarding representation, up to and including the representation of the bloc as a minority in the new CEC, elected at the 1927 Convention. Of the 13 minority representatives on the new committee, we got 6 and the Foster group got 7, giving them the odd one.

The opposition bloc seemed to grow out of the logic of the situation as it developed in Moscow in 1927. But I believe it would be fair to say that Foster pressed hardest for it and made the most concessions. It did not signify that Weinstone had become a Fosterite in any sense whatever or that our 1925 split with Foster had been healed. It was more of a marriage of convenience.

The Eighth Plenum of the Comintern, Summer of 1927. Weinstone and I traveled to Moscow together and arrived on the last day of the Plenum. We had no part in any of its proceedings or in the voting, as I recall, as this right was reserved to members of the Executive Committee of the Comintern. We were in Moscow not as delegates to the Plenum but only on a special mission on the American question.

The German Ewart (Braun) was in charge of the American Commission. Ewart impressed me as an honest, straightforward communist, a former worker who was one of the second and third-line men who eventually were brought into the leadership of the German party after the Comintern demolished, first, the traditional leadership of Brandler-Thalheimer, and then that of the leftists—Fischer-Maslow—who succeeded them. I don't know how he happened to get chosen for the job of heading the American Commission. I think he was close to Bukharin and carried out Bukharin's wishes in the matter.

I do not remember that Weinstone and I saw any of the top leaders of the Russian party on that occasion. In general Lovestone was far ahead of us in playing the Moscow game in that period. To begin with he had the help of Pepper, who was ensconced in the apparatus of the Comintern, and knew all the angles and prevailing winds and whom to see and whom to keep away from.

Here I might as well frankly state that I never was worth a damn on a mission to Moscow after my first trip in 1922. Then everything was open and aboveboard. A clear-cut political issue was presented by both sides in open debate and it was settled straightforwardly, on a political basis, without discrimination or favoritism to the factions involved, and without undisclosed reasons, arising from internal Russian questions, motivating the decision and determining the attitude toward the leaders of the contending factions. That was the Lenin-Trotsky Comintern, and I did all right there. But after 1924 everything was different in the Comintern, and I never seemed to be able to find my way around.

I detested the business of going around to see one person after another like a petitioner, and sort of groping in the dark without knowing what was going to be decided by others without our participation. The only time I ever felt at ease in Moscow was in the Commission meetings where the representatives of different factions could confront each other in open debate. But by the time the Commission meetings got under way they were mere formalities. Everything had been settled behind the scenes; the word had been passed and all the secondary leaders and functionaries in the Comintern were falling into line.

I felt, with considerable reason, that I was no good in that whole business. I left Moscow each time with a feeling of futility, and my resistance to going again increased steadily until in 1928 I at first flatly refused to go. It was only the insistent urging and pressure of factional associates that finally induced me to give it one more try in 1928.

I was then already deeply troubled by the developments in the Russian party, but did not expect that anything would be done to change anything at the Sixth Congress of the Comintern. I had no idea that I would be propelled into the fight and come out of it a convinced Trotskyist, breaking all previous relations and connections on that issue.

I think the Ruthenberg-Lovestone group gained their initial advantage in Moscow by jumping earlier and more enthusiastically into the fight against Trotskyism, way back in 1924, and that this was always in the minds of the Russian leaders in the subsequent years. Foster and Bittelman did everything they could to make up for the earlier sluggishness of the Foster-Cannon faction on the Trotsky question, but I never did anything but go along silently. This may have been noted in Moscow and may account in part for my disfavor there, but I am not sure about that.

You are right in your "impression that there was literally no one in the American party in 1927 who might be considered a 'Trotskyite' or even a sympathizer of Trotsky's position." I know of no one who openly took such a position in the party prior to my return from the Sixth Congress in 1928. I personally had been deeply disturbed and dissatisfied by the expulsion of Trotsky and Zinoviev, but I could not have been called a "Trotskyite" or even a sympathizer, at that time. And the atmosphere in the party was such that it was not wise to express such sentiments or disgruntlements unless one intended to do something about it. By that time the issue of Trotskyism posed the immediate threat of expulsion in all parties of the Comintern.

After our expulsion we did discover a small group of expelled Hungarian communists, headed by Louis Basky, who had previously adopted the platform of the Russian Opposition on their own account. But they had come to this position after their expulsion, which had taken place on some other grounds, trumped up in the course of the Lovestoneites' campaign to cinch up their factional control in the Hungarian Federation. The Hungarian comrades were a great comfort and strength to us in the difficult and stormy pioneer days of our movement under the Trotskyist banner.

Lore was never a Trotskyist in the political sense and never cooperated with our group after we were expelled. The first American Trotskyist was undoubtedly Max Eastman, but he had never been formally a member of the party. On his own responsibility as an individual he published a book called *The Real Situation in Russia*, by Leon Trotsky, in 1928. But this came out about the time we were in Moscow at the Sixth Congress and I did not see it until our return. It contained the Platform of the Left Opposition in the Russian party and a number of other documents of the Left Opposition. Eastman cooperated with us and gave us quite a bit of help in the first days of our existence as an expelled group publishing *The Militant*.

The Comintern decision in 1927 did not specifically provide that the Lovestoneites should have a majority in the next CEC. All the successive decisions and cables were slanted to aid that result but did not specifically provide for it. What Lovestone got from the Comintern on this occasion was the help he needed to secure a majority but not enough to enable him to exterminate or exclude the minority. Moreover, the slanted support he got was accompanied by a provision that the party must be united and peace established.

That's the sense in which Ewart, the Comintern representative, acted during his stay in this country at that time. After the Convention—and of course within the framework of its decisions—he seemed to work always for peace and moderation, and we never found any reason to complain that he was unfair. It may be assumed that he was working according to instructions but such conduct would have been natural for him. He was undoubtedly a sincere communist; my memory of him is not unfriendly.

I believe it would be correct to say that Lovestone was given conditional support from Moscow in 1927; that he was put on trial, so to speak; and that provisions were made to conserve the minority, in case the experiment did not work out to the satisfaction of Moscow. As previously stated, the American question was not decided at the Comintern Plenum at that time at all. Everything was done afterward—formally through the American Commission, but actually in behind-the-scene arrangements among the Russian leaders.

The Lovestone regime

FEBRUARY 3, 1956

The February, 1928 Plenum was notable, not so much for what was formally decided there, but as a new turning point in the evolution of the party leadership. The full effect of the death of Ruthenberg was registered at this Plenum for the first time.

At the Fifth National Convention in August, 1927, Lovestone and Wolfe had won the majority—with the help of the Comintern—on their claim to be the heirs of Ruthenberg.

They had also scared up some votes on their promise to unify the party and dissolve the factions. During the intervening six months the Lovestoneites had been in full control of the party, and the February Plenum provided an occasion to review the results.

It was already quite evident that the party regime was new and different from anything the party had known before. Ruthenberg had never been the "one" leader of the party, or even of his own faction, as he was represented; he was only a part of the so-called Ruthenberg group. Nevertheless, the Ruthenberg regime had borne the stamp of his personal qualities. He was a devoted communist, fully committed to the cause—I don't think anyone ever doubted that. Moreover, he was a man of responsibility, concerned about the progress of party work in all departments. His political inclination was somewhat leftist.

The new regime was a Lovestone regime—and that was not the same thing. The change was becoming manifest in both political and party organizational policy. In the past Lovestone and Wolfe had adapted themselves to Ruthenberg, in order to advance behind the shield of his personal influence and authority. Now, freed of the old restraints, they had begun to impose their own political ideas, which were decidedly more conservative, and their own organizational methods, which were far less responsible, than those of Ruthenberg.

They were fascinated by the expanding strength of American capitalism. They pictured it as entering its "Victorian Day," and drew from that perspective their theory of "American exceptionalism." They foresaw no economic crisis on the American horizon and consequently no prospects for a radicalization of the American working class.

On the party organizational side, as per Comintern instructions, the Lovestoneites had continued to talk softly about unity. But under cover of this chatter they were moving organizationally, wherever they could find a soft spot, to cinch up their factional control of the party apparatus, far more aggressively than had been the case in Ruthenberg's time.

The "Ruthenberg regime" (in the party) in reality had been a coalition of factions. The Ruthenberg group held a dominant position, but the other factions always exerted a strong influence on important party decisions and had plenty of leeway in their own departments of work. The Fosterites had a pretty free hand in practical trade-union affairs and the Cannonites in the International Labor Defense—the two principal fields of the party's mass work. Now, with Ruthenberg out of the way, Lovestone was moving, smoothly but relentlessly, to break up this coalition modus operandi and replace it by a monolithic Lovestoneite control in all departments and corners of the party.

The two opposition groups, after several months of watchful waiting, began to take note of the new political trend of the Lovestoneites and to react against it. The February Plenum witnessed the beginning of opposition criticism of the theory of "American exceptionalism" and the rightward swing of the Lovestoneites in general.

It had also become evident to us, by the time of the February Plenum, that the Lovestoneites' peace and unity ballyhoo was only a formula for the assimilation of weaker elements of the opposition groups into the Lovestone faction and the isolation and eventual elimination of the others. There was no choice but to fight. The beginning of opposition to the Lovestoneite policy on political grounds at the February Plenum was accompanied by the beginning of a re-consolidation of the opposition factions organizationally.

Any illusions about the possible liquidation of all the factions in a united leadership were pretty well dissipated at the February Plenum. Weinstone and Ballam made the Plenum the occasion for their return to the Lovestone group, but that didn't change much in the relation of forces. All the other leading people, who had stood in opposition at the August, 1927 Convention, began to harden into irreconcilable opposition to the Lovestone regime on both political and organizational grounds.

We did not trust Lovestone. Nothing was decided or settled definitively at this plenum; it simply marked the first skirmishes in the new factional war.

One item on the agenda of the February Plenum was the report by Wolfe on the expulsion of the Left Opposition in the Russian party. Wolfe was the "specialist" on this question. This whole business was handled rather perfunctorily, since the issues seemed to be settled and dead. Nobody got excited about it and the resolution was adopted for the record.

As I reported in my *History of American Trotskyism*, I did not speak on this issue at the February Plenum. This disturbed Bill Dunne and some of the other members of our faction, who feared that my silence would be noticed and used against us. The Lovestoneites certainly would have used it against me if they had suspected the reason for it. But my abstention seemed to get lost in the shuffle at the plenum and I heard no comment about it outside our own group.

Maurice Spector was present at this plenum as the

representative of the Canadian party. He was as much discontented about the expulsion of Trotsky and Zinoviev as I was. We spent an evening together talking about it, and I confided my own feeling to him. Neither of us had any idea of what we could do about it, and we made no plans to do anything at that time.

This confidential conversation, however, did prepare the way for our getting together later at the Sixth Congress, and the eventual agreement we made there to come out for the cause of Trotsky when we returned home from the Congress. Spector was the only one to whom I spoke frankly about my feelings on the Russian question before the Sixth Congress.

As far as I can recall, the Russian question did not come up at the May, 1928 Plenum. And no objection was raised in the Central Committee to my election as a delegate to the Sixth Congress, as would certainly have been the case if they had suspected me of Trotskyist inclinations.

A note on Zinoviev

JULY 26, 1955

I have long been thinking and promising to write an appreciation of Zinoviev in the form of a condensed political biography. A comrade who is thoroughly familiar with the Russian language and the history of the Russian movement has promised to collaborate with me in preparing the material.* But I don't know when, if ever, we will get

---

* This refers to John G. Wright, who had begun work on this project before his recent untimely death.

around to it. It is too big and serious an undertaking to sandwich in between other tasks.

I was greatly influenced by Zinoviev in the early days of the Comintern, as were all communists throughout the world. I have never forgotten that he was Lenin's closest collaborator in the years of reaction and during the First World War; that he was the foremost orator of the revolution, according to the testimony of Trotsky; and that he was the Chairman of the Comintern in the Lenin-Trotsky time.

It was Zinoviev's bloc with Trotsky and his expulsion, along with Trotsky, that first really shook me up and started the doubts and discontents which eventually led me to Trotskyism. I have always been outraged by the impudent pretensions of so many little people to deprecate Zinoviev, and I feel that he deserves justification before history.

I have no doubt whatever that in all his big actions, including his most terrible errors, he was motivated fundamentally by devotion to the higher interests of the working class of the whole world—to the communist future of humanity. I believe that his greatest fault as a politician was his reliance on maneuverism when principled issues were joined in such a way as to exclude the efficacy of maneuver.

I do not think Zinoviev capitulated to Stalin either out of conviction or for personal reasons, but primarily because he thought he could serve the cause by such a stratagem. He wanted himself and the other opposition leaders to live and be on hand when a change in the situation would create a new opportunity for the overthrow of Stalin and the restoration of a revolutionary leadership of the Russian party and the Comintern.

In the exigencies of the political struggle it has not been convenient for the Trotskyist movement to make a full and objective evaluation of this man's life; and others have shown no interest in it. But historical justice cries out for it and it will be done sometime by somebody. In spite of all, Zinoviev deserves restoration as one of the great hero-martyrs of the revolution.

As far as I know, Zinoviev did not have any special favorites in the American party. The lasting personal memory I have of him is of his patient and friendly efforts in 1925 to convince both factions of the necessity of party peace and cooperation, summed up in his words to Foster which I have mentioned before: "Frieden ist besser." ("Peace is better.")

Some people in the party

1. BILL DUNNE

JULY 19, 1955

It is true, as you surmise, that Dunne was very close to me in those days, both personally and politically. I am still somewhat inhibited emotionally from writing an adequate objective account of the personality and career of this tragic figure. He and I were "together" before we ever met; we both came from the "industrial" wing of the movement and knew about each other. He was the editor of the *Butte Daily Bulletin* in the tough post-war times of the mine strikes and mob violence before the formal organization of the CP, while I was the editor of a left-wing paper, *The Workers' World,* in Kansas City.

Bill had a big and well-deserved reputation in the Northwest and was especially popular in Minneapolis, where his brothers lived, and where he was a featured speaker for the Central Labor Union on Labor Days and similar occasions. It was on my motion that he was brought to New York in 1921 as a member of the delegation to the Profintern in that year.

He and I were close friends and political associates from the very start of our acquaintance, and remained such until we parted in Moscow at the Sixth Congress in 1928 over the Trotsky issue. He supported me from the first in 1923 in the fight against Pepperism, and also later in the conflict with Foster. After the national office was moved to New York in 1927 the two couples—Bill and Margaret and Rose and I—lived together, sharing an apartment. We were good friends and boon companions all the time, and the separation in 1928 left an emotional wound that never healed.

The tragedy was compounded in 1928 when Bill's split with me brought a split with his own brothers in Minneapolis. All three of them—Vincent, Miles and Grant—took a stand for Trotskyism in the break and remained firm Trotskyists in all the vicissitudes of the struggle that followed. Bill was a victim of Stalinism. He was never the same man after 1928. We grieved more over him than any of the others. Revolutionary politics takes a lot out of people who take it seriously.

2. LUDWIG LORE

MARCH 22, 1955

I didn't know Lore very well personally and never had close relations with him, but I always thought he was a very likeable fellow. His tradition was that of the pre-war left Social Democracy. I don't think he ever felt really at home in the Comintern, or that he ever became an all-out communist in the sense that the rest of us did. As I recall it, he interpreted the united front policy of the Comintern favorably as a step toward reconciliation and reunification with the Second International and not as, among other things, a means of struggle against the Social Democrats.

I think his opposition to the "Third Party Alliance" was determined by his left social-democratic orthodoxy on the question of the peasantry. I don't know whether he was influenced by Trotsky in his position or whether he knew what stand Trotsky was taking in Moscow on this question. I doubt it.

Lore's political tendency in general was to the right. In the first stages of the fight in the Russian party, Lore, like some others in Europe, supported Trotsky under the mistaken impression that his opposition represented a revolt against the "leftism" of Zinoviev. Lore's later evolution showed very clearly that he was no "Trotskyist" in a political sense. Looking back now, there is little doubt that the Comintern blasts against Lore were motivated by his original declaration in favor of Trotsky and not, as alleged, by his policies in American affairs.

I don't think the La Follette policy was the only or main reason for Lore's opposition to the Ruthenberg-Pepper group and his support of the Foster-Cannon group. He was decidedly anti-Pepper and against "maneuverism" in general. He was also anti-Zinoviev, but whether he considered Pepper Zinoviev's agent or not, I do not know.

Lore was popular in the party ranks in New York but not decisively influential in a factional showdown. He was a supporter of the Foster-Cannon faction but was never a decisive member of its inner councils. The two strong factions between them completely dominated the party. This state of affairs confronted Lore and his sub-group with the necessity of making a choice; there was no prospect whatever for his group to contest with the others for party control.

I think his determining reasons for supporting us were that he considered us more American, more proletarian trade-unionist, and therefore more capable of establishing the party as a factor in the real life of the country.

MARCH 31, 1955

I don't recall that anybody in the top caucus of our faction got excited about the Comintern's criticisms of Lore. He had been with us, so to speak, but not of us; we did not feel responsible for him as an all-out member of our faction. It is true that he had supported us in the 1923 Convention, but in his daily practice he acted pretty much as a free lance. He had his own little principality in the *Volkszeitung,* and his own ideas, and he expounded them freely from day to day without consulting us.

We took the Comintern's political criticisms of Lore, like all its other political pronouncements, for good coin and thought it was up to Lore to straighten himself out with the Comintern. At the same time, it can be safely said that we would have paid no attention to Lore's "deviations," and most probably would not have noticed them, if they had not been pounced on in Moscow. I am sure that it did not occur to any of us at the time that the strictures against Lore were in reality motivated by factional considerations in the struggle against Trotsky in the Russian party and in the Comintern.

3. ANTOINETTE KONIKOW

OCTOBER 16, 1956

The "Red" socialist woman "from Boston," whom Max Eastman remembers as one of those present at the meeting with Solntsev at Lore's apartment in the winter of 1928, must certainly have been Dr. Antoinette Konikow. She had always been friendly to Lore.

This remarkable woman had been a socialist since 1888. She was one of the pioneer members of the Communist Party and also one of the pioneers of the Trotskyist movement in 1928. In fact, she was a little ahead of us, because, after her expulsion from the party on other grounds, she had formed a little group in Boston before we were expelled in October 1928. This group published one issue of a little paper known as *Bulletin No. 1,* dated December 1928, just about the time the first issue of *The Militant* came off the press. The Boston group became part of our new organization, and Antoinette remained with us until her death at the age of 77 in July 1946. She was an honorary member of our National Committee.

The Militant for July 13, 1946, contains extensive biographical material about her, as well as a photostat of the first page of her *Bulletin No. 1. The Militant* for July 27, 1946, printed the beautiful memorial address by her daughter, Edith Konikow, who was also a member of our organization until her own death in 1954.

The biographical account in *The Militant* relates that Antoinette was born in Russia in 1869. She joined the Russian socialist movement in Switzerland in 1888, becoming a member of the "Emancipation of Labor" group founded by Plekhanov. She emigrated to America in 1893. Although not Jewish herself, she learned to speak Yiddish to facilitate her work among the Jewish workers in Boston, and was one of those instrumental in founding the Workmens' Circle. She was a member of the Socialist Labor Party, was active as a lecturer, served on the Massachusetts State Committee, and held other leading posts. In 1897 she joined the Debs' wing of the socialist movement, which presently fused with other groups to found the Socialist Party.

Antoinette was a graduate of Tufts College. As a doctor she became prominent as one of the founders of the movement for planned families through birth control. She practiced medicine all the time, but her chief interest and activity were in the movement for Socialism.

4. ISRAEL AMTER

DECEMBER 18, 1956

This is a delayed answer to your inquiries of November 21. After I wrote my last letter, I turned off the switch connecting my thoughts to the affairs of the distant past, and it requires a real effort to switch back again. In my peculiar method of thinking I am an extremist, as in everything else; once I get really "concentrated" on a given subject, everything else gets blotted out of my mind for the time being. When I finally got rolling on the track of reminiscence under your persistent prodding, I put current affairs out of my mind and really began to relive the old days, and to be confident that I was relating them with a very high degree of factual accuracy.

It was a fortunate coincidence that the stagnant condition of the American radical movement at the time made it possible for me to make that long excursion into the past with a clear conscience. I have to thank you in the first place for putting me on that track and keeping me on it until I finally got my recollections down on paper. My two pamphlets—about the IWW and Debs—which I believe have a value to the movement and which, in any case, have given me great personal satisfaction, were by-products of this concentration on the days of long ago. I have to thank you for that too.

Now I am at the other extreme. The stormy events of the last few months in Poland and Hungary have blotted out the old memories again and I have to make my way back to the factual points raised in your letter of November 21 with considerable difficulty.

This is the best I can do:

Amter's role. I did not attend the Fifth Congress of the Comintern in 1924. Amter was not only a delegate to the Congress, but he had been the standing representative of the American CP at the Executive Committee of the Communist International for a long time before that. That did not signify, however, that he was playing a more important role then than he played subsequently or previously.

Amter's appointment to Moscow was a typical illustration of Pepper's inner party politics. Amter played his biggest role in the party as one of the chief leaders of the leftist "Goose Caucus" in 1921–1922. Amter (Ford) was co-author of the "Ford-Dubner Thesis," Dubner being Jakira. This caucus was defeated so catastrophically by the decision of the Communist International on party legalization at the end of 1922 that the prestige of all its leaders was badly shattered. Pepper then went to work to break up the "Goose Caucus" by discrediting and isolating the more stiff-necked leaders on the one hand, and by rehabilitating and assimilating the others into his own new personal faction.

Katterfeld and Lindgren were two of the most prominent "Goose Caucus" leaders whom Pepper destroyed. Amter and Gitlow were rehabilitated as "Pepperites." Wagenknecht and others found protection from Pepper's proscription in the newly-forming Foster-Cannon group. Amter's appointment as delegate of the American party to the Executive Committee of the Comintern was his reward for becoming a Pepper lieutenant.

That is the true explanation of how he appears in the formal record as playing a more important role in the period prior to the Fifth Congress, when his personal influence as an independent leader of the party, which he had strongly exerted in 1922, had been obliterated and he had become and was to remain henceforth merely a lieutenant, first of Pepper and later of Lovestone.

American CP politics, beginning with Pepper, was a devious and vicious business.

5. KUCHER

DECEMBER 18, 1956

In your letter of November 21 you also inquire about "Kucher" who turned up in your research as a dissident delegate to the Fifth Congress of the Comintern, also the Fourth Congress. Kucher was his real name. I remember him well.

He was an active trade unionist and a principled, even fanatical, exponent of independent unionism and an independent union federation. Prior to Foster's entry into the party in 1921 and the concurrent switch to a pro-AFL policy, a number of small local unions in New York and New Jersey, which had seceded from the AFL or had been expelled, or had arisen independently, were joined together in an independent union council under the leadership of Kucher. He fought vigorously for his policy against the new Foster line adopted by the party and was allowed to go to Moscow twice to defend his position before the Comintern. He lost the fight there and his movement eventually disintegrated. I lost track of him after that.

What is most significant about this episode in retrospect

is the way it illustrates the fairness and democracy prevailing in the movement at that time, the recognition of the right of a small group to maintain a dissident point of view, not only in the party here but also to have representation at the Comintern debates on the disputed questions.

6. THE LENINIST LETTS

MARCH 20, 1959

Your reference to Robert Zelms in connection with the Dozenberg affair evoked a pleasant memory of the old days. I knew him well. He was the full time New England organizer of the ILD during the whole period of the Sacco-Vanzetti campaign and I had many dealings with him. He was another one of those all-out Lettish Bolsheviks like Charlie Scott and Dozenberg. As a still unreconstructed Wobbly, I liked those people and felt a kinship with them. I like to think that the American workers' movement to come will throw up a breed comparable to the Leninist Letts who were always reliable and ready for anything. The American revolution will need them, as the Russian did.

7. MAGIL'S RUTHENBERG

FEBRUARY 6, 1959

I happen to remember reading A. B. Magil's poem on the death of Ruthenberg, "Go to Sleep, Charlie," at the time it was published in the *Daily Worker*—perhaps because it struck me on the funny bone in the midst of all the memorial services. Magil was then only a young staff contributor on the *Worker* and could scarcely have seen Ruthenberg, except at a distance. Yet he blithely calls him "Charlie," as if Ruthenberg and he had been old pals, or at least, that Ruthenberg was such a hail-fellow-well-met as to invite familiarity from all and sundry.

I saw Ruthenberg from day to day over a period of years and never heard anybody, not even his most intimate collaborators, call him Charlie, or even so much as Charles. That sort of undue chumminess was unthinkable in the presence of the austere and aloof Ruthenberg. He was strictly "Comrade Ruthenberg" until you got to know him well for several years. Then you could go as far as "C.E.", but no further. He invariably called the rest of us Comrade Foster, Comrade Cannon, etc. We never did get a Bill or a Jim out of him, although everybody else took it for granted that those were the names we were born with. Magil's "Charlie" was definitely not the palsy-walsy type.

Before the Sixth Congress of the Comintern

JANUARY 27, 1956

The period from the victory of the Lovestone faction in 1927 until the Sixth Congress of the Comintern in the summer of 1928 has been overshadowed in my mind by the new struggle I started after the Congress. Many of the details of the earlier 1928 period are blurred in my memory. I was away from the party center nearly all the time between the February and May Plenums of the party. I went on a big national tour for the International Labor Defense right after the February 1928 Plenum and returned to New York only shortly before the May Plenum. On the tour I tried to put the factional squabbles out of mind and didn't keep track of internal party developments very closely. Your questions show a much greater familiarity with the events of that time.

We were aware in 1928 that the Comintern was making a left turn and that this was producing a more favorable climate for the Opposition in the American party. Just how much this influenced me at the time is hard to say now in retrospect. We were all predominantly concerned with the American struggle. I didn't begin to get a real international orientation until after the Sixth Congress of the Comintern.

It is clear now that all Stalin's moves were strongly influenced by Trotsky. Stalin's method was to smash the Opposition organizationally and then to expropriate its ideas and apply them in his own way. It was Trotsky who first saw the coming of the new period of capitalist stabilization after the big post-war revolutionary upsurge had subsided. This was shown already in his polemics against the leftists in 1921. Somewhat later the official policy of the Comintern caught up with the new reality and overdid the emphasis on the new capitalist "stabilization." This was the period of the Comintern's swing to the right—1924–1928—which helped the Lovestoneites so much in the American party.

Just about the time the Comintern was going overboard on this theme, Trotsky saw the contradictions in the new stabilization and the opening up of new revolutionary perspectives. His fight against the official policy on the Anglo-Russian Committee and the British General Strike reflected his thinking in that time. So also did his book *Whither England?* and his speech of February 15, 1926, on

"Europe and America" (republished in *Fourth International* in the April and May issues, 1943).

Simultaneously with the expulsion of the Left Opposition, in December 1927, Stalin began to appropriate a large part of Trotsky's program on the international field as well as in Russia. This is what brought him into the conflict with Bukharin.

As I have said before, this was all a mystery to me at the time. Then we only noted the indications of a left turn. It began at a time when Lovestone and Wolfe were divesting themselves of the leftist baggage they had inherited from Ruthenberg to give free play to their own political instincts, which were always decidedly conservative. The "left turn" of the Comintern caught them off guard.

The formal record could give the impression that the factional conflict in the American party in the year 1928 centered mainly around the trade-union question, with Foster and Lovestone lining up on one side and Bittelman-Cannon on the other. The documentary material may support this view, but it is not really correct. The main feature of Foster-Cannon-Bittelman relations at that time was their agreement on irreconcilable opposition to the Lovestone regime in the party and its conservative perspectives in general. The trade-union question was only one of the items in the struggle.

And even though Foster, at the May 1928 Plenum, was closer to the Lovestoneites on this one point, he was definitely with us on an over-all factional basis in the fight against the Lovestone regime. It was Foster who first approached me when I returned to New York, shortly before the May Plenum, with a proposal that we get together for a more aggressive fight against the Lovestoneites. Pepper, it appeared, had returned to this country in the spring of 1928 with a special mission to promote "unity" of the Lovestone-Foster groups. The Lovestoneites were trying hard, at the instigation of Pepper, to win over or neutralize Foster, but he was not receptive.

At the May Plenum the Lovestoneites centered their attacks on me and Bittelman and made a big play for "unity" with Foster. I remember ridiculing their sudden discovery of Foster's virtues by asking if they meant to kill him with kindness, and quoting the Latin adage: "De mortuis nil nisi bonum." The aptness of the remark was pretty well understood in the whole assembly, and Foster joined in the general laughter. The Lovestoneites wanted to make a captive of Foster, but their maneuver was fruitless. Foster was dead set against their control of the party and rejected all their overtures.

Foster's approach to the trade-union question was not the same as that of Lovestone and Wolfe. The position of the latter on that, as on other national questions, was determined by their basically conservative view of American perspectives. They were sure that American capitalism was entering its "Victorian" period, and they seemed to be downright happy about it. These people simply did not believe any more in the perspective of revolution in this booming country.

Foster's trade-union position was differently motivated. He was the prisoner of his own fetish of "boring from within" the AFL, which had dominated his thinking since his break with the IWW in 1911. His whole career seemed to be bound up with that specific tactic, and he was tied to it by the possibly unconscious need of self-justification.

I had never fully agreed with Foster on the trade-union

question. I had started out in the IWW and I never disavowed my work in that field. I had come to recognize the error in the IWW attempt to build brand-new revolutionary unions all up and down the line. But in my own thinking I never went to the extreme AFL-ism that Foster did.

At the 1920 Convention of the United Communist Party, where an anti-AFL position was adopted, I had spoken for a more flexible policy of working within the existing AFL unions and of supporting independent unions in fields neglected by the AFL. The Convention report of the speech of "Dawson" refers to me. (*The Communist*, official organ of the United Communist Party, Vol. I, No. I, June 12, 1920, page 4.)

In the exigencies of the faction fight that began in 1923 there was no special occasion, and it was not appropriate, for this difference of emphasis to show itself openly in the party. But as early as the December, 1925 Plenum, both Dunne and I differed with the Fosterites on the Passaic campaign. Dunne's support of Losovsky at the Fourth Congress of the RILU was the natural expression of our real sentiment about the necessity of building independent unions in fields neglected or sabotaged by the AFL. That could be considered a real difference between us and Foster; but we considered it then as a difference of emphasis, and it was overshadowed all the time, even at the May 1928 Plenum, by our general agreement in opposition to the Lovestone regime and its conservative outlook in general.

Bittelman's role in these new developments was a special one. Bittelman was never a "Fosterite" any more than I was. He was first, last and all the time a Moscow man, and the line from Moscow was law for him. He had the advantage of reading Russian and that put him one jump ahead of the others whenever new winds began to blow in Moscow. Moreover, inside the party Bittelman always had his own personal sub-faction in the Jewish Federation. It was always necessary to deal with him not merely as an individual but as the representative of a factional following.

The final decision made by the party—after our expulsion in October 1928—to go all out for a policy of independent unionism, and to transform the TUEL into a new trade-union center under the name of the Trade Union Unity League, was swallowed by Foster, but it must have been a bitter pill for him. It constituted, in effect, a repudiation of his whole course since his break with the IWW.

When Zack was expelled from the CP and came over to us for a while, in the fall of 1934, he told me that he had been to see Foster shortly before that. He found him very ill, helpless and discouraged. Zack said that Foster had enjoined him not to take any steps that would give Browder the pretext to expel him from the party. In connection with that, he told Zack that he had never believed in the program of the TUUL but felt that he had to go along with it to prevent his own expulsion.

I doubt that Foster's failure to attend the Fourth Congress of the Profintern in the winter of 1928 had any special significance. He was deeply preoccupied with the miners' campaign at that time and was in the field constantly. I don't recall any special discussion between me and Dunne before his departure for this Profintern Congress. My memory about the whole thing is rather hazy—perhaps because I was on tour all that time. I think there is no doubt, however, that the initiative for the sharp turn came from Losovsky and not from us. But it was very easy for us to go along with it, because it was becoming more and more obvious to us that the organization of the unorganized required more emphasis on independent unions in certain fields.

My trade-union article in the July 1928 *Communist* was published at my own insistence. I felt rather strongly about the question and wanted to make my position clear. It was considered somewhat "irregular" already then to have conflicting views appear in the press. The Lovestoneites objected, but they probably thought it was better to print it than to have a fuss with me on that kind of an issue at that particular time. I do not recall any discussion with Foster about it. To be sure, the Lovestoneites thought they were playing a clever game by putting Foster forward to defend the official policy. But Foster was playing his own game in coming to the defense of his fetish.

The difference between me and Foster on the trade-union question at the May Plenum did not seriously disturb relations in the bloc of the two factions. It remained, as before, a touch-me-not alliance of convenience. I recall that we had a joint social gathering of the two groups shortly before our departure for Moscow for the Sixth Congress. The general understanding was that we were going to make common cause there.

I do not recall the division among the Fosterites becoming manifest at the May Plenum. They kept it bottled up in the family for a while. The furious internal fight of the Fosterites, in which Foster was isolated, was revealed to us only when the fight broke out into the open at a joint meeting of the delegates of the two opposition groups in Moscow.

Our group, which was strongly represented at the

Congress—Dunne, Cannon, Hathaway, Gomez and several others attending the Lenin School in Moscow—did not intervene on the side of Bittelman-Browder-Johnstone. We kept hands off and let the Fosterites fight it out among themselves.

Lovestone's reaction to the Losovsky line in 1928 was not determined primarily by any fanatical conviction about trade-union policy. The trade-union question was not his main interest—not by a long shot. Lovestone was far more concerned to justify the policy of the majority of the party in the past, and thus to protect its prestige, than about any line he would have to take in the future. His main concern was to keep control of the party.

For that he was willing to adapt himself to almost any kind of a new directive from Moscow. I feel quite sure he had the illusion that Losovsky himself was out on a limb and that, with the support of Bukharin, he could get around him in Moscow. Losovsky was the one who forced the fight and left Lovestone no alternative but to fight back.

It is difficult to describe my feeling and expectations in this period before the Sixth Congress of the Comintern, without coloring the recollections by what I learned and did afterward—after I read Trotsky's *Criticism of the Draft Program* during the Congress.

The new signs from Moscow in the early months of 1928 were undoubtedly more favorable for the Opposition, but I think the Fosterites took more courage from it than I did. We had had so many disappointments in Moscow that I couldn't get up any real enthusiasm about better luck the next time.

Also, as I have explained in my *History of American Trotskyism,* I was deeply oppressed by the developments in the Russian party and the expulsion of the Opposition. But with the limited understanding of the disputed questions I had at that time, I didn't know what I could do about it, and had no definite idea of trying to do anything. In that mood I really did not want to go to the Congress at all, and would not have gone if my factional associates had not insisted on it.

I did not communicate my inner thoughts and doubts to them at that time, since I had no definite proposals to make. Their mood, contrary to mine, was rather optimistic about the prospects of support for our factional struggle in Moscow. That, I suppose, is why they wouldn't hear of my withdrawal from the Congress delegation.

Lovestone's troubles in Moscow

MAY 31, 1955

I remember the session of the American Commission at the Sixth Congress which you refer to. The incident was highlighted in my memory by the particularly impudent attacks which Lovestone and others made on Losovsky. Referring to Losovsky's opposition to Lenin's policy in 1917, Lovestone said: "Nobody in our party ever fought Lenin," etc. This was the first time, as far as I know, that any American delegate had ventured to attack any of the Russian leaders.

The Lovestone leadership was under very heavy fire for its trade-union policy, and the vicious attacks of Lovestone and the others on Losovsky represented rather desperate defensive actions.

Further proof that Losovsky's view really prevailed was indicated by the sharp turn which the party made on the trade-union question after the Congress, heading straight into the policy of building rival unions to the AFL. That happened soon after we were expelled, and we objected to making a principle of independent unions.

While it is true that Lovestone seemed to have a slight shade of advantage in Moscow in 1928, it was by no means complete and unconditional. Losovsky was unrestrained in his attacks and this could not possibly have occurred without the permission of Stalin. Looking back on it now, one can surmise that he "unleashed" Losovsky on purpose to encourage the Foster group, and then softened the blow in personal conversations to postpone the showdown with Lovestone. He was preparing the break with Bukharin, but was not yet ready to bring it into the open at the Sixth Congress.

Soon after that Foster was called to a private interview with Stalin. He reported it to me and, later, to the joint meeting of the opposition groups. This report of Foster's was later made into a factional document circulated in the party, which compelled Stalin to left-handedly disavow it. I remember distinctly the main point of Foster's report: that Stalin told him he had no confidence in the Lovestone group; that he had said to him in so many words: "No good can come from the Lovestone group."

This undoubtedly encouraged the Fosterites to renew the factional struggle after the Sixth Congress. Their confidence that they would get support from Moscow was certainly borne out when the C.I. delegation at the Party Convention a few months later came out openly against the Lovestone majority. After that Lovestone was called to

Moscow and given the works there. His disaster was one of the comical by-products of the fall of Bukharin.

Stalin's devious design

JULY 6, 1955

This refers to your letter of June 29. . . .

What really happened after Ruthenberg's death was that the ECCI, in successive decisions, first prohibited the majority at the May 1927 Plenum—Foster-Weinstone-Cannon—from exercising its right to elect a successor to Ruthenberg as General Secretary; and then, by the later decisions following the Eighth Plenum of the ECCI, deliberately helped the Lovestone faction to win a majority at the party convention by presenting it to the party membership as the faction most favored by the ECCI. Lovestone convinced the majority of the party members that he had the support of the Comintern. That was the principal reason why he won the majority of the delegates in the pre-convention contest.

Ironically—and this point is important for interpretation—the specific 35 to 13 provision [for the composition of the new Central Committee] in the 1927 decision of the Comintern was not and could not have been directed exclusively or even primarily against the Foster-Weinstone-Cannon minority. It was designed, of course, to assure the convention majority—which it was assumed, but not specifically stated, would be the Lovestoneites—a safe working majority in the new CEC. But the primary purpose was to guarantee the convention minority sufficient representation in the new CEC to permit its leading people to function freely in the party, and to protect it against elimination by the majority. The prohibition of "any disciplinary measures against [the] opposition"—which you quote—should also be read in this light.

The importance of this point cannot be overstressed for an understanding of the Moscow policy on the American question, as it was evolving in the 1925-1928 period. I couldn't fathom the devious design of the Comintern at the time. I see it more clearly now in retrospect. The policy of the Russians in that period was not to base themselves exclusively on one faction and to eliminate the others, but simply to favor one and keep the others in reserve, just in case.

There is no doubt that Bukharin, who was then Chairman of the Comintern, was a partisan of the Lovestone group and used his position to help them. This was the time of the Stalin-Bukharin bloc, and Bukharin most probably was still able to exert a measure of independent influence in Comintern affairs. Lovestone got the benefit of this transitory situation.

It was not until 1929 that Stalin took full command of the Comintern and eliminated Bukharin, as he had previously eliminated Zinoviev. Then he adopted the policy of assuring the monopolistic party leadership of a single faction and eliminating all others. And this single faction by that time turned out to be none of the old indigenous groups with more or less independent leaders, but a new faction synthetically put together out of parts of all the others and proclaiming allegiance exclusively to Stalin, not to any specific American leader.

In 1927 Moscow was not yet ready for such a drastic settlement of the American question. I think it is extremely important to interpret the 1927 decision of the ECCI from that view. Lovestone was helped to get a majority but he was not permitted to eliminate the opposition. He was saddled with a strong minority, which was guaranteed one-third representation in the Central Committee and permitted to function freely in party work. I am sure it would be a misinterpretation of the 1927 decision to see in it only the support given to the Lovestone majority and not to recognize the provisions for the protection of the minority.

We can see the same pattern again in the 1928 decision. The Lovestone majority was still slightly favored in the official decision, but this was counterbalanced by Stalin's calling Foster to a private interview and telling him that he had no confidence in the Lovestone group. "No good can come from the Lovestone group"—those were Stalin's exact words as Foster reported them to me in Moscow at the Sixth Congress. I am absolutely sure that that was one time Foster did not lie.

At the Sixth World Congress of the Comintern

FEBRUARY 1, 1956

There is very little I can add to what I have already written about the Sixth World Congress of the Comintern (1928) in the *History of American Trotskyism*. That report on the Congress as a whole is meager enough, and the reason for it is frankly explained there. The simple truth is that in the first period after our arrival in Moscow, I, like all the other American delegates, was far more concerned about the fight over the American question than the work of the Congress in general. Then, after I got hold of a copy of Trotsky's *Criticism of the Draft Program,* my interest and attention was concentrated on that and what I would do about it after I got back home.

Maurice Spector, a top leader of the Canadian party, read the *Criticism* at the same time and his reaction to it was the same as mine. Thereafter we lost interest in the official proceedings. We made a compact to fight for Trotsky's cause, but we knew that it would be futile and tactically unwise to begin our fight in Moscow. We held a continuous "Congress" of our own about Trotsky's great document and its implications. As I said in the *History,* "We let the caucus meetings and the Congress sessions go to the devil while we studied this document."

I realize that this puts me down as a poor reporter and convicts me of one-sidedness. This quality, however, is sometimes useful in a political worker. It certainly was so in this case; the "one side" represented by Trotsky's criticism of the draft program was far more important than all the rest of the Congress put together.

My *History of American Trotskyism* will have to stand as my recollection of that time. Everything was fresher in my mind when it was written 14 years ago, and I can't think of anything important to add to it. This book had a curious history. Like practically all my writing, it happened more or less by chance, incident to other work in the movement. It was not planned at all. In the winter of 1942 the comrades in charge of the party school in New York asked me to give a couple of lectures on party history to fill out some open dates on their forum schedule. I thought that would be a small chore and I agreed rather light-mindedly, having nothing more in mind than to relate a few reminiscences about the main points.

Then, when I sat down to make the notes for the first lecture, it occurred to me that I should explain how our movement originated in the Communist Party. But the story of this experience in the CP also required some explanatory background. Before I fully realized what I was undertaking to do I was back in the beginning, making notes about the early days of American communism. I got so bogged down in notes about that period that it took me three lectures to get out of the Communist Party, before I could start on the subject of our independent activities after our expulsion.

The interest of the attending audience stimulated me to keep going along that line until the course was strung out to 12 lectures. The lectures were not written, but spoken free-style, from notes usually made on the day of the lecture. The only research I did was to leaf through the bound volumes of *The Militant* to fix the various events in their proper order of continuity. All the rest came from my memory at the time.

The eventual publication of the lectures also happened without prior design on my part. Sylvia Caldwell, who was my secretary at that time, took the lectures down in shorthand on her own initiative, and later transcribed her notes. There was some casual talk among us of publishing the lectures some time, but I did nothing about it and left the typescripts sleeping in the file for another year and a half. They would still be there, probably, except for another incident over which I had no control.

In November, 1943, we got notice that our appeal from our conviction in the 1941 trial at Minneapolis had been denied by the Supreme Court, and that we would have about a month to get ready to go to Sandstone Prison. Then, under pressure of time, I hastily corrected some of the grammatical mistakes in the typescripts of the lectures and handed them over to Pioneer Publishers just under the deadline. The accidental book was finally published the following spring. Others have to judge what the book is worth. All I know for sure is that it is all true.

My comment on Stalin's policy at the time of the Sixth World Congress must be qualified by the observation that I know more now about what was going on in the Russian party and the Comintern, than I did then. Consequently I have to be on guard against coloring my recollections of various incidents by interpretations I arrived at later.

It is safe to say that all of us in the American opposition were aware of the muted struggle going on against the right wing in the Russian party; and that we drew the conclusion that in one way or another this would be advantageous to us in the factional struggle at home. I don't think we realized at that time how deep the cleavage had become between Stalin and Bukharin. This was obscured by the fact that Bukharin was put forward as the leader of the Congress to make the chief political report.

There was a great deal of speculation as to what was really going on in the Russian party, but no one seemed to know. I personally got a good deal of information from Hathaway, a member of our faction, who had just finished a three-year term in Moscow as a student in the Lenin School. Hathaway, like all the other students of this misnamed institution, had been trained to scent the wind in the Russian party, and he was a fully indoctrinated Stalinist. He parroted the official line against Rykov, Tomsky and a number of others whom he designated as right-wingers in the Russian party, but I can't recall that he was very definite about Bukharin.

Stalin evidently wanted to utilize the Congress as a

final mopping-up operation against the Left Opposition before bringing the fight against Bukharin into the open. The American opposition delegates were cagey about getting out on a limb in connection with the internal affairs of the Russian party. They denounced the Lovestoneites as representatives of the right-wing tendency in the International without specifying who were the Russian leaders in this right wing. I cannot recall that Bittelman or any other member of the American opposition attacked Bukharin openly. I am pretty sure it didn't happen.

We were told that rumors of the fight in the Russian party had been taken up in the Senioren Konvent, but I do not recall any report that Lovestone had raised the question. (This Senioren Konvent was a sort of advisory body made up of the heads of delegations. I think it also included some other especially prominent delegates. If I am not mistaken Foster was also a member of the Senioren Konvent. It was translated as "Council of Elders.")

What sticks in my mind is the report that Stalin, at a special session of the Senioren Konvent, had denied any conflict in the Russian leadership, and that this had a restraining influence on any delegates in the Congress who might have been inclined to press the question.

The Congress was buzzing all the time with rumors about the differences in the Russian party; but I heard nothing about any organized or semi-organized movement that could be considered a "Corridor Congress." I am inclined to think this expression was manufactured by the Lovestoneites after their expulsion, when they no longer had anything to lose. My personal testimony, of course, is not conclusive; my standing in Moscow was such that I could not have been invited into such a cabal.

But Foster would have been considered eligible; and I never heard anything from Foster to indicate that he was part of any "Corridor Congress." If he had been so connected, it seems almost certain that he would have reported it. He reported the even more confidential matter of his personal talk with Stalin, on the latter's invitation, in which Stalin told him that he did not trust Lovestone, as I related in a previous letter.

As far as I know, Stalin's devious method of political manipulation was absolutely unique. There was no criterion by which to estimate what he was driving at at any particular moment. In one of his comments about the early days of the struggle of the Left Opposition in the Russian party—perhaps it was in his autobiography—Trotsky said the party functionaries were kept in the dark as to what the majority faction intended by this or that action. They were required to "guess" what it meant and to adapt themselves in time. Selections of people and promotions were made by the accuracy of their guesses at each stage of development in the factional struggle. Those who guessed wrong or didn't guess at all were discarded. This guessing game was played to perfection in the period of Stalin's preparation to dump Bukharin. I don't think many people knew what was really going on and what was already planned at the time of the Sixth Congress. Everybody was guessing, and it is quite evident that the Lovestoneites guessed wrong.

Here an interesting speculation arises. If Lovestone and Wolfe had *known* about the so-called "Corridor Congress," and had also known that Stalin was behind it—would they still have clung to Bukharin as the representative of an obviously losing cause? Permit me to doubt it—or rather, permit me to say categorically, No.

The main concern of Lovestone and Wolfe was not the general direction of policy in the Russian party and the Comintern, but their own stake in the leadership of the American party. When the showdown came at the party convention the following year, their attempt to propitiate Stalin by proposing the expulsion of Bukharin, was a revealing gesture. Their failure to cut loose from Bukharin at the time of the Sixth Congress really doesn't deserve to be considered as a sign of their quixotic devotion to Bukharin's cause. It was just a bad guess.

As I have previously reported [Letter of May 31, 1955], I do remember the meeting during the Sixth Congress referred to in Lovestone's cable to his factional supporters in America, submitted by Gitlow to one of the hearings of the Un-American Activities Committee. I recall it rather as a meeting of the American Commission than as a joint meeting of the American and Russian delegations. However that may be, I definitely do not remember Stalin being present and speaking. It is highly doubtful that I could have forgotten that, because Stalin's personal appearances at such gatherings were rare events, and were apt to be remembered. What fixes the memory of this meeting in my mind was Lovestone's unprecedented action in making a rude and angry attack on Losovsky, and his remark in obvious reference to Losovsky's differences with Lenin in the October days: "Nobody in our party ever fought Lenin."

It could be that the Lovestone faction had private meetings with Stalin and Bukharin and that Stalin at such a meeting gave them some grounds to think they could count on his support. That could have been part of his devious game of putting Bukharin off guard until he was ready to cut his throat. But that, of course, is speculation. Nothing was clear to anybody then. And all that's clear now is that Stalin at the time of the Sixth Congress, was planning to open fire on Bukharin and to finish off his supporters in the International in the process, but that he wasn't ready to disclose his whole plan at that time.

The opposition platform entitled "The Right Danger in the American Party" was submitted to the American Commission by the official Congress delegates of the opposition bloc. The signatures—J.J. Johnstone, M. Gomez, W.F. Dunne, J.P. Cannon, Wm. Z. Foster, Alex Bittelman and G. Siskind—were apparently the signatures of the regularly designated delegates. (A number of other oppositionists such as Browder, Hathaway and others, present at the Congress, were evidently not regular delegates.) The document was presented in the name of the opposition delegation as a whole. As far as I know there were no dissenters. The chief author of the document was Bittelman. The order of the signatures had no significance.

I do not remember the American oppositionists' protest against Paragraph 49 of the Congress Theses on the ground that it failed to emphasize sufficiently the "growing contradictions confronting American imperialism, etc." In any case, it could not be considered as a serious conflict but rather as an attempt to put a little pressure to have the American resolution brought into line more precisely with the new orientation of the Comintern and, to help the opposition in its fight in the American party. It was a custom in these faction fights in the Comintern for every faction to demand a little more than it expected to get in the hope that it would get something by way of compromise.

At the time we submitted the platform of the opposition on "The Right Danger" everything was still more or less normal in the opposition bloc. There was not the slightest sign of objection by the Fosterites to my participation, since there could be no hope of winning a majority in the party unless the bloc held together. The objection to me, rather, was that I was not sufficiently active and aggressive in the struggle before the American Commission. This discontent with my conduct became accentuated after I read Trotsky's *Criticism of the Draft Program*. Then I began to slow down and lose interest in the faction fight altogether. The others may have known, or suspected the reasons, but I am sure they could not bring themselves to believe that I would do anything foolishly impractical about it. They didn't care what anyone's secret thoughts might be as long as they were not compromised by some overt action.

The delegates of the "Cannon group" were especially discontented with my increasing indifference to the factional struggle in Moscow and what it might portend; their own positions in the party stood to be affected adversely by my default. They started a pressure campaign to induce me to snap out of it and get back into the fight in earnest. The repudiation of Foster by his own faction had created a sort of vacuum in the leadership of the combined opposition and they felt, not without some justification, as things were at that time, that I was far better qualified to fill it than any of the other members of the Foster group. All this led to an incident which is perhaps worth reporting, since it compelled me to make the decision which was to have far-reaching consequences.

A meeting was called of all the members and sympathizers of our faction in Moscow. About a dozen, all told, were there, including our Congress delegates, the students in the Lenin School and a number of others. Spector was also present. There the proposition was flatly put to me—that if I would quit dragging my feet and go all-out in the factional struggle, they would pledge me their support all the way to the end as the logical candidate for the central position of leadership in the party when the Lovestone regime was overthrown.

I did not give a definite answer at the meeting. Spector and I held our own caucus on the question for a couple of days. We discussed it solely from the point of view of how best to serve the cause of Trotsky, to which we were by then fully committed. The proposal had an attractive glitter. In the first place, even though we were less optimistic than the others, we recognized that the objective outlined in the meeting was not unrealistic. If the indications of a Comintern swing to the left were fully developed there was good ground to think that the opposition's chances for gaining the majority in the party would steadily improve.

Secondly, with Foster discredited and repudiated by his own former supporters, it was obvious that my claim to a more important role as the central leader of the opposition, and eventually of the party, was far stronger than that of Bittelman or any of the others in the Foster faction. Bittelman suffered from a number of disqualifications, which he himself was well aware of. He was distinctively an internal party man, not a mass worker and orator suited to the role of public leader. Browder had no standing as a political leader and was not even thought of in that connection. The other people of the Foster group were of even lesser caliber.

We speculated that if I could secure the central position in the official apparatus of the party, I would be in a position to swing far more substantial support for the International Left Opposition when the time came to make a decisive open break. The fly in the ointment was that in order to carry out such a maneuver I would have to adapt myself to the official Comintern line against Trotskyism, and even make up for previous derelictions by excessive zeal in this respect. I would, in effect, be winning the party for the program of Stalinism.

Could I then, at some indefinite future time, reveal my own secret program and overcome the effect of the miseducation which I had helped to disseminate? Was there not a danger that I myself would become compromised and corrupted in the process and find it impossible to extricate myself at some future time?

I must state frankly that Spector and I discussed the proposition between ourselves very seriously before deciding against it. Only after thorough consideration of the maneuver from all sides, did we finally decide to reject the proposition. We came to the conclusion that the cause of Trotskyism would be served better in the long run if we frankly proclaimed his program and started the education of a new cadre on that basis, even though it was certain to mean our own expulsion and virtual isolation at the start of the new fight.

The choice of alternatives would present no difficulties to people who have been raised and educated in the Trotskyist school of principled politics, which our movement has consistently represented since 1928. The decision we made at that time would seem to be an easy one, to be made out of hand. It was not so easy for us in those days. Since the death of Lenin, the politics of the Comintern had become a school of maneuverism, and we ourselves had been affected by it. Trotsky's document on the Draft Program was a great revelation of the meaning of principled politics. But for us at that time it was a new revelation. We were profoundly influenced by it, but we were only beginning to assimilate its full significance.

That accounts for our hesitation, for our toying for a day or two with the possibility of a self-deceiving maneuver which might well have gravely injured the cause of genuine communism in this country. And not only in this country, for the expelled and slandered defenders of the banner everywhere were then in their darkest hour. They needed to hear an American voice in their support. Our demonstrative action in publicly unfurling the banner of Trotsky in 1928—at a time when he was exiled and isolated in Alma Ata—greatly encouraged the scattered forces of the International Left Opposition throughout the world.

The Fosterites had never talked to us about their own family affairs. Consequently, the big explosion at the joint caucus of the delegates of the two groups in Moscow came as somewhat of a surprise to us. To judge from the intensity of the feelings expressed, the revolt against Foster must have been brewing for a long time; it could hardly have been caused by the difference on trade-union tactics alone. It is more likely that the trade-union dispute, in which Bittelman and Browder could draw courage from being on Losovsky's side, triggered an explosion built up out of many accumulated grievances.

One of Foster's traits which I especially detested, after I got to know him well, was his different manner and attitude in dealing with different people. To those whom he thought he needed, such as Bittelman and myself, he was always careful and at times even a bit deferential. To those who needed him, such as Browder and Johnstone, he was brusque and dictatorial. They must have stored up many resentments against that.

I remember one rather dramatic incident during the discussion. Foster stood over Johnstone threateningly, with his fist clenched, and tried his old trick of intimidation with the snarling remark: "You're getting pretty bold!" Johnstone, almost hysterical, answered: "You have been trampling on me for years, but you're not going to trample on me any more." Johnstone and Browder gave the impression at this meeting of people who had broken out of long confinement and were running wild.

Bittelman's conduct was more difficult for me to understand. During all the time that we had been together in one group, and I had known everything that was going on with respect to personal relations, Foster had never presumed to bulldoze Bittelman. Yet at this meeting Bittelman's tone and language seemed to be that of a man who was out to settle personal scores long overdue. He was absolutely ruthless in his attack on Foster, and even contemptuous of his arguments.

It was remarkable that not a single person in the meeting spoke up in defense of Foster. The whole faction was in revolt against him, with Bittelman in the lead and Browder and Johnstone close behind him. The funny thing about the whole business was that this fight, of almost unprecedented violence, which ordinarily would signify a complete break of personal and political relations between the participants, was apparently carried on with no thought of such consequences.

The Fosterites in revolt were still dependent on Foster's

name and prestige whether they liked it or not. At that time they had no prospect of playing a big role in the party without him. Foster, for his part, had nowhere else to go except to become a captive of the Lovestoneites, and that was impossible for him. So the whole stew blew up violently and then receded and continued to simmer and sizzle in the same pot. We, the "Cannonites," stood aside and let the Fosterites fight it out among themselves. From a personal standpoint I felt a certain sympathy for the slaves in hysterical rebellion. But from a political standpoint I couldn't see any sense whatever in encouraging a split with a view to realignment in the form of a bloc between our faction and the Fosterites, minus Foster.

Foster's name and prestige, and his dogged persistence and outstanding ability as a mass worker, were always the bigger half of the assets of the Foster group, and remained so even after he had been defeated and isolated within the group. This was shown quite conclusively a short time later. When Stalin wanted to convey a message—with more than a hint of future support—to the American opposition, he sent for Foster and gave it to him personally.

It is quite possible that Browder and Johnstone could have had illusions of going on without Foster as if nothing had happened, for they were notorious for their political unrealism and ineptitude. But I could not imagine Bittelman entertaining such illusions. He had always been pretty realistic in his estimate of the forces in the party and of his own impediments. He knew that he had to be allied with others who had what he lacked, and he relied on combinations in which he could play a strategic part. The original Foster-Bittelman-Cannon combination was made to order for him to play a role in the party that he never could have played by himself. His importance declined when one-third of the combination broke off. And he cannot have failed to understand that it would decline still more if he came to an open break with Foster.

I had known Bittelman as a man of reserve, who kept his personal feelings under control far better than most—a quality which I admired; and to this day I can't understand what drove him to such violence in the attack on Foster as to risk the danger of an irreparable split. That he had any idea of fighting for the leadership of the party in his own name is in my opinion the one hypothesis that has to be excluded.

There is one small postscript to my recollections of this family fight among the Fosterites, which was soon swallowed up in my preoccupation with the immeasurably larger subject of Trotsky's *Criticism of the Draft Program*, and all that it implied for my own future course.

After the meeting, in a personal conversation with Bill Dunne and me, Foster complained of the treatment he had received and intimated—without saying so directly—that he would like to have better personal relations with us for collaboration in the future. But my own mind was already turning to far bigger things than the old factions and faction squabbles in the American party, and I couldn't get up any interest in them any more.

On critics and criticism

APRIL 6, 1959

I received your letter of March 31 and the current issue of *Political Affairs* at the same time. So far I have only had time and interest to skim through the Oakley Johnson article and to note its grossly malicious and mendacious—typically Stalinist—criticism of your first volume. I have developed the automatic habit of putting all this kind of literature aside, in a separate bundle, to read through all at once when I have the time and mood for hard work at disagreeable chores. Is it prejudice, or merely my finicky taste for honest writing with a reasonably clear style, that makes it such an onerous duty for me to keep track of the Stalinist press?

My experience, and a habit I acquired as I gradually became a case-hardened politician ready for anything, might be worth while for you, as a writer, to consider. I eventually learned to hear all criticism attentively, if not gladly, and to examine it carefully—to see if I had left any exposed targets which might be covered next time.

My critics, including the foolishly mistaken and the deliberately crooked, have never suspected how attentively I listened and how much I profited from their efforts—after my tender, sensitive skin finally got calloused and toughened up enough to bounce off everything from pin-pricks to dagger-thrusts.

You might try looking at Johnson's article with this philosophy.

The 'Third Period'

MARCH 20, 1959

The "Third Period," promulgated at the Sixth Congress of the Comintern in 1928, was the over-all title given to the whole era of frenzied ultra-radicalism—in Russia, and on an international scale—which lasted for five years. Everything was done under the sign of the "Third Period." The words became a slogan to explain everything and justify everything the party did. They even once advertised a "Third Period Dance." (I am not spoofing; it is literally true.)

Stalin's left turn (1928–33) was not merely a device for his factional war against Bukharin, Tomsky and Rykov. It was also used with diabolic efficiency to out-flank the Left Opposition. But there was another, and still more compelling, motivation: the turn was not by any means simply a capricious decision of Stalin in his factional struggles.

As with so many of his later swings, it was imposed on him by circumstances which had crept up on him and been fostered by his previous policy. By 1928, the kulaks, who had prospered under the previous right-wing policy during the war against the Left Opposition, had grown bold enough to start a grain strike which threatened the bread supply of the cities and would have made the execution of the first Five Year Plan impossible.

It became a matter of self-preservation for the Stalinist regime to strike back and break the power of the kulaks. The comparatively moderate policy previously advocated by the Left Opposition, of squeezing and taxing the kulaks to get funds to promote the industrialization program, was now taken up by the Stalinists and executed with all the exaggerated frenzy of desperation. Bukharin and the others, who tried to resist the turn or at least to moderate it, had to be crushed in the stampede. Trotsky wrote extensively about these basic compelling reasons for the "left turn" at the time. If I am not mistaken, he referred to the causative circumstances as the "unarmed kulak uprising," which caught the Stalinist regime by surprise and threw it into a panic.

I recall that Trotsky, in the early Thirties, wrote a devastating criticism of this ultra-radical policy—applied everywhere uniformly, regardless of national conditions. Trotsky called his article "The Third Period of the Comintern's Mistakes."* The "Third Period" culminated, as you have noted, in the fascist catastrophe in Germany in 1933. Soon after that the right swing toward the People's Front policy got under way.

Foster's last stand

JANUARY 22, 1958

Foster's evolution in his twilight hours is strictly in accord with the evaluation of him which I have made in previous letters to you. Foster is fighting to the last twitch to justify himself, to protect his prestige, his place in history, which, as he sees it, long ago became completely dependent on the historical vindication of Stalinism.

But in the true sense of the word, Foster is not a "Stalinist Mohican" and still less a "Bourbon." Foster is a Fosterite—a fame fetishist—who adapted himself to the Stalinist power as he had previously adapted himself to Fitzpatrick, and even to Gompers, with the calculation that in doing so he could serve his own ends and his own career.

The big difference is that when his adaptation to Gompers, in order to serve his own purposes, ran up against the difficulty which always arises in such cases—that Gompers insisted on using the adaptation for *his* purposes—Foster

---

* See *Writings of Leon Trotsky, 1930* (Pathfinder Press, 1974).

could find an alternative field of operations, still within the labor movement, by adapting himself to Moscow, which eventually became an adaptation to Stalinism. But after that there was no third road open to him.

Foster was stuck with Stalinism. He could not hope to go back to Gompers and Fitzpatrick and find the necessary elbow room to advance his own fame and prestige. He could not go over to the side of American capitalism; his role, his fame, and even more than that, his whole life, were irrevocably tied to the working class movement.

To be sure, he might have considered the alternative of breaking with Stalinism and undertaking to create a new revolutionary movement from scratch. But for that he would have had to sacrifice his popularity, his prestige, his position and some kind of authority—or a simulacrum of it. It was not in Foster's character to do that. So there he is, as his last sands run out, still clinging to his illusion that in trying to outwit history he is in some way or other making history.

Foster and the later Stalinists

JANUARY 31, 1958

I do think it rather important, if one is to probe the phenomenon of American Stalinism to the bottom, to recognize the difference between Foster and that generation of young idealists who came into the party after it had become completely Stalinized and who never knew any other school. Foster was past 40 when he came to the CP in 1921. His character, his general conceptions and his ambitions had been fully formed in the previous movements.

There is no doubt that he had learned something from the Russians and changed a little. But his primary strategy was to adapt himself to the new power in order to serve his original ambition to rearrange things in the American trade-union movement and advance his own career in the process. The savage irony in the whole affair is that the Stalinist power, which he had set out to use, used him instead and used him up and is still using him in his last hour. Who can feel sorry when the biter gets bit? Not me.

You raise an interesting question when you say: "It's better that he should be a fake Stalinist than a real one." I personally find it easier at least to try to have a sympathetic understanding of the young men who joined the party in the early Thirties with full conviction that they were serving the cause of communism. Gates' articles in the *New York Post*, which I have just read, unknowingly draw a poignant picture of this deceived and betrayed generation of young idealists. Their story remains to be written, but I suppose it would take a deep-seeing artist to do justice to the theme. There is a profounder tragedy in their aspirations and defeat than in the career of Foster who came to Stalinism with tongue in cheek.

Spector's role

JANUARY 22, 1958

Your interview with Maurice Spector will enable you to fill a gap in the information I have previously given to you. According to my recollection, Spector's account of his part in the early development of the Trotskyist movement is factually correct on every point.

Referring to your letter of December 25, I will comment briefly on the numbered paragraphs:

1. I had indeed heard about Spector's reluctance to condemn Trotsky as far back as 1925. His open manifestation of sympathy for Trotsky, or at least of doubts on the question, thus antedated mine by three years. However, I had no communication with him and did not know what the evolution of his thinking had been until I talked with him in New York in the early part of 1928.

2. I remember well my meeting with Spector in New York in 1928 prior to the Sixth World Congress of the Comintern. I am pretty certain that this was in February, on the occasion of his attendance at the American party plenum at that time as fraternal delegate of the Canadian party. We spent an entire evening together, frankly discussing our doubts and dissatisfaction with the way things were going in Russia. But neither of us knew what to do about it and made no plan or decision to do anything at that time. I think it can be safely said, however, that the thoughts we confided to each other at this meeting in February 1928 prepared the way for our getting together in Moscow at the Sixth World Congress.

In fact, this earlier meeting with Spector in New York had remained so fresh in my memory, and I had mentioned it so often, that when I got your letter I was sure I had reported it fully in one of my previous letters to you. But a check of the letters since I got back from the desert discloses only a brief reference (February 3, 1956). I think it is most fortunate, in the interest of historical accuracy, that your interview with Spector brought out this important detail about the origins of American Trotskyism, and I am very glad that you have given me the opportunity to make good my omission and to confirm Spector's report. The only difference between his recollection and mine seems to concern the time of our New York meeting, but there is no doubt whatever about the meeting itself.

3. Spector's report of our collaboration in Moscow is identical with my account in the *History of American Trotskyism* and in one or more of my letters to you. I didn't remember that Spector had also succeeded in bringing a copy of Trotsky's criticism of the program out of Russia, but I would take his own statement on that without question.

4. I don't remember that Shachtman and Abern were "deeply shocked" when I showed them Trotsky's criticism of the program and informed them of my stand on it, after my return from the Sixth Congress. Trotsky's document itself seemed to convince them of its correctness. My own announcement that I was going to take a stand for Trotsky in any case may have helped them to make up their minds to come along without delay. As far as I can recall, a very short time, not more than two or three days, elapsed before we had made a solid agreement to start the fight together.

I can imagine that you are having difficulty in trying to compress the whole story from 1923 to 1945 in one volume. It seems to me that there are at least three good-sized stories there: the faction battles of the Twenties which ended with the expulsion of the Lovestoneites in 1929; then "The Third Period" of ultra-leftism to the end of 1933; and after that the big swing to the "People's Front" when Browder rose on a mushroom cloud and thought he was headed for control of outer space. One could almost say that these three stages of development were represented by three different parties. Well, that's your problem, and I can't give you anything but sympathy.

Our trial for 'Trotskyism'

FEBRUARY 3, 1956

Our "trial" for "Trotskyism" before the joint session of the Political Committee and the Central Control Commission of the Communist Party took place in October, 1928. In a way it was a rehearsal for our other trial under the "Smith Act" at Minneapolis 13 years later. The nature of the alleged crime and the method of prosecution was the same in both trials. In each case we were charged, not with overt acts, but with "conspiracy to advocate" certain proscribed ideas.

I described our 1928 trial in my *History of American Trotskyism* (page 291) as follows:

"Up until the end of the long trial, when we read our declaration and put a stop to all ambiguity, they had been trying to 'prove' a case of 'Trotskyism' against us by any kind of 'circumstantial evidence' they could get. (We had not admitted that we were a Trotskyist faction for tactical reasons, as I have already explained.) They brought in a lot of witnesses, very much in the manner of the prosecutors at our recent trial in Minneapolis, to bring corroborative and circumstantial evidence of our guilt. One little stool pigeon would run in and say he heard this, and another would say he heard that. But the star witness was the manager of the Communist Party bookshop. He said he could swear that Shachtman was a Trotskyist. Why? How did he know? 'Because he is always coming into the bookstore, trying to get books on China, and I know China is a Trotskyist question.' The little weasel wasn't so far wrong at that. China was indeed a Trotskyist question, as were all questions of world import."

We were stalling for time and we used up a lot of it in cross-examining this and other witnesses. The Lovestoneites, for reasons of their own, seemed to be willing to let the trial drag out endlessly. They wanted to compromise the Fosterites as our accomplices. The Fosterites were especially nervous about this and were anxious to bring the trial to a close.

I remember two small incidents on the last day: Foster, with righteous indignation, made the statement: "It is absolutely clear already that there is a Trotskyite faction in the party and that the three leaders of it are sitting right here." Then Stachel, the inveterate and most unscrupulous factionalist, suddenly got a twinge of conscience—or maybe it was something he had eaten—and said rather solemnly: "These comrades have been a long time in the movement and we must proceed very carefully before we make a decision."

It was just about then that we decided to bring the thing to a head. I got up and read our statement of allegiance to the Russian Opposition, which was printed on the first page of Volume I, Number 1 of *The Militant*. We were expelled and out of there a few minutes later. The "jury" didn't bother to leave the box.

In reply to your question:

I was not surprised or disappointed by the behavior of Foster, Bittelman and the other Fosterites during this period. By that time they, like all other functionaries in all the parties of the Comintern, could exist only by the grace of Stalin. Their own heads were at stake.

I had only one brief discussion with Foster—on the morning the trial opened. We had coffee together at a cafeteria on the way to the session. It was an accidental meeting; several others were present. Foster and I faced each other across a table. He told me that he had preferred the charges against us. I did not tell him what my answer would be.

His thoughts must have been on the immediate situation and the new blow my defection had dealt to his hopes and dreams of getting a party majority—another blow on top of all the other blows. My break with him in 1925 had been the one big blow that shattered his ambitions. He had never recovered from that, and it was on the tip of my tongue to ask him: "Do you think you are going to get revenge today?" But I refrained. I was looking far ahead to the great new struggle we were starting, and I had no disposition to talk with him in the old factional terms.

On 'The Birth of American Trotskyism'

MAY 27, 1959

It seems to me that I have already written myself out on "The Birth of American Trotskyism"—in which I played the central role because I just happened to be standing there at the time and there was no one else to do it. I couldn't add much to what I have already written in the *History of American Trotskyism,* in my letters to you, and in the big article—"The Degeneration of the Communist Party—and the New Beginning"*—in the Fall, 1954 issue of *Fourth International*. That's my case. If I were to write about it again I could only repeat what I have already said.

You'll find a better and fuller exposition there than I could write again today. I have the faculty, which for me is a happy one, of pushing things to the back of my mind once I have written them out. In order to write a fresh report on the origin of American Trotskyism, I would have to force myself back into a semi-coma, recalling and reliving the struggle of 31 years ago. That is too much for me to undertake again.

The only thing I left out of my extensive writing about that period, which I try to leave out of all my writing, was the special element of personal motivation for my action—which cynics would never believe and research workers never find in the files and cross-indexes. That is the compulsion of *conscience* when one is confronted by an obligation which, in given circumstances, is his alone to accept or to evade.

In the summer of 1928 in Moscow, in addition to the theoretical and political revelation that came to me when I read Trotsky's *Criticism of the Draft Program* of the Comintern, there was another consideration that hit me where I live. That was the fact that Trotsky had been expelled and deported to far-away Alma Ata; that his friends and supporters had been slandered and expelled and imprisoned; and that the whole damned thing was a *frame-up!*

Had I set out as a boy to fight for justice for Moyer and Haywood in order to betray the cause of justice when it was put squarely up to me in a case of transcendent importance

---

* Republished as the introduction to this volume.

to the whole future of the human race? A copy-book moralist could easily answer that question by saying: "Of course not. The rule is plain. You do what you have to do, even if it costs you your head." But it wasn't so simple for me in the summer of 1928. I was not a copy-book moralist. I was a party politician and factionalist who had learned how to cut corners. I knew that at the time, and the self-knowledge made me uneasy.

I had been gradually settling down into an assured position as a party official with an office and staff, a position that I could easily maintain—as long as I kept within definite limits and rules which I knew all about, and conducted myself with the facility and skill which had become almost second nature to me in the long drawn-out factional fights.

I knew that. And I knew something else that I never told anybody about, but which I had to tell myself for the first time in Moscow in the summer of 1928. The foot-loose Wobbly rebel that I used to be had imperceptibly begun to fit comfortably into a swivel chair, protecting himself in his seat by small maneuvers and evasions, and even permitting himself a certain conceit about his adroit accommodation to this shabby game. I saw myself for the first time then as another person, as a revolutionist who was on the road to becoming a *bureaucrat*. The image was hideous, and I turned away from it in disgust.

I never deceived myself for a moment about the most probable consequences of my decision to support Trotsky in the summer of 1928. I knew it was going to cost me my head and also my swivel chair, but I thought: What the hell—better men than I have risked their heads and their swivel chairs for truth and justice. Trotsky and his associates were doing it at that very moment in the exile camps and prisons of the Soviet Union. It was no more than right that one man, however limited his qualifications, should remember what he started out in his youth to fight for, and speak out for their cause and try to make the world hear, or at least to let the exiled and imprisoned Russian Oppositionists know that they had found a new friend and supporter.

In the *History of American Trotskyism,* pp. 92–93, I wrote:

"The movement which then began in America brought repercussions throughout the entire world; overnight the whole picture, the whole perspective of the struggle changed. Trotskyism, officially pronounced dead, was resurrected on the international arena and inspired with new hope, new enthusiasm, new energy. Denunciations against us were carried in the American press of the party and reprinted throughout the whole world, including the Moscow *Pravda*. Russian Oppositionists in prison and exile, where sooner or later copies of *Pravda* reached them, were notified of our action, our revolt in America. In the darkest hour of the Opposition's struggle, they learned that fresh reinforcements had taken the field across the ocean in the United States, which by virtue of the power and weight of the country itself, gave importance and weight to the things done by the American communists.

"Leon Trotsky, as I remarked, was isolated in the little Asiatic village of Alma Ata. The world movement [outside Russia] was in decline, leaderless, suppressed, isolated, practically non-existent. With this inspiring news of a new detachment in far-away America, the little papers and bulletins of the Opposition groups flared into life again. Most inspiring of all to us was the assurance that our hard-pressed Russian comrades had heard our voice. I have always thought of this as one of the most gratifying aspects of the historic fight we undertook in 1928—that the news of our fight reached the Russian comrades in all corners of the prisons and exile camps, inspiring them with new hope and new energy to persevere in the struggle."

In Moscow, in the summer of 1928, I foresaw such a possible consequence of my decision and action. And I thought that that alone would justify it, regardless of what else might follow. Many things have changed since then, but that conviction has never changed.

The Negro question

APRIL 6, 1959

I am enclosing herewith a copy of an article on the evolution and results of CP policy on the Negro question in the earlier days.* You can check my views and conclusions against your own to see whether there is anything useful for you in your account of this experience.

I had a lot of trouble with this thing. My first intention was to avoid discussion of this chapter of communist history. I was afraid that, if I undertook to answer your questions, I would get so deeply involved in the whole subject that it would consume a great deal of time—and throw me off schedule in my other work. Then temptation lured me and I kept playing hooky from other tasks, and going back to your letter—until I finally did what I was afraid I would do in the first place.

The article contains a number of thoughts and impressions about the results of CP intervention in the Negro

---

* "The Russian Revolution and the American Negro Movement." Published in *International Socialist Review,* Summer 1959. Included in this volume as Part 2.

movement in the early days which have been rattling around in my head for quite a while. I have never seen them stated before, but I had no design to write on the question. It is fairly safe to say that I never would have written anything about it if your questions hadn't propelled me.

But that's the way it has been with all my writing on the first ten years of American communism. Reading that material over again, in preparation for the publication of the collection, I see nothing to change. I am mighty glad I got it out of my system, and I think it will serve a good purpose. I have to thank you in large measure for this.

It is true that the Communist Party influence among the Negroes in the first ten years didn't amount to very much, regardless of its policy. This fact, standing by itself, could perhaps justify a negative critical treatment of the whole experience in your second volume. But your research has established another important fact—that the party recruited substantial numbers of Negroes in the next decade. Why and how could this have happened with such a false policy? In my opinion, you should say something about this to provide a springboard for fuller treatment in the third volume when the results of CP activity in the Negro field began to show up in a big way.

And above all, I believe it is necessary to bring out more clearly, and to emphasize, the profound differences wrought by Russian influence on CP policy in the Twenties, in contrast to that of the traditional socialist position.

I am assuming that, having involved and committed yourself so deeply already, you will write the next volume dealing with the Thirties—if you survive the ordeal and your strength holds out. I recoil from the thought that the history of that tragic and terrible time, when Stalinism really became Stalinism, will be put together by a team of professorial non-participants. The time of the Communist Party in the Thirties was *your own time,* and you are probably the only person who can write about it as one who was there. Trotsky wrote some very wise words, in his recently published *Diary,* about writing in general: "Only a participant can be a *profound* observer"—or words to that effect.

Of course, one can write history as well as fiction with the perception and depth of a participant without having been physically present in the events he describes. But he has to be deeply involved, and see and feel it anyway, if he is to report it truly. That takes more than research; and it is not a task that can be *assigned* to someone, or some team.

Please pardon my sermonizing. It's a habit I got into. I wasn't fooling when I called my book: "Notebook of an *Agitator.*"*

---

* A collection of Cannon's articles from 1926–54. The British edition appeared in 1958. American edition: Pathfinder Press, 1973.

Part 2

The Russian Revolution and the American Negro movement

Top: (Left) William Z. Foster in 1919. (Right) Earl Browder in 1917.
Bottom: (Left) Jay Lovestone in 1924. (Right) Bertram D. Wolfe in 1924.

The Russian Revolution and the American Negro movement

All through the first ten years of American communism, the party was preoccupied with the Negro question, and gradually arrived at a policy different and superior to that of traditional American radicalism. Yet in my published recollections of this period, the Negro question does not appear anywhere as the subject of internal controversy between the major factions. The reason for this was that none of the American leaders came up with any new ideas on this explosive problem on their own account; and none of the factions, as such, sponsored any of the changes in approach, attitude and policy which were gradually effected by the time the party finished its first decade.

The main discussions on the Negro question took place in Moscow, and the new approach to the problem was elaborated there. As early as the Second Congress of the Comintern in 1920, "The Negroes in America" was a point on the agenda, and a preliminary discussion of the question took place. Historical research will prove conclusively that CP policy on the Negro question got its initial impulse from Moscow, and also that all further elaborations of this policy, up to and including the adoption of the "self-determination" slogan in 1928, came from Moscow.

Under constant prodding and pressure from the Russians in the Comintern, the party made a beginning with Negro work in its first ten years; but it recruited very few Negroes and its influence in the Negro community didn't amount to much. From this it is easy to draw the pragmatic conclusion that all the talk and bother about policy in that decade, from New York to Moscow, was much ado about nothing, and that the results of Russian intervention were completely negative.

That is, perhaps, the conventional assessment in these days of the cold war when aversion to all things Russian is the conventional substitute for considered opinion. But it is not true history—not by a long shot. The first ten years of American communism are too short a period for definitive judgment of the results of the new approach to the Negro question imposed on the American party by the Comintern.

Historical treatment of Communist Party policy and action on the Negro question, and of Russian influence in shaping it in the first ten years of the party's existence, however exhaustive and detailed, cannot be adequate unless the inquiry is projected into the next decade. It took the first ten years for the young party to get fairly started in this previously unexplored field. The spectacular achievements in the Thirties cannot be understood without reference to this earlier decade of change and reorientation. That's where the later actions and results came from.

A serious analysis of the whole complex process has to begin with recognition that the American communists in the early Twenties, like all other radical organizations of that and earlier times, had nothing to start with on the Negro question but an inadequate *theory,* a false or indifferent *attitude* and the adherence of a few individual Negroes of radical or revolutionary bent.

The earlier socialist movement, out of which the Communist Party was formed, never recognized any need for a special program on the Negro question. It was considered purely and simply as an economic problem, part of the struggle between the workers and the capitalists; nothing could be done about the special problems of discrimination and inequality this side of socialism.

The best of the earlier socialists were represented by Debs, who was friendly to all races and purely free from prejudice. But the limitedness of the great agitator's view on this far from simple problem was expressed in his statement: "We have nothing special to offer the Negro, and we cannot make separate appeals to all the races. The Socialist Party is the party of the whole working class, regardless of color—the whole working class of the whole world." (Ray Ginger: *The Bending Cross.*) That was considered a very advanced position at the time, but it made no provision for active support of the Negro's special claim for a little equality here and now, or in the foreseeable future, on the road to socialism.

And even Debs, with his general formula that missed the main point—the burning issue of ever-present discrimination against the Negroes every way they turned—was far superior in this regard, as in all others, to Victor Berger, who was an outspoken white supremacist. Here is a summary pronouncement from a Berger editorial in his Milwaukee paper, the *Social Democratic Herald:* "There can be no doubt that the Negroes and mulattoes constitute a lower race." That was "Milwaukee socialism" on the

Negro question, as expounded by its ignorant and impudent leader-boss. A harried and hounded Negro couldn't mix that very well with his Milwaukee beer, even if he had a nickel and could find a white man's saloon where he could drink a glass of beer—at the back end of the bar.

Berger's undisguised chauvinism was never the official position of the party. There were other socialists, like William English Walling who was an advocate of equal rights for the Negroes, and one of the founders of the National Association for the Advancement of Colored People in 1909. But such individuals were a small minority among the socialists and radicals before the First World War and the Russian Revolution.

The inadequacy of traditional socialist policy on the Negro question is amply documented by the historians of the movement, Ira Kipnis and David Shannon. The general and prevailing attitude of the Socialist Party toward the Negroes is summed up by Shannon as follows:

"They were not important in the party, the party made no special effort to attract Negro members, and the party was generally disinterested in, if not actually hostile to, the effort of Negroes to improve their position in American capitalist society." And further: "The party held that the sole salvation of the Negro was the same as the sole salvation of the white: 'Socialism.'"

In the meantime, nothing could be done about the Negro question as such, and the less said about it the better. Sweep it under the rug.

Such was the traditional position inherited by the early Communist Party from the preceding socialist movement out of which it had come. The policy and practice of the trade-union movement was even worse. The IWW barred nobody from membership because of "race, color or creed." But the predominant AFL unions, with only a few exceptions, were lily-white job trusts. They also had nothing special to offer the Negroes; nothing at all, in fact.

The difference—and it was a *profound* difference—between the Communist Party of the Twenties and its socialist and radical ancestors, was signified by its break with this tradition. The American communists in the early days, under the influence and pressure of the Russians in the Comintern, were slowly and painfully learning to change their *attitude;* to assimilate the new theory of the Negro question as a *special* question of doubly-exploited second-class citizens, requiring a program of special demands as part of the over-all program—and to start doing something about it.

The true importance of this profound change, in all its dimensions, cannot be adequately measured by the results in the Twenties. The first ten years have to be considered chiefly as the preliminary period of reconsideration and discussion, and change of attitude and policy on the Negro question—in preparation for future activity in this field.

The effects of this change and preparation in the Twenties, brought about by the Russian intervention, were to manifest themselves explosively in the next decade. The ripely favorable conditions for radical agitation and organization among the Negroes, produced by the great depression, found the Communist Party ready to move in this field as no other radical organization in this country had ever done before.

Everything new and progressive on the Negro question came from Moscow, after the revolution of 1917, and as a result of the revolution—not only for the American communists who responded directly, but for all others concerned with the question.

By themselves, the American communists never thought of anything new or different from the traditional position of American radicalism on the Negro question. That, as the above quotations from Kipnis' and Shannon's histories show, was pretty weak in theory and still weaker in practice. The simplistic formula that the Negro problem was merely economic, a part of the capital-labor problem, never struck fire among the Negroes—who knew better even if they didn't say so; they had to live with brutal discrimination every day and every hour.

There was nothing subtle or concealed about this discrimination. Everybody knew that the Negro was getting the worst of it at every turn, but hardly anybody cared about it or wanted to do anything to try to moderate or change it. The 90 percent white majority of American society, including its working class sector, North as well as South, was saturated with prejudice against the Negro; and the socialist movement reflected this prejudice to a considerable extent—even though, in deference to the ideal of human brotherhood, the socialist attitude was muted and took the form of evasion. The old theory of American radicalism turned out in practice to be a formula for inaction on the Negro front, and—incidentally—a convenient shield for the dormant racial prejudices of the white radicals themselves.

The Russian intervention changed all that, and changed it drastically, and for the better. Even before the First World War and the Russian Revolution, Lenin and the Bolsheviks were distinguished from all other tendencies in the international socialist and labor movement by their concern with the problems of oppressed nations and national minorities, and affirmative support of their struggles for freedom, independence and the right of self-determination. The Bolsheviks gave this support to all "people without equal rights" sincerely and earnestly, but there was nothing "philanthropic" about it. They also recognized the great revolutionary potential in the situation of oppressed peoples and nations, and saw them as important allies of the international working class in the revolutionary struggle against capitalism.

After November, 1917 this new doctrine—with special emphasis on the Negroes—began to be transmitted to the American communist movement with the authority of the Russian Revolution behind it. The Russians in the Comintern started on the American communists with the harsh, insistent demand that they shake off their own unspoken prejudices, pay attention to the special problems and grievances of the American Negroes, go to work among them, and champion their cause in the white community.

It took time for the Americans, raised in a different tradition, to assimilate the new Leninist doctrine. But the Russians followed up year after year, piling up the arguments and increasing the pressure on the American communists until they finally learned and changed, and went to work in earnest. And the change in the attitude of the American communists, gradually effected in the Twenties, was to exert a profound influence *in far wider circles* in the later years.

The Communist Party's break with the traditional position of American radicalism on the Negro question coincided with profound changes which had been taking place among the Negroes themselves. The large-scale migration from the agricultural regions of the South to the industrial centers of the North was greatly accelerated during the First World War, and continued in the succeeding years. This brought some improvement in their conditions of life over what they had known in the Deep South, but not enough to compensate for the disappointment of being herded into ghettoes and still subjected to discrimination on every side.

The Negro movement, such as it was at the time, patriotically supported the First World War "to make the world safe for democracy"; and 400,000 Negroes served in the armed forces. They came home looking for a little democratic pay-off for themselves, but couldn't find much anywhere. Their new spirit of self-assertion was answered by a mounting score of lynchings and a string of race riots across the country, North as well as South.

All this taken together—the hopes and the disappointments, the new spirit of self-assertion and the savage reprisals—contributed to the emergence of a new Negro movement in the making. Breaking sharply with the Booker T. Washington tradition of accommodation to a position of inferiority in a white man's world, a new generation of Negroes began to press their demand for equality.

What the emerging new movement of the American Negroes—a ten percent minority—needed most, and lacked almost entirely, was effective support in the white community in general and in the labor movement, its necessary ally, in particular. The Communist Party, aggressively championing the cause of the Negroes and calling for an alliance of the Negro people and the militant labor movement, came into the new situation as a catalytic agent at the right time.

It was the Communist Party, and no other, that made the Herndon and Scottsboro cases national and world-wide issues, and put the Dixiecrat legal-lynch mobs on the defensive—for the first time since the collapse of Reconstruction. Party activists led the fights and demonstrations to gain fair consideration for unemployed Negroes at the relief offices, and to put the furniture of evicted Negroes back into their empty apartments. It was the Communist Party that demonstratively nominated a Negro for Vice-President in 1932—something no other radical or socialist party had ever thought about doing.

By such and similar actions and agitation in the Thirties, the party shook up all more or less liberal and progressive circles of the white majority, and began to bring about a radical change of attitude on the Negro question. At the same time, the party became a real factor among the Negroes, and the Negroes themselves advanced in status and self-confidence—*partly as a result of the Communist Party's aggressive agitation on the issue.*

The facts are not disposed of by saying: The communists had their own axe to grind. All agitation for Negro rights is grist to the mill of the Negro movement; and the agitation of the communists was more energetic and more effective than any other at that time—by far.

These new developments appear to contain a contradictory twist which, as far as I know, has never been confronted or explained. The expansion of communist influence in the Negro movement in the Thirties happened despite the fact that *one* of the new slogans imposed on the party by the Comintern—the slogan of "self-determination"—about which the most to-do was made and the most theses and resolutions were written, and which was even touted as the main slogan, never seemed to fit the actual situation. The slogan of "self-determination" found little or no acceptance in the Negro community; after the collapse of the separatist movement led by Garvey, their trend was mainly toward integration, with equal rights.

In *practice* the CP jumped over this contradiction. When the party adopted the slogan of "self-determination," it did not drop its aggressive agitation for *Negro equality and Negro rights on every front*. On the contrary, it intensified and extended this agitation. That's what the Negroes wanted to hear, and that's what made the difference. It was the CP's agitation and action under the *latter* slogan that brought the results, without the help, and probably despite, the unpopular "self-determination" slogan and all the theses written to justify it.

The communists turned Stalinists, in the "Third Period" of ultra-radicalism, carried out their activity in the Negro field with all the crooked demagogy, exaggerations and distortions which are peculiar to them and inseparable from them. But in spite of that the main appeal to equal rights came through and found an echo in the Negro community. For the first time since the abolitionists, the Negroes saw an aggressive, militant dynamic group of white people championing their cause. Not a few philanthropists and pallid liberals this time, but the hard-driving Stalinists of the Thirties, at the head of a big, upsurging radical movement generated by the depression. There was power in their drive in those days, and it was felt in many areas of American life.

The first response of many Negroes was favorable; and the party's reputation as a revolutionary organization identified with the Soviet Union, was probably more a help than a hindrance. The Negro upper crust, seeking respectability, tended to shy away from anything radical; but the rank and file, the poorest of the poor who had nothing to lose, were not afraid. The party recruited thousands of

Negro members in the Thirties and became, for a time, a real force in the Negro community. The compelling reason was their policy on the issue of equal rights and their general *attitude,* which they had learned from the Russians, and their activity on the new line.

In the Thirties, Communist Party influence and action were not restricted to the issue of "civil rights" in general. They also operated powerfully to re-shape the labor movement and help the Negro workers gain a place in it which had previously been denied. The Negro workers themselves, who had done their share in the great struggles to create the new unions, were pressing their own claims more aggressively than ever before. But they needed help, they needed allies.

The Communist Party militants stepped into this role at the critical point in the formative days of the new unions. The policy and agitation of the Communist Party at that time did more, ten times over, than any other to help the Negro workers to rise to a new status of at least semi-citizenship in the new labor movement created in the Thirties under the banner of the CIO.

It is customary to attribute the progress of the Negro movement, and the shift of public opinion in favor of its claims, to the changes brought about by the First World War. But the biggest thing that came out of the First World War, the event that changed everything, including the prospects of the American Negro, was the Russian Revolution. The influence of Lenin and the Russian Revolution, even debased and distorted as it later was by Stalin, and then filtered through the activities of the Communist

Party in the United States, contributed *more than any other influence from any source* to the recognition, and more or less general acceptance, of the Negro question as a *special* problem of American society—a problem which cannot be simply subsumed under the general heading of the conflict between capital and labor, as it was in the pre-communist radical movement.

It adds something, but not much, to say that the Socialist Party, the liberals and the more or less progressive labor leaders went along with the new definition, and gave some support to the claims of the Negroes. That's just what they did; they went along. They had no independent, worked-out theory and policy of their own; where would they get it—out of their own heads? Hardly. They all followed in the wake of the CP on this question in the Thirties.

The Trotskyists and other dissident radical groups—who also had learned from the Russians—contributed what they could to the fight for Negro rights; but the Stalinists, dominating the radical movement, dominated the new developments in the Negro field too.

Everything new on the Negro question came from Moscow—after the Russian Revolution began to thunder its demand throughout the world for freedom and equality for all national minorities, all subject peoples and all races—for all the despised and rejected of the earth. This thunder is still rolling, louder than ever, as the daily headlines testify.

The American communists responded first, and most emphatically, to the new doctrine from Russia. But the *Negro people,* and *substantial segments of American white society,* responded indirectly, and are still responding—whether they recognize it or not.

The present official leaders of the "civil rights" movement of the American Negroes, more than a little surprised at its expanding militancy, and the support it is getting in the white population of the country, scarcely suspect how much the upsurging movement owes to the Russian Revolution which they all patriotically disavow.

The Reverend Martin Luther King did remark, at the time of the Montgomery boycott battle, that their movement was part of the world-wide struggle of the colored peoples for independence and equality. He should have added that the colonial revolutions, which are indeed a powerful ally of the Negro movement in America, got their starting impulse from the Russian Revolution—and are stimulated and strengthened from day to day by the continuing existence of this revolution in the shape of the Soviet Union and the new China, which white imperialism suddenly "lost."

Indirectly, but all the more convincingly, the most rabid anti-sovieteers, among them the liberal politicians and the official labor leaders, testify to this when they say: The Little Rock scandal and things like that shouldn't happen because it helps communist propaganda among the dark-skinned colonial people. Their fear of "communist propaganda," like some other people's fear of the Lord, makes them virtuous.

It is now conventional for labor leaders and liberals—in the North—to sympathize with the Negro struggle for a few elementary rights as human beings. It is the Right Thing To Do, the mark of civilized intelligence. Even the ex-radicals, turned into anti-communist "liberals" of a sort—a very poor sort—are all now pridefully "correct" in their formal support of "civil rights" and their opposition to Negro segregation and other forms of discrimination. But how did they all get that way?

It never occurs to the present-day liberals to wonder why their counterparts of a previous generation—with a few notable individual exceptions—never thought of this new and more enlightened attitude toward the Negroes before Lenin and the Russian Revolution upset the apple cart of the old, well-established and complacently accepted separate-but-unequal doctrine. The American anti-communist liberals and labor officials don't know it, but some of the Russian influence they hate and fear so much even rubbed off on them.

Of course, as everybody knows, the American Stalinists eventually fouled up the Negro question, as they fouled up every other question. They sold out the struggle for Negro rights during the Second World War, in the service of Stalin's foreign policy—as they sold out striking American workers, and rooted for the prosecution in the first Smith Act trial of the Trotskyists at Minneapolis in 1941, for the same basic reason.

Everybody knows that now. The chickens finally came home to roost, and the Stalinists themselves have felt impelled to make public confessions of some of their treachery and some of their shame. But nothing, neither professed repentance for crimes that can't be concealed, nor boasts of former virtues that others are unwilling to remember, seem to do them any good. The Communist Party, or rather what is left of it, is so discredited and despised that it gets little or no recognition and credit today for its work in the Negro field in those earlier days—when it had far-reaching and, in the main, progressive consequences.

It is not my duty or my purpose to help them out. The sole aim of this condensed review is to set straight a few facts about the early days of American communism—for the benefit of inquiring students of a new generation who want to know the whole truth, however the chips may fall, and to learn something from it.

The new policy on the Negro question, learned from the Russians in the first ten years of American communism, enabled the Communist Party in the Thirties to advance the cause of the Negro people; and to expand its own influence among them on a scale never approached by any radical movement before that time. These are facts of history; not only of the history of American communism, but of the history of the Negro struggle for emancipation too.

For those who look to the future these facts are important; an anticipation of things to come. By their militant activity in earlier years, the Stalinists gave a great impetus to the new Negro movement. Then, their betrayal of the Negro cause in the Second World War cleared the way for the inch-at-a-time gradualists who have been leading the movement unchallenged ever since.

The policy of gradualism, of promising to free the Negro within the framework of the social system that subordinates and degrades him, is not working out. It does not go to the root of the problem. The aspirations of the Negro people are great and so are the energies and emotions expended in their struggle. But the concrete gains of their struggle up to date are pitifully meager. They have gained a few inches, but the goal of real equality is miles and miles away.

The right to occupy a vacant seat on a bus; the token integration of a handful of Negro children in a few public schools; a few places open for individual Negroes in public office and some professions; fair employment rights on the books, but not in practice; the formally and legally recognized right to equality which is denied in practice at every turn—that's the way it is today, 96 years after the Emancipation Proclamation.

There has been a big change in the outlook and demands of the Negroes' movement since the days of Booker T. Washington, but no fundamental change in their actual situation. This contradiction is building up to another explosion and another change of policy and leadership. In the next stage of its development, the American Negro movement will be compelled to turn to a more militant policy than gradualism, and to look for more reliable allies than capitalist politicians in the North who are themselves allied with the Dixiecrats of the South. The Negroes, more than any others in this country, have reason and right to be revolutionary.

An honest workers' party of the new generation will recognize this revolutionary potential of the Negro struggle, and call for a fighting alliance of the Negro people and the labor movement in a common revolutionary struggle against the present social system.

Reforms and concessions, far more important and significant than any yet attained, will be by-products of this revolutionary alliance. They will be fought for and attained at every stage of the struggle. But the new movement will not stop with reforms, nor be satisfied with concessions. The movement of the Negro people and the movement of militant labor, united and coordinated by a revolutionary party, will solve the Negro problem in the only way it can be solved—by a social revolution.

The first efforts of the Communist Party along these lines a generation ago will be recognized and appropriated. Not even the experience of the Stalinist betrayal will be wasted. The memory of this betrayal will be one of the reasons why the Stalinists will not be the leaders next time.

Part 3

The forerunners

Top: (Left) April 1928 cartoon announcing James P. Cannon's tour for the International Labor Defense. (Right) Cannon as secretary of the ILD in January 1926.
Bottom: William F. Dunne and Charles A. Ruthenberg in 1921.

Eugene V. Debs

and the socialist movement of his time

1. LABOR AND SOCIALISM TODAY

The centennial of the birth of Debs coincided with the merger of the AFL and CIO in a year of standstill, which appears to present a mixed picture of progress and reaction.

The organized labor movement as it stands today, with industrial unionism predominant, owes a lot to Debs, but his name was not mentioned at the merger convention. Debs was the greatest of the pioneers of industrial unionism who prepared the way—but that was yesterday. The smug bureaucrats who ran the convention are practical men who live strictly in the present, and they are convinced that progress is something you can see and count, here and now.

They counted approximately 15 million members in the affiliated organizations, and even more millions of dollars in the various treasuries, and found the situation better than ever. The official mood was never more complacent and conservative.

On the other hand, various groups and organizations calling themselves socialists, taking the numerical size of the present-day movement of political radicalism as their own criterion, found nothing to cheer about in Debs' centennial year. They compared the present membership and support of all the radical organizations with the tens of thousands of members and hundreds of thousands of votes of the Socialist Party in Debs' time, and concluded that things were never so bad. Their celebrations of the Debs Centennial were devoted mainly to nostalgic reminiscences about the "Golden Age of American Socialism" and sighs and lamentations for a return to "the way of Debs."

In my opinion, both of these estimates derive from a misunderstanding of the present reality of the labor movement and of its perspectives for the future. The changes since the time of Debs are not all progressive as the complacent trade-union bureaucrats imagine, and not all reactionary as some others assume, but a combination of both.

The organization of 15 million workers in the AFL-CIO, plus about two million more in the independent unions—and the acquisition of a trade-union consciousness that has come with it—represents in itself a progressive achievement of incalculable significance. And more than trade-union expansion is involved in this achievement.

There has been a transformation of the position of the working class in American capitalist society, which is implicitly revolutionary. Properly understood, the achievements on the trade-union field represent a tremendous advance of the cause of American socialism; since the socialist movement is a part of the general movement of the working class, and has no independent interests or meaning of its own.

In addition to that—and no less important—the revolutionary socialist movement of the present, although numerically smaller, is ideologically richer than its predecessors. Insofar as it has assimilated the experience of the past, in this and other countries, and incorporated their lessons in its program, it is better prepared to understand its tasks. That represents progress for American socialism in the highest degree, for in the last analysis the program decides everything.

At the same time, it is obvious that the progressive growth of the industrial labor movement has not been accompanied by a corresponding development of the class consciousness of the workers. On the contrary, the recent years have seen a decline in this respect; and this is reflected in the numerical weakness of socialist political organization.

That is certainly a reactionary manifestation, but it is far outweighed by the other factors in the situation. The over-all picture is one of tremendous progress of the American working class since the time of Debs. And the present position is a springboard for another forward leap.

In their next advance the organized trade unionists will become class-conscious and proceed to class political organization and action. That will be accomplished easier than was the first transformation of a disorganized, atomized class into the organized labor movement of the present day. And most probably it will take less time.

The same conditions and forces, arising from the contradictions of the class society, which produced the one will produce the other. We can take it for granted without fear of going wrong, that the artificial prosperity of present-day American capitalism will explode sooner and more devastatingly than did the more stable prosperity of expanding capitalism in the time of Debs; and that the next explosion will produce deeper changes in the consciousness of the workers than did the crisis of the Thirties, which brought about the CIO.

In the light of that perspective, the work of revolutionary socialists in the present difficult period acquires an extraordinary historical significance. With that prospect in view, the present momentary lull in the class struggle, which gives time for thought and reflection, can be turned to advantage. It can be, and probably will be, one of the richest periods in the history of American socialism—a period of preparation for great events to come. A study of the socialist movement of the past can be a useful part of this preparation for the future.

That is the only sensible way to observe the Debs Centennial. It should be an occasion, not for nostalgic reminiscence, not for moping and sighing for the return of times and conditions that are gone beyond recall, but for a thorough-going examination and critical evaluation of the early socialist movement. It should be seen as a stage of development, not as a pattern to copy. The aim should be to study its defeats as well as its victories, in order to learn something from the whole experience.

The first rule for such an inquiry should be to dig out the truth and to tell it; to represent the Debsian movement as it really was. Debs deserves this, and he can stand it too. Even his mistakes were the mistakes of a giant and a pioneer. In an objective survey they only make his monumental virtues stand out more sharply in contrast.

2. THE MAKING OF A SOCIALIST

The real history of America is the history of a process leading up to socialism, and an essential part of that process is the activity of those who see the goal and show it to others. From that point of view Eugene V. Debs is a man to remember. The day of his birth one hundred years ago—November 5, 1855—was a good day for this country. Debs saw the future and worked for it as no one else has been privileged to do. On the honor roll of the socialist pioneers his name leads all the rest.

The life of Debs is a great American story; but like everything else American, it is partly foreign. He was truly indigenous, about as American as you can get, and he did far more than anyone else to "Americanize" socialism. But he was not, as he is sometimes pictured, the exponent of a peculiar home-made socialism, figured out all by himself, without benefit of "foreign" ideas and influences.

Debs was the perfect example of an American worker whose life was transformed by the ideas of others, and imported ideas at that. Many influences, national and international, his own experiences and the ideas and actions of others at home and abroad, conspired to shape his life, and then to transform it when he was already on the threshold of middle age.

The employers and their political tools did all they could to help. When President Cleveland sent federal troops to break the strike of the American Railway Union in 1894, and a federal judge put Debs in jail for violating an injunction, they made a great, if unintended, contribution to the auspicious launching of the native American socialist movement.

The inspired agitator began to "study socialism" in Woodstock jail. That was the starting point of the great change in the life of Debs, and thereby in the prospects of socialism in this country. It was to lead a little later to the organization of the first indigenous movement of American socialism under the name of the Socialist Party.

The transformation of Debs, from a progressive unionist and Populist into a revolutionary socialist, didn't happen all at once, as if by a sudden revelation. It took him several more years after he left Woodstock jail, carefully checking the new idea against his own experiences in the class struggle, and experimenting with various reformist and utopian conceptions along the route, to find his way to the revolutionary socialism of Marx and Engels.

But when he finally got it, he got it straight and never changed. Debs learned the basic essentials from Kautsky, the best popularizer of Marxism known in this country in the epoch before the First World War. Thereafter the Marxist theory of the class struggle was the central theme of all his agitation. He scornfully denounced the Gompers theory that the interests of capital and labor are identical. And he would have no truck with the delusive theory that capitalism will grow into socialism through a series of reforms.

Debs campaigned for the overthrow of capitalism by workers' revolution, and refused to settle for anything less. As he himself expressed it, he "determined to stick to the main issue and stay on the main track, no matter how alluring some of the by-ways may appear."

Debs was the main influence and most popular attraction making possible the formation of the Socialist Party of America at the "Unity Convention" in 1901, and the party became an important factor in American life mainly because of him.

There had been socialists and socialist organizations in this country for a half century before that; but they had been derailed every time by a combination of objective circumstances and their own misunderstanding of the doctrine they espoused. The original socialists had been mainly utopians of various kinds, or German immigrants who brought their socialist ideas with them and never learned to relate them to American conditions.

Engels who, like Marx, was foreign to no country, saw no future for that kind of socialism in the United States. In his letters to friends in this country, up to the time of his death in 1895, he continuously insisted that American socialism would never amount to anything until it learned to "speak English" and find expression through the native workers.

In Debs the movement finally found a man who really spoke the language of the country, and who knew how to explain the imported idea of socialism to the American workers in relation to their own experiences.

3. THE ROLE OF THE AGITATOR

When he came to socialism, Debs had already attained national fame as a labor leader. He brought to the new party the rich benefits of his reputation and popularity, the splendor of his oratorical gifts, and a great good will to work for the cause. Debs made the difference; Debs, plus conditions at the time which produced an audience ready to respond. With Debs as its outstanding spokesman after the turn of the century, socialism began for the first time to get a hearing in this country.

Part of what I have to say about Debs and the movement he symbolized is the testimony of a witness who was there at the time. The rest is afterthought. My own appreciation of Debs goes all the way back to the beginning of my conscious life as a socialist. I never knew Debs personally, but I heard him speak several times and he loomed large in my life, as in the lives of all other radicals of my generation.

Debs was an ever-present influence in the home where I was raised. My father was a real Debs man—all the way through. Of all the public figures of the time, Debs was his favorite. Debs' character and general disposition, his way of life—his whole radiant personality—appealed strongly to my father.

Most of the pioneer socialists I came to know were like that. They were good people, and they felt warmly toward Debs as one of their own—the best representative of what they themselves were, or wanted to be. It would not be an exaggeration to say that they loved Debs as a man, as a fellow human being, as much as they admired and trusted him as a socialist leader and orator.

My father's political evolution had been along the same line as that of Debs. He had been a "labor man" since the old Knights of Labor days, then a Populist, then a Bryanite in the presidential campaign of '96, and he finally came to socialism, along with Debs, around the turn of the century.

The *Appeal to Reason,* for which Debs was then the chief editorial writer, came to our house in the little town of Rosedale, Kansas, every week. When Moyer and Haywood, then leaders of the Western Federation of Miners, were arrested in 1906 on a framed-up charge of murder, the *Appeal,* with Debs in the lead, opened up a tremendous campaign for their defense. Debs called for revolutionary action to prevent the judicial murder, with his famous declaration: "If they hang Moyer and Haywood, they will have to hang me!"

That was when I first began to take notice of the paper and of Debs. From week to week I was deeply stirred by the thunderous appeals of Debs and the dispatches of George H. Shoaf, the *Appeal's* "war correspondent" in the Western mine fields. My father and other local socialists chipped in to order extra bundles of the paper for free distribution. I was enlisted to help in that work. My first activity for the movement—in the memory of which I still take pride—was to distribute these special Moyer-Haywood editions of the *Appeal* from house to house in Rosedale. I was then 16 years old.

The campaign for the defense of Moyer and Haywood was the biggest socialist action of the time. All the agitation seemed to center around that one burning issue, and it really stirred up the people. I believe it was the action itself, rather than the political arguments, that influenced me most at first. It was an action for justice, and that always appeals powerfully to the heart of youth. My commitment to the action led to further inquiry into the deeper social issues involved in the affair.

It was this great Moyer-Haywood campaign of Debs and the *Appeal to Reason* that started me on the road to socialism while I was still a boy, and I have always remembered them gratefully for that. In later years I met many people all around the country whose starting impulse had been the same as mine. Debs and the *Appeal to Reason* were the most decisive influences inspiring my generation of native radicals with the great promise of socialism.

Debs was a man of many talents, but he played his greatest role as an agitator, stirring up the people and sowing the seed of socialism far and wide. He was made for that and he gloried in it. The enduring work of Debs and the *Appeal to Reason,* with which he was long associated, was to wake people up, to shake them loose from habits of conformity and resignation, to show them a new road.

Debs denounced capitalism with a tongue of fire, but that was only one side of his agitation. He brought a message of hope for the good time coming. He bore down heavily on the prospect of a new social order based on cooperation and comradeship, and made people see it and believe in it. The socialist movement of the early days was made up, in the main, of people who got their first introduction to socialism in the most elementary form from Debs and the *Appeal to Reason*.

That's a long time ago. In the meantime history has moved at an accelerated pace, here and everywhere else. Many things have happened in the world of which America is a part—but only a part—and these world events have had their influence on American socialism. The modern revolutionary movement has drawn its inspiration and its ideas from many sources and many experiences since the time of Debs, and these later acquisitions have become an essential part of its program.

But for all that, the movement of the present and the future in the United States is the lineal descendant of the earlier movement for which Debs was the outstanding spokesman, and owes its existence to that pioneering endeavor. The Debs Centennial is a good time to take a deeper look at the movement of his time.

4. THE DOUBLE STORY

Those of the younger generation who want to study the ancestral origins of their movement, can easily find the necessary material already assembled. A group of conscientious scholars have been at work reclaiming the record as it was actually written in life and pointing it up with all the necessary documentation.

The published results of their work are already quite substantial. Almost as though in anticipation of the Debs Centennial, we have seen the publication of a number of books on the theme of Debs and American socialism within the last decade.

The Forging of American Socialism, by Howard H. Quint, gives an account of the tributary movements and organizations in the nineteenth century and ends with the launching of the Socialist Party at the Unity Convention in 1901.

The American Socialist Movement—1897–1912, by Ira Kipnis, takes the story up to the presidential campaign of 1912, and gives an extensive report of the internal conflicts in the Socialist Party up to that time. The reformist leaders of the party come off badly in this account. The glaring contrast between them and Debs is fully documented on every point.

Following that, the Debs Centennial this year coincides with the publication of a rather concise history of *The Socialist Party of America* by David A. Shannon. Professor Shannon's research has evidently been thoroughgoing and his documentary references are valuable. In his interpretation, however, he appears to be moved by a tolerance for the party reformists, who did an efficient job of exploiting the popularity of Debs and countering his revolutionary policy at the same time.

On top of these historical works, Debs speaks for himself in *Writings and Speeches of Eugene V. Debs.* This priceless volume, published in 1948, contains an "explanatory" introduction by Arthur Schlesinger Jr. which in simple decency had better been left out.

Schlesinger, the sophisticated "liberal" apologist of American imperialism, has no right to introduce Debs, the thorough-going and fully committed revolutionary socialist; and still less right to "explain" him because he can't begin to understand him. Schlesinger's ruminations stick out of this treasury of Debs' own speeches and writings like a dirty thumb; but everything else in the book is clean and clear. It is the real Debs, explained in his own words.

Finally, there is the truly admirable biography of Debs by Ray Ginger, entitled *The Bending Cross*. Following after earlier biographies by David Karsner and McAlister Coleman, Ginger gives a more complete and rounded report. This is a sweet book if there ever was one; the incomparable Gene comes to life in its pages. All the lights and shadows in that marvelous life as it was actually lived are there, the shadows making the lights shine brighter.

Out of this imposing mass of documentary material—allowing for the shadings of opinion and interpretation by the authors—emerges a pretty clear picture of what the Socialist Party was and what Debs was. Debs was by far the most popular socialist in the heyday of the party, and in the public mind he stood for the party. But the history of American socialism in the first two decades of this century is a double story.

It is the story of the party itself—its official policies and actions—and the story of the unofficial and largely independent policies and actions of Debs. They were related to each other and they went on at the same time, but they were not the same thing. Debs was in and of the party, but at the same time he was bigger than the party—bigger and better.

5. THE DEBS LEGEND

Ray Ginger, the biographer of Debs, remarks that he was a legendary figure while he was still alive. Many stories—some of them of doubtful authenticity—were told about him, and many people professed devotion to him for different and even contradictory reasons.

Debs was a many-sided man, the like of which the movement has not seen, and this gave rise to misinterpretations by some who saw only one facet of his remarkable personality; and to misrepresentations by others who knew the whole man but chose to report only that part which seemed to serve their purpose. This business of presenting fragmentary pictures of Debs is still going on.

There is no doubt that Debs was friendly and generous, as befits a socialist, and that he lived by the socialist ideal even in the jungle of class society. For that he was praised more than he was imitated, and attempts were often made to pass him off as a harmless saint. It was the fashion to say that Debs was a good man, but that's not what they put him in prison for. There was nothing saintly about his denunciation of the exploiters of the workers and the labor fakers who preached the brotherhood of workers and exploiters.

For all the complexity of his personality, Debs was as rigidly simple in his dedication to a single idea, and in suiting his actions to his words, as was John Brown, his acknowledged hero. His beliefs and his practices as a socialist agitator were related to each other with a singular consistency in everything he said and did. The record is there to prove it.

He was a famous labor organizer and strike leader—a man of action—long before he came to socialism, and he never lost his love and feel for the firing line of the class struggle after he turned to the platform. Striking workers in trouble could always depend on Gene. He responded to every call, and wherever there was action he was apt to turn up in the thick of it.

Debs was a plain man of the people, of limited formal education, in a party swarming with slick lawyers, professional writers and unctuous doctors of divinity. It was customary for such people to say—flattering themselves by implication—that Debs was a good fellow and a great orator, but not the "brains" of the party; that he was no good for theory and politics.

The truth is, as the documentary record clearly shows, that as a political thinker on the broad questions of working-class policy in his time, Debs was wiser than all the pretentious intellectuals, theoreticians and politicians in the Socialist Party put together. On practically all such questions his judgment was also better than that of any of the left-wing leaders of his time, most of whom turned to syndicalism to one degree or another.

Debs' own speeches and writings, which stand up so well even today, make the Socialist Party for which he spoke appear better than it really was. The simplicity, clarity and revolutionary vigor of Debs were part of the party's baggage—but only a part. The Socialist Party, by its nature and composition, had other qualities and the other qualities predominated.

6. THE ALL-INCLUSIVE PARTY

The political law that every workers' party develops through internal struggles, splits and unifications is vividly illustrated in the stormy history of the Socialist Party—from start to finish. There is nothing obscure about this history; it is quite fully documented in the historical works previously mentioned.

The Socialist Party came into existence at the "Unity Convention" of 1901, but it had roots in the movements of the past. The new unity followed from and was made possible by a split in the old Socialist Labor Party, which was left on the sidelines in dogmatic isolation; a split in the original, short-lived "Social Democracy," in which Debs and Berger broke away from the utopian colonist elements of that organization; and an earlier split of thousands of native radicals—including Debs and J.A. Wayland, the famed publisher of the *Appeal to Reason*—from the Populist movement, which in its turn, had been "united" with the Democratic Party and swallowed up by it.

These currents of different origins, plus many other local groups and individuals who had begun to call themselves socialists, were finally brought together in one camp in the Socialist Party.

Revolutionists and reformists were present at the first convention, and even after, until the definitive split in 1919. In addition, the new organization made room for a wide variety of people who believed in socialism in general and had all kinds of ideas as to what it really meant and how it was to be achieved. All hues of the political rainbow, from dogmatic ultra-radicalism to Christian Socialism, showed up in the party from the start.

The mixed assemblage was held together in uneasy unity by a loose organizational structure that left all hands free from any real central control. The principle of "States' Rights" was written into the constitution by a provision for the complete autonomy of the separate state organizations; each one retained the right to run its own affairs and, by implication, to advocate its own brand of socialism. Decentralization was further reinforced by the refusal to sanction a national official organ of the party. This measure was designed to strengthen the local and state publications—and incidentally, the local bosses such as Berger—in their own bailiwicks.

The party's principle of the free press included "free enterprise" in that domain. The most influential national publications of large circulation—*Appeal to Reason*,

Wilshire's Magazine, The Ripsaw, and *The International Socialist Review*—were all privately owned. The individual owners interpreted socialism as they saw fit and the party members had no say, and this was accepted as the natural order of things.

To complete the picture of a socialist variety store, each party speaker, writer, editor and organizer, and—in actual practice—each individual, promoted his own kind of socialism in his own way; and the general unification, giving rise to the feeling of greater strength, stimulated all of them to greater effort. The net result was that socialism as a general idea got a good work-out, and many thousands of people heard about it for the first time, and accepted it as a desirable goal.

That in itself was a big step forward, although the internal conflict of tendencies was bound to store up problems and difficulties for the future. Such a heterogeneous party was made possible, and perhaps was historically justified as an experimental starting point, by the conditions of the time.

The socialist movement, such as it was, was new in this country. In its experiences, as well as in its thinking, it lagged far behind the European movement. The different groups and tendencies espousing socialism had yet to test out the possibility of working out a common policy by working together in a single organization. The new Socialist Party provided an arena for the experiment.

The trade unions embraced only a narrow stratum of the skilled and privileged workers; the problem of organizing the basic proletariat in the trustified industries—the essential starting point in the development of a real class movement—had not yet been seriously tackled. It was easier to organize general centers of radicalism, in the shape of socialist locals, than industrial unions which brought down the direct and immediate opposition of the entrenched employers in the basic industries.

In the country at large there was widespread discontent with the crude brutalities of expanding capitalism, just entering into its first violent stage of trustification and crushing everything in its path. Workers, exploited without the restraints of union organization; tenant and mortgaged farmers waging an unequal struggle to survive on the land; and small businessmen squeezed to the wall by the trend to monopoly—they all felt the oppression of the "money power" and were looking about for some means of defense and protest.

The ruling capitalists, for their part, were happy with things as they were. They thought everything was fine and saw no need of ameliorating reforms. The two big political parties of capitalism had not yet developed the flexibility and capacity for reformist demagogy which they displayed in later decades; they stood pat on the status quo and showed little interest in the complaints of its victims. The collapse of the Populist Party had left a political vacuum.

7. THE YEARS OF GROWTH AND EXPANSION

The stage was set in the first decade of the present century for a general movement of social protest. And the new Socialist Party, with its appeal to all people with grievances, and its promise of a better deal all the way around in a new social order, soon became its principal rallying center.

With Debs as its presidential candidate and most popular agitator, and powerfully supported by the widely-circulated *Appeal to Reason,* the new party got off to a good start and soon began to snowball into a movement of imposing proportions. Already in 1900, as the presidential candidate of the new combination of forces before the formal unification in the following year, Debs polled nearly 100,000 votes. This was about three times the vote for a presidential candidate of any previous socialist ticket.

In 1904 the Debs vote leaped to 402,283, a sensational four-fold increase; and many people, calculating the *rate* of growth, began to predict a socialist majority in the foreseeable future. In 1908 the presidential vote remained stationary at 420,713; but this electoral disappointment was more than counter-balanced by the organizational growth of the party.

In the intervening four years the party membership had doubled, going from 20,763 in 1904 to 41,751 in 1908. (Official figures cited by Shannon.) The party still had the wind in its sails, and the next four years saw spectacular advances all along the line.

Socialist mayors were elected all the way across the country from Schenectady, New York, to Berkeley, California, with Milwaukee, the home of small-time municipal reform socialism—almost as famous and even milder than its beer—the shining light in between.

We had a socialist mayor in New Castle, Pennsylvania, when I was there in 1912–1913, working on *Solidarity,* eastern organ of the IWW. Ohio, a center of "red socialism," had a number of socialist mayors in the smaller industrial towns. On a tour for the IWW Akron rubber strike in 1913, I spoke in the City Hall at St. Marys, Ohio, with Scott Wilkins, the socialist mayor of the town, as chairman of the meeting. Scott was a "red socialist," friendly to the IWW.

By 1912, according to official records cited by Kipnis, the party had "more than one thousand of its members elected to political office in 337 towns and cities. These included 56 mayors, 305 aldermen and councilmen, 22 police officials, 155 school officials and four pound-keepers."

If the transformation of society from capitalism to socialism was simply a process of electing enough socialist mayors and aldermen, as a great many leaders of the Socialist Party—especially its candidates for office—fervently believed, the great change was well under way by 1912.

In the campaign of 1912 the socialist cause was promoted by 323 papers and periodicals—five dailies, 262 weeklies and 10 monthlies, plus 46 publications in foreign languages, of which eight were dailies. *The Appeal to Reason,* always the most widely read socialist paper, reached a circulation of over 600,000 in that year. The party membership from a claimed 10,000 (probably an exaggeration) at the formation of the party 11 years earlier, had climbed to an average of 117,984 dues payers for 1912, according to official records cited by Shannon.

In the 1912 presidential election Debs polled 897,000 votes on the Socialist ticket. This was before woman suffrage, and it was about six percent of the total vote that year. Proportionally, this showing would represent more than four million votes in the 1960 election.

Considering that Debs, as always, campaigned on a program of straight class-struggle socialism, the 1912 vote was an impressive showing of socialist sentiment in this country at that time, even though a large percentage of the total must be discounted as protest, rather than socialist, votes, garnered by the reform socialists working the other side of the street.

But things were not as rosy as this statistical record of growth and expansion might seem to indicate. The year 1912 was the Socialist Party's peak year, in terms of membership as well as votes, and it never reached that peak again. The decline, in fact, had already set in before the votes were counted. This was due, not to public disfavor but to internal troubles.

At the moment of its greatest external success the contradictions of the "all-inclusive party" were beginning to catch up with it and tear it apart. After 1912 the Socialist Party's road was downhill to catastrophe.

8. INTERNAL CONFLICT AND DECLINE

The Socialist Party was more radical in its first years than it later became. The left wing was strong at the founding convention and still stronger at the second convention in 1904. As we see it now, the original left wing was faulty in some of its tactical positions; but it stood foursquare for industrial unionism, and took a clear and definite stand on the basic principle of the class struggle—the essential starting point of any real socialist policy. The class struggle was the dominant theme of the party's pronouncements in its first—and best—period.

A loose alliance of the left and center constituted the party majority at that time. The right-wing faction led by Berger, the Milwaukee, slow-motion, step-at-a-time municipal reformer, was a definite minority. But the opportunists fought for control of the party from the very beginning. As a pressure tactic in the fight, Berger threatened, at least once a year, to split off his Wisconsin section.

Soon after the 1904 convention the centrists led by Hillquit combined with the Milwaukee reformists against the proletarian left wing. Thereafter the policy of Berger—with a few modifications provided by Hillquit to make it go down easier—became the prevailing policy of the party. With this right-wing combination in control, "political action" was construed as the pure and simple business of socialists getting elected and serving in public office, and the party organization became primarily an electoral machine.

The fight for industrial unionism—the burning issue of the labor movement championed by Debs and the left wing—was abandoned and betrayed by the opportunists in the hope of propitiating the AFL bureaucracy and roping in the votes of conservative craft unionists. The doctrine of socialism was watered down to make it more acceptable to "respectable" middle-class voters. The official Socialist Party turned more and more from the program of the class struggle to the scramble for electoral success by a program of reform.

This transformation did not take place all at once and without internal convulsions. The battle between left and right—the revolutionists and the reformists—raged without let-up in all sections of the party. Many locals and state organizations were left-wing strongholds, and there is little room for doubt that the majority sentiment of the rank and file leaned toward the left.

Debs, who voiced the sentiments of the rank and file more sensitively and accurately than anyone else, always stood for the class-struggle policy, and always made the same kind of speeches no matter what the official party platform said. But Debs poured out all his energies in external agitation; the full weight of his overwhelming influence was never brought to bear in the internal struggle.

The professional opportunists, on the other hand, worked at internal party politics all the time. They wangled their way into control of the national party machinery, and used it unscrupulously in their unceasing factional maneuvers and manipulations. They fought, not only to impose their policy on an unwilling party, whose majority never trusted them, but also to drive out the revolutionary workers who consciously opposed them.

In 1910 Victor Berger, promoting the respectable reformist brand of socialism, was elected as the first socialist congressman; and a socialist city administration was swept into office in Milwaukee in the same year. These electoral victories had the double effect of strengthening the reformist influence in the party and of stimulating the hunger and thirst for office in other parts of the country by the Milwaukee method. Municipal elections, in which the opportunist wing of the party specialized, on a program of petty municipal reform, yielded many victories for socialist office-seekers, if not for socialism.

Says Kipnis: "Few of these local victories were won on the issue of capitalism versus socialism. In fact, this issue was usually kept well in the background. The great majority of Socialists elected to office between 1910 and 1912 were ministers and professional men who conducted their successful campaigns on reform questions that appeared crucial in their own communities; local option, prohibition, liquor law enforcement; corruption, inefficiency, maladministration, graft, and extravagance; bipartisan combinations, boss and gang rule, and commission government; public improvements, aid to schools, playgrounds, and public health; municipal ownership, franchises, and equitable taxation; and, in a small minority of the elections, industrial depression and labor disputes."

The steady shift of the official policy from the class struggle to reformist gradualism, and the appeal to moderation and respectability that went with it, had its effects on the social composition of the party. Droves of office-hunting careerists, ministers of the gospel, businessmen, lawyers and other professional people were attracted to the organization which agreeably combined the promise of free and easy social progress with possible personal advantages for the ambitious. In large part they came, not to serve in the ranks but to take charge and run the show. Lawyers, professional writers and preachers became the party's most prominent spokesmen and candidates for office.

At a Christian Socialist Congress in 1908 it was claimed that more than 300 preachers belonged to the Socialist Party. The preachers were all over the place; and in the nature of things they exerted their influence to blunt the edge of party policy. Kipnis pertinently remarks: "Since the Christian Socialists based their analysis on the brotherhood of man rather than on the class struggle, they aligned themselves with the opportunist, rather than the revolutionary, wing of the party."

The revolutionary workers in the party ranks were repelled by this middle-class invasion, as well as by the policy that induced it. Thousands left the party by the other door. Part of them, recoiling against the parliamentary idiocy of the official policy, renounced "politics" altogether and turned onto the by-path of syndicalism. Others simply dropped out. Thousands of revolutionary-minded workers, first-class human material out of which a great party might have been built, were scattered and lost to the movement in this period.

The revolutionary militants who remained in the party found themselves fighting a losing battle as a minority, without adequate leadership. In a drawn-out process the "all-inclusive" Socialist Party was being transformed into a predominantly reformist organization in which revolutionary workers were no longer welcome.

At the 1912 convention the right-wing majority mobilized to finish the job. They pushed through an amendment to the constitution committing the party to bourgeois law and order, and proscribing the advocacy of any methods of working-class action which might infringe upon it. This amendment—the notorious "Article 11, Section 6"—which later was included almost verbatim in the "Criminal Syndicalism" laws adopted by various states to outlaw the IWW—read as follows:

"Any member of the party who opposes political action or advocates crime, sabotage, or other methods of violence as a weapon of the working class to aid in its emancipation shall be expelled from membership in the party. Political action shall be construed to mean participation in elections for public office and practical legislative and administrative work along the lines of the Socialist Party platform."

This trickily worded amendment was deliberately designed to split the party by forcing out the revolutionary workers. This aim was largely realized. The convention action was followed by the recall of Bill Haywood, the fighting leader of the left wing, from the National Executive Committee, and a general exodus of revolutionary workers from the party.

The reformist bosses had also calculated that their demonstration of respectability would gain more recruits and more votes for the Socialist Party, if not for socialism. But in this they were sadly disappointed. The party membership declined precipitately after that, and so did the votes. By 1916 the party membership was down to an average of 83,138, a drop of close to 35,000 from the 1912 average. And the party vote that year—with Benson, a reformist, as presidential candidate in place of Debs—fell to 588,113, a decline of one-third from the Debs vote of 1912.

The Socialist Party never recovered from the purge of 1912, and came up to the First World War in a weakened condition. The war brought further mass desertions—this time primarily from the right-wing elements, who were finding the struggle for socialism far more difficult and dangerous than the program of reformist gradualism had made it appear. At the same time, the war, and then the Russian Revolution, also brought a new influx of foreign-born workers who swelled the membership of the language federations and provided a new base of support for a reinvigorated left wing.

This new left wing, armed with the great ideas of the Russian Revolution, fought far more effectively than its predecessor. There was no disorganized withdrawal and dispersal this time. The opportunist leaders, finding themselves in a minority, resorted to wholesale expulsions, and the split became definitive. The new left wing emerged from the internal struggle and split as the Communist Party.

The new Communist Party became the pole of attraction for all the vital elements in American radicalism in the next decade. The Socialist Party was left on the sidelines; after the split it declined steadily. The membership in 1922 was down to 11,277; and by 1928 it had declined to 7,793, of which almost half were foreign-language affiliates. (All figures from official records cited by Shannon.)

Debs remained a member of the shattered organization, but that couldn't save it. Nothing could save it. The Socialist Party had lost its appeal to the rebel youth, and not even the magic name of Debs could give it credit any more. The great agitator died in 1926. In the last years of his life the Socialist Party had less members and less influence—less everything—than it had started with a quarter of a century before.

9. THE ROLE OF DEBS IN THE INTERNAL CONFLICT

The Socialist Party was bound to change in any case. It could begin as an all-inclusive political organization, hospitably accommodating all shades and tendencies of radical thought; but it could not permanently retain the character of its founding days. It was destined, by its nature, to move toward a more homogeneous composition and a more definite policy. But the direction of the change, and the eventual transformation of the party into a reformist electoral machine, were not predetermined. Here individuals, by their actions and omissions, played their parts, and the most decisive part of all was played by Debs.

The role of Debs in the internal struggles of the Socialist Party is one of the most interesting and instructive aspects of the entire history of the movement. By a strange anomaly, the conduct of this irreproachable revolutionist was the most important single factor enabling the reformist right wing to control the party and drive out the revolutionary workers.

He didn't want it that way, and he could have prevented it, but he let it happen just the same. That stands out clearly in the record, and it cannot be glossed over without falsifying the record and concealing one of the most important lessons of the whole experience.

Debs was by far the most popular and influential member of the party. If he had thrown his full weight into the internal conflict there is no doubt that he could have carried the majority with him. But that he would never do. At every critical turning point he stepped aside. His abstention from the fight was just what the reformists needed to win, and they could not have won without it.

Debs never deviated from the class-struggle line in his own public agitation. He fought steadfastly for industrial unionism, and he never compromised or dodged that issue as the official party did. He had no use for vote-catching nostrums. He was opposed to middle-class intellectuals and preachers occupying positions of leadership in the party. His stand against the war was magnificent. He supported the Russian Revolution and proclaimed himself a Bolshevik.

On all these basic issues his sympathies were always consistently with the left wing, and he frequently took occasion to make his own position clear in the *International Socialist Review,* the organ of the left wing. But that's as far as he would go. Having stated his position, he withdrew from the conflict every time.

This seems paradoxical, for Debs certainly was no pacifist. In the direct class struggle of the workers against the capitalists Debs was a fighter beyond reproach. Nothing and nobody could soften him up or cool his anger in that domain. He didn't waste any of his good nature on the capitalist-minded labor fakers either.

Debs' blind spot was the narrower, but no less important, field of internal party politics and organization. On that field he evaded the fight. This evasion was not inspired by pacifism; it followed from his own theory of the party.

As far as I know, Debs' theory of the party was never formally stated, but it is clearly indicated in the course he consistently followed in all the internal conflicts of the party—from beginning to end. He himself always spoke for a revolutionary program. But at the same time he thought the party should have room for other kinds of socialists; he stood for an all-inclusive socialist party, and party unity was his first consideration.

Debs was against expulsions and splits from either side. He was opposed to the split in 1919 and saddened by it. Even after the split had become definitive, and the Rights and Lefts had parted company for good, he still appealed for unity.

Debs believed that all who called themselves socialists should work together in peace and harmony in one organization. For him all members of the party, regardless of their tendency, were comrades in the struggle for socialism, and he couldn't stand quarreling among comrades.

This excellent sentiment, which really ought to govern the relation between comrades who are united on the basic principles of the program, usually gets lost in the shuffle when factions fight over conflicting programs which express conflicting class interests. The reformists see to that, if the revolutionists don't. That's the way it was in the Socialist Party. Debs held aloof from the factions, but that didn't stop the factional struggles. And there was not much love lost in them either.

Debs' course in the internal conflicts of the party was also influenced by his theory of leadership, which he was inclined to equate with bureaucracy. He deliberately limited his own role to that of an agitator for socialism; the rest was up to the rank and file.

His repeated declarations—often quoted approvingly by thoughtless people—that he was not a leader and did not want to be a leader, were sincerely meant, like everything else he said. But the decisive role that leadership plays in every organization and every collective action cannot be wished away. Debs' renunciation of leadership created a vacuum that other leaders—far less worthy—came to fill. And the program they brought with them was not the program of Debs.

Debs had an almost mystic faith in the rank and file, and repeatedly expressed his confidence that, with good will all around, the rank and file, with its sound revolutionary instincts, would set everything straight. Things didn't work out that way, and they never do. The rank and file, in the internal conflicts of the party, as in the trade unions, and in the broader class struggle, can assert its will only when it is organized; and organization never happens by itself. It requires leadership.

Debs' refusal to take an active part in the factional struggle, and to play his rightful part as the leader of an organized left wing, played into the hands of the reformist politicians. There his beautiful friendliness and generosity played him false, for the party was also an arena of the struggle for socialism. Debs spoke of "the love of comrades"—and he really meant it—but the opportunist sharpers didn't believe a word of it. They never do. They waged a vicious, organized fight against the revolutionary workers of the party all the time. And they were the gainers from Debs' abstention.

Debs' mistaken theory of the party was one of the most costly mistakes a revolutionist ever made in the entire history of the American movement.

The strength of capitalism is not in itself and its own institutions; it survives only because it has bases of support in the organizations of the workers. As we see it now, in the light of what we have learned from the Russian Revolution and its aftermath, nine-tenths of the struggle for socialism is the struggle against bourgeois influence in the workers' organizations, including the party.

The reformist leaders were the carriers of bourgeois influence in the Socialist Party, and at bottom the conflict of factions was an expression of the class struggle. Debs obviously didn't see it that way. His aloofness from the conflict enabled the opportunists to dominate the party machine and to undo much of his great work as an agitator for the cause.

Debs' mistaken theory of the party was one of the most important reasons why the Socialist Party, which he did more than anyone else to build up, ended so disgracefully and left so little behind.

10. DEBS AND LENIN

Here we can make an instructive comparison between the course of Debs—to whom we owe so much—and that of Lenin—to whom we owe even more.

As we see them in their words and works, which were always in harmony, they were much alike in character—honest and loyal in all circumstances; unselfish; big men, free from all pettiness. For both of them the general welfare of the human race stood higher than any concerns of self. Each of them, in his own way, has given us an example of a beautiful, heroic life devoted to a single idea which was also an ideal. There was a difference in one of their conceptions of method to realize the ideal.

Both men started out from the assumption that the transformation of society requires a workers' revolution. But Lenin went a step farther. He saw the workers' revolution as a concrete actuality of this epoch; and he concerned himself particularly with the question of how it was to be prepared and organized.

Lenin believed that for victory the workers required a party fit to lead a revolution; and to him that meant a party with a revolutionary program and leadership—a party of revolutionists. He concentrated the main energies of his life on the construction of just such a party, and on the struggle to keep it free from bourgeois ideas and influences.

Lenin recognized that this involved internal discussion and conflict, and he never shirked it. The Menshevik philistines—the Russian counterparts of the American Bergers and Hillquits—hated him for that, especially for his single-minded concentration on the struggle for a revolutionary program, and for his effectiveness in that struggle, but that did not deter him. Lenin believed in his bones that the internal problems of the party were the problems of the revolution, and he was on top of them all the time.

After 1904 Debs consistently refused to attend party conventions, where policy was decided, and always declined nomination for the National Committee, where policy was interpreted and put into practice. Lenin's attitude was directly opposite. He saw the Party Congress as the highest expression of party life, and he was always on hand there, ready to fight for his program. He regarded the Central Committee as the executive leadership of the movement, and he took his place at the head of it.

Lenin wrote a whole book about the conflict at the Second Congress of the party in 1903, where the first basic division between the Bolsheviks and the Mensheviks took place. He was in his element there, in that internal struggle which was to prove so fateful for the Russian Revolution and the future of all mankind.

Contrasting his own feeling about it to that of another delegate dismayed by the conflict, Lenin wrote:

"I cannot help recalling in this connection a conversation I happened to have at the Congress with one of the 'Centre' delegates. 'How oppressive the atmosphere is at our Congress!' he complained. 'This bitter fighting, this agitation one against the other, this biting controversy, this uncomradely attitude . . .'

"'What a splendid thing our Congress is,' I replied. 'A free and open struggle. Opinions have been stated. The shades have been brought out. The groups have taken shape. Hands have been raised. A decision has been taken. A stage has been passed. Forward! That's the stuff for me! That's life! That's not like the endless, tedious, word-chopping of intellectuals which terminates not because the question has been settled, but because they are too tired to talk any more . . .'

"The comrade of the 'Centre' stared at me in perplexity and shrugged his shoulders. We were talking in different languages." (*One Step Forward, Two Steps Back*, p. 225 footnote.)

In her book, *Memories of Lenin*, Krupskaya, his widow, quoted those words of Lenin with the remark: "That quotation sums up Ilyich to a 't'."

The practical wiseacres in Lenin's time looked disdainfully at the ideological conflicts of the Russian emigrés, and regarded Lenin as a sectarian fanatic who loved factional squabbling for its own sake. But Lenin was not fighting over trifles. He saw the struggle against opportunism in the Russian Social Democratic Party as an essential part of the struggle for the revolution. That's why he plunged into it.

It is important to remember that the Bolshevik Party, constructed in the course of that struggle, became the organizer and leader of the greatest revolution in history.

11. THE MOST IMPORTANT LESSON

Debs and Lenin, united on the broad program of revolutionary socialism, were divided on the narrower question of the character and role of the party. This turned out to be the most important question of our epoch for socialists in this country, as in every other country.

The Russian Revolution of 1917 clarified the question. Lenin's party of revolutionists stood up and demonstrated its historical rightness at the same time that the all-inclusive party of Debs was demonstrating its inadequacy.

This is the most important lesson to be derived from the experiences in the two countries, so far apart from each other yet so interdependent and alike in their eventual destiny.

The validity of the comparison is not impaired by reference to the well-known fact that Russia came to a revolutionary situation before America, which hasn't come to it yet. Lenin's greatest contribution to the success of the Russian Revolution was the work of *preparation* for it. That began with the construction of a revolutionary party in a time of reaction, *before* the revolution; and the Bolshevik Party, in turn, began with *Lenin's theory of the party*.

The Socialist Party of Debs' time has to be judged, not for its failure to lead a revolution, but for its failure to work with that end in view and to select its membership accordingly. Socialism signifies and requires the revolutionary transformation of society; anything less than that is mere bourgeois reform. A socialist party deserves the name only to the extent that it acts as the conscious agency in preparing the workers for the necessary social revolution. That can only be a party of revolutionists; an all-inclusive party of diverse elements with conflicting programs will not do.

The achievements of American socialism in the early years of the present century are not to be discounted, but it would be well to understand just what these achievements were. The movement, of which the party was the central organizing force, gave many thousands of people their first introduction to the general perspective of socialism; and it provided the arena where the main cadres of the revolutionary movement of the future were first assembled. These were the net results that remained after everything else became only a memory, and they stand to the historic credit of the early Socialist Party—above all to Debs.

But these irrevocable achievements were rather the by-products of an experimental form of socialist organization which, by its nature, could only be transitory. By including petty-bourgeois reformists and proletarian revolutionists in one political organization, the Socialist Party, presumed to be an instrument of the class struggle of the workers against the capitalists, was simply introducing a form of the class struggle into its own ranks. The result was unceasing internal conflict from the first day the party was constituted. The eventual breakup of the party, and the decision of the revolutionary elements to launch a party of their own, was the necessary outcome of the whole experiment.

In the Russian movement Lenin saw all that beforehand, and the revolution was the gainer for it. After the Russian Revolution, the left wing of the American Socialist Party, and some of the syndicalists too, recognized the superiority of Lenin's method. Those who took the program of socialism seriously had no choice but to follow the path of Lenin. The Bolshevik Party of Lenin rightly became the model for the revolutionary workers in all countries, including this country.

The launching of the Communist Party in 1919 represented, not simply a break with the old Socialist Party, but even more important a break with the whole conception of a common party of revolutionists and opportunists. That signified a new beginning for American socialism, far more important historically than everything that had happened before, including the organization of the Socialist Party in 1901. There can be no return to the outlived and discredited experiment of the past.

The reconstituted movement has encountered its own difficulties and made its own mistakes since that new beginning in 1919. But these are of a different order from the difficulties and mistakes of the earlier time and have to be considered separately. In any case, the poor ideological equipment of the old movement cannot help in their solution.

The struggle against the crimes and betrayals of Stalinism, the prerequisite for the construction of an honest revolutionary party, requires weapons from a different arsenal. Here also the Russians are our teachers. The programmatic weapons for the fight against Stalinist treachery were given to us by Trotsky, the coequal and successor of Lenin.

There can be no return to the past of the American movement. In connection with the Debs Centennial some charlatans, who measure the worth of a socialist movement by its numerical strength at the moment, have discovered new virtues in the old Socialist Party, which polled so many votes in the time of Debs, and have recommended a new experiment on the same lines. Besides its worthlessness as advice to the socialist vanguard that prescription does an injustice to the memory of Debs.

He deserves to be honored for his great positive contributions to the cause of socialism, not for his mistakes. The life work of Debs, as the foremost agitator for socialism we have ever had, as the man of principle who always stood at his post in the class struggle in times of danger and difficulty, will always remain a treasured heritage of the revolutionary workers.

It is best—and it is enough—to honor him for that. The triumph of the cause he served so magnificently will require a different political instrument—a different kind of party—than the one he supported. The model for that is the party of Lenin.

The IWW

The great anticipation

1. THE BOLD DESIGN

When the Founding Convention of the IWW—the Industrial Workers of the World—assembled in Chicago in June, 1905, the general strike movement initiating the first Russian revolution was already under way, and its reverberations were heard in the convention hall. The two events coincided to give the world a preview of its future. The leaders at Chicago hailed the Russian revolution as their own. The two simultaneous actions, arising independently with half a world between them, signalized the opening of a revolutionary century. They were the anticipations of things to come.

The defeated Russian revolution of 1905 prepared the way for the victorious revolution of 1917. It was the "dress rehearsal," as Lenin said, and that evaluation is now universally recognized. The Founding Convention of the

IWW was also a rehearsal; and it may well stand out in the final account as no less important than the Russian action at the same time.

The founders of the IWW were indubitably the original inspirers and prime movers of the modern industrial unions in the mass production industries. That is commonly admitted already, and that's a lot. But even such a recognition of the IWW, as the precursor of the present CIO, falls far short of a full estimate of its historic significance. The CIO movement, at its present stage of development, is only a small down payment on the demands presented to the future by the pioneers who assembled at the 1905 Convention to start the IWW on its way.

The Founding Convention of the IWW brought together on a common platform the three giants among our ancestors—Debs, Haywood and De Leon. They came from different backgrounds and fields of activity, and they soon parted company again. But the things they said and did, that one time they teamed up to set a new movement on foot, could not be undone. They wrote a Charter for the American working class which has already inspired and influenced more than one generation of labor militants. And in its main essentials it will influence other generations yet to come.

They were big men, and they all grew taller when they stood together. They were distinguished from their contemporaries, as from the trade-union leaders of today, by the immensity of their ambition which transcended personal concerns, by their far-reaching vision of a world to be remade by the power of the organized workers, and by their total commitment to that endeavor.

The great majority of the other delegates who answered the call to the Founding Convention of the IWW were people of the same quality. They were the non-conformists, the stiff-necked irreconcilables, at war with capitalist society. Radicals, rebels and revolutionists started the IWW, as they have started every other progressive movement in the history of this country.

In these days when labor leaders try their best to talk like probationary members of the Junior Chamber of Commerce, it is refreshing to turn back to the reports of men who spoke a different language. Debs, Haywood and De Leon, and those who stood with them, did not believe in the partnership of capital and labor, as preached by Gompers and Co. at the time. Such talk, they said in the famous "Preamble" to the Constitution of the IWW, "misleads the workers." They spoke out in advance against the idea of the permanent "co-existence" of labor unions and the private ownership of industry, as championed by the CIO leaders of the present time.

The men who founded the IWW were pioneer industrial unionists, and the great industrial unions of today stem directly from them. But they aimed far beyond industrial unionism as a bargaining agency recognizing the private ownership of industry as right and unchangeable. They saw the relations of capital and labor as a state of war.

Brissenden puts their main idea in a nutshell in his factually correct history of the movement: "The idea of the class conflict was really the bottom notion or 'first cause' of the IWW. The industrial union type was adopted because it would make it possible to wage this class war under more favorable conditions." (*The IWW: A Study of American Syndicalism,* by Paul Frederick Brissenden, p. 108.)

The founders of the IWW regarded the organization of industrial unions as a means to an end; and the end they had in view was the overthrow of capitalism and its replacement by a new social order. This, the heart and soul of their program, still awaits its vindication in the revolution of the American workers. And the revolution, when it arrives, will not neglect to acknowledge its anticipation at the Founding Convention of the IWW. For nothing less than the revolutionary goal of the workers' struggle was openly proclaimed there 50 years ago.

The bold design was drawn by Bill Haywood, General Secretary of the Western Federation of Miners, who presided at the Founding Convention of the IWW. In his opening remarks, calling the convention to order, he said:

"This is the Continental Congress of the working class. We are here to confederate the workers of this country into a working class movement that shall have for its purpose the emancipation of the working class from the slave bondage of capitalism." (*Proceedings of the First Convention of the Industrial Workers of the World,* p. 1.)

The trade unions today are beginning to catch up with the idea that Negroes are human beings, that they have a right to make a living and belong to a union. The IWW was 50 years ahead of them on this question, as on many others. Many of the old Gompers unions were lily-white job trusts, barring Negroes from membership and the right to employment in their jurisdictions. Haywood, in his opening speech, indignantly denounced the policy of those unions "affiliated with the A.F. of L. which in their constitution and by-laws prohibit the initiation of or conferring the obligation on a colored man." He followed, in his speech at the public ratification meeting, with the declaration that the newly-launched organization "recognizes neither race, creed, color, sex or previous condition of servitude." (*Proceedings,* p. 575.)

And he wound up with the prophetic suggestion that the American workers take the Russian path. He said he hoped to see the new movement "grow throughout this country until it takes in a great majority of the working people, and that those working people will rise in revolt against the capitalist system as the working class in Russia are doing today." (*Proceedings*, p. 580.)

Debs said: "The supreme need of the hour is a sound, revolutionary working class organization. . . . It must express the class struggle. It must recognize the class lines. It must, of course, be class conscious. It must be totally uncompromising. It must be an organization of the rank and file." (*Proceedings*, pp. 144, 146.)

De Leon, for his part, said: "I have had but one foe—and that foe is the capitalist class. . . . The ideal is the overthrow of the capitalist class." (*Proceedings*, pp. 147, 149.)

De Leon, the thinker, was already projecting his thought beyond the overthrow of capitalism to "the form of the governmental administration of the Republic of Labor." In a post-convention speech at Minneapolis on "The Preamble of the IWW" he said that the industries, "regardless of former political boundaries, will be the constituencies of that new central authority the rough scaffolding of which was raised last week in Chicago. Where the General Executive Board of the Industrial Workers of the World will sit there will be the nation's capital." (*Socialist Reconstruction of Society*, by D. De Leon.)

The speeches of the others, and the official statement adopted by the Convention in the Preamble to the Constitution, followed the same line. The Preamble began with the flat affirmation of the class struggle: "The working class and the employing class have nothing in common." Following that it said: "Between these two classes a struggle must go on until all the workers come together on the political, as well as on the industrial field, and take and hold" the industries of the country.

These were the most uncompromising, the most unambiguous declarations of revolutionary intention ever issued in this country up to that time. The goal of socialism had been previously envisioned by others. But at the Founding Convention of the IWW the idea that it was to be realized through a struggle for power, and that the power of the workers must be organized, was clearly formulated and nailed down.

The men of 1905 spoke truer than they knew, if only as anticipators of a historical work which still awaits its completion by others. Between that date of origin and the beginning of its decline after the First World War, the IWW wrote an inerasable record in action. But its place as a great progressive factor in American history is securely fixed by the brave and far-seeing pronouncements of its founding convention alone. The ideas were the seed of the action.

The IWW had its own forebears, for the revolutionary labor movement is an unbroken continuum. Behind the convention assembled in Chicago fifty years ago stood the Knights of Labor; the eight-hour movement led by the Haymarket martyrs; the great industrial union strike of the American Railway Union; the stormy battles of the Western Federation of Miners; and the two socialist political organizations—the old Socialist Labor Party and the newly-formed Socialist Party.

All these preceding endeavors were tributary to the first convention of the IWW, and were represented there by participants. Lucy Parsons, the widow and comrade-in-arms of the noble martyr, was a delegate, as was Mother Jones, the revered leader of the miners, the symbol of their hope and courage in trial and tribulation.

These earlier movements and struggles, rich and tragic experiences, had prepared the way for the Founding Convention of the IWW. But Debs was not far wrong when he said, in a speech a few months later: "The revolutionary movement of the working class will date from the year 1905, from the organization of the Industrial Workers of the World." (*Writings and Speeches of Eugene V. Debs*, p. 226.)

2. AN ORGANIZATION OF REVOLUTIONISTS

The IWW set out to be an industrial union movement uniting all workers, regardless of any differences between them, on the simple proposition that all unions start with—the defense of their immediate interests against the employers. As an industrial union, the IWW in its heyday led some memorable battles on the economic field, and set a pattern of organization and militant strike strategy for the later great struggles to build the CIO.

The CIO became possible only after and because the IWW had championed and popularized the program of industrial unionism in word and deed. That alone—the teaching and the example in the field of unionism—would be sufficient to establish the historical significance of the IWW as the initiator, the forerunner of the modern industrial unions, and thereby to justify a thousand times over all the efforts and sacrifice put into it by so many people.

But the IWW was more than a union. It was also—at the same time—a revolutionary organization whose simple and powerful ideas inspired and activated the best young militants of its time, the flower of a radical generation. That, above all, is what clothes the name of the IWW in glory.

The true character of the IWW as a revolutionary organization was convincingly demonstrated in its first formative year, in the internal conflict which resulted in a split at its second convention. This split occurred over questions which are normally the concern of political parties rather than of unions. Charles O. Sherman, the first general president of the IWW, was an exponent of the industrial-union form of organization. But that apparently was as far as he wanted to go, and it wasn't far enough for those who took the revolutionary pronouncements of the First Convention seriously. They were not satisfied with lip service to larger principles.

When the Second Convention of the IWW assembled in Chicago in September, 1906, Haywood was in jail in Idaho awaiting trial for his life; and Debs, never a man for factionalism, was standing aside. Vincent St. John, himself a prominent figure in the Western Federation of Miners, and a member of its delegation to the Second Convention of the IWW, came forward as the leader of the anti-Sherman forces, in alliance with De Leon.

As is customary in factional fights, all kinds of secondary charges were thrown about. But St. John stated the real issue motivating him and his supporters in his own invariably forthright manner. This resolute man was on the warpath at the Second Convention because, as he said:

"The administration of the IWW was in the hands of men who were not in accord with the revolutionary program of the organization. . . . The struggle for control of the organization formed the Second Convention into two camps. The majority vote of the convention was in the revolutionary camp. The reactionary camp, having the Chairman, used obstructive tactics in their effort to gain control of the convention. . . . The revolutionists cut this knot by abolishing the office of President and electing a chairman from among the revolutionists." (*The IWW: History, Structure and Methods,* by Vincent St. John.)

That action precipitated the split and consigned Sherman to a niche in history as a unique figure. He was the first, and is so far the only, union president on record to get dumped because he was *not* a revolutionist. There will be others, but Sherman's name will live in history as the prototype.

This split at the Second Convention also resulted in the disaffiliation of the Western Federation of Miners, the only strongly organized union the IWW had had to start with. The other members of the WFM delegation, already turning to conservatism, supported Sherman in the split. But St. John, as was his nature and consistent practice, took his stand on principle.

Faced with a choice of affiliation between the widely advertised and well-heeled WFM, of which he was a paid officer, and the poverty-stricken, still obscure IWW, with its program and its principles, he unhesitatingly chose the latter. For him, as for all the others who counted in making IWW history, personal interests and questions of bread and butter unionism were secondary. The first allegiance was to revolutionary principle.

Sherman and his supporters, with the help of the police, seized the headquarters and held on to the funds of the organization, such as they were. St. John remarked that the newly elected officials "were obliged to begin work after the Second Convention without the equipment of so much as a postage stamp." (Brissenden, p. 144.) The new administration under the leadership of St. John, who was thereafter to be the dominating influence in the organization for the next decade, had to start from scratch with very little in the way of tangible assets except the program and the ideal.

That, plus the indomitable spirit of Vincent St. John, proved to be enough to hold the shattered organization together. The Sherman faction, supported by the Western Federation of Miners, set up a rival organization. But it didn't last long. The St. John wing prevailed in the post-convention conflict and proved itself to be the true IWW. But in the ensuing years it existed primarily, not as a mass industrial union of workers fighting for limited economic demands, but as a revolutionary organization proclaiming an all-out fight against the capitalist system.

As such, the IWW attracted a remarkable selection of young revolutionary militants to its banner. As a union, the organization led many strikes which swelled the membership momentarily. But after the strikes were over, whether won or lost, stable union organization was not maintained. After every strike, the membership settled down again to the die-hard cadre united on principle.

3. THE DUALITY OF THE IWW

The IWW borrowed something from Marxism; quite a bit, in fact. Its two principal weapons—the doctrine of the class struggle and the idea that the workers must accomplish their own emancipation through their own organized power—came from this mighty arsenal. But for all that, the IWW was a genuinely indigenous product of its American environment, and its theory and practice ought to be considered against the background of the class struggle as it had developed up to that time in this country.

The experience of the American working class, which did not yet recognize itself as a distinct class, had been limited; and the generalizing thought, even of its best representatives, was correspondingly incomplete. The class struggle was active enough, but it had not yet developed beyond its primary stages. Conflicts had generally taken the form of localized guerrilla skirmishes, savagely conducted on both sides, between separate groups of workers and employers. The political power brought to bear on the side of the employers was mainly that of local authorities.

Federal troops had broken the ARU strike of the railroaders in '94—"the Debs Rebellion," as the hysterical press described it—and had also been called out against the metal miners in the West. But these were exceptional cases. The intervention of the federal government, as the executive committee of all the capitalists—the constant and predominant factor in capital-labor relations in modern times—was rarely seen in the local and sectional conflicts half a century ago. The workers generally made a distinction between local and federal authorities, in favor of the latter—as do the great majority, in a delayed hangover from earlier times, even to this day.

The all-embracing struggle of all the workers as a class, against the capitalist class as a whole, with political power in the nation as the necessary goal of the struggle, was not yet discernible to many when the IWW made its entrance in 1905. The pronouncements of the founders of the IWW, and all the subsequent actions proceeding from them, should be read in that light. The restricted and limited scope of the class struggle in America up to that time, from which their program was derived, makes their prevision of 50 years ago stand out as all the more remarkable.

In the situation of that time, with the class struggle of the workers still in its most elementary stages, and many of its complications and complexities not yet disclosed in action, the leaders of the IWW foresaw the revolutionary goal of the working class and aimed at one single, overall formula for the organization of the struggle. Putting everything under one head, they undertook to build an organization which, as Vincent St. John, its chief leader and inspirer after the Second Convention, expressed it, would be "all-sufficient for the workers' needs." One Big Union would do it all. There was an appealing power in the simplicity of this formula, but also a weakness—a contradiction—which experience was to reveal.

One of the most important contradictions of the IWW, implanted at its first convention and never resolved, was the dual role it assigned to itself. Not the least of the reasons for the eventual failure of the IWW—as an organization—was its attempt to be both a union of all workers and a propaganda society of selected revolutionists—in essence a revolutionary party. Two different tasks and functions, which, at a certain stage of development, require separate and distinct organizations, were assumed by the IWW alone; and this duality hampered its effectiveness in both fields. All that and many other things are clearer now than they were then to the leading militants of the IWW—or anyone else in this country.

The IWW announced itself as an all-inclusive union; and any worker ready for organization on an everyday union basis was invited to join, regardless of his views and opinions on any other question. In a number of instances, in times of organization campaigns and strikes in separate localities, such all-inclusive membership was attained, if only for brief periods. But that did not prevent the IWW agitators from preaching the revolutionary overthrow of capitalism in every strike meeting.

The strike meetings of the IWW were in truth "schools for socialism." The immediate issues of the strike were the take-off point for an exposition of the principle of the class struggle, for a full-scale indictment of the capitalist system all up and down the line, and the projection of a new social order of the free and equal.

The professed "non-political" policy of the IWW doesn't stand up very well against its actual record in action. The main burden of its energies was devoted to agitation and propaganda—in soap-box speeches, press, pamphlets and songbooks—against the existing social order; to defense campaigns in behalf of imprisoned workers; and to free-speech fights in numerous localities. All these activities were in the main, and in the proper meaning of the term, political.

The IWW at all times, even during strikes embracing masses of church-going, ordinarily conservative workers, acted as an organization of revolutionists. The "real IWW's," the year-round activists, were nicknamed Wobblies—just when and why nobody knows—and the criterion of the Wobbly was his stand on the principle of the class struggle and its revolutionary goal; and his readiness to commit his whole life to it.

In truth, the IWW in its time of glory was neither a union nor a party in the full meaning of these terms, but something of both, with some parts missing. It was an uncompleted anticipation of a Bolshevik party, lacking its rounded-out theory, and a projection of the revolutionary industrial unions of the future, minus the necessary mass membership. It was the IWW.

4. VINCENT ST. JOHN

The second split of the IWW, which broke off De Leon and SLP elements at the Fourth (1908) Convention, likewise occurred over a doctrinal question. The issue this time was "political action" or, more correctly, conflicting conceptions of working class action in the class struggle which—properly understood—is essentially political.

The real purpose of the split was to free the IWW from the Socialist Labor Party's ultra-legalistic, narrowly restricted and doctrinaire conception of "political action" at the ballot box; and to clear the way for the St. John conception of overthrowing capitalism by the "direct action" of the organized workers. This, by a definition which was certainly arbitrary and inexact, was declared to be completely "non-political."

In a negative gesture, the 1908 Convention merely threw the "political clause" out of the Preamble. Later, going overboard, the IWW explicitly disavowed "politics" altogether, and political parties along with it. The origin of this trend is commonly attributed to the influence of French syndicalism. That is erroneous; although the IWW later imported some phrase-mongering anti-political radicalism from Europe, to its detriment. Brissenden is correct when he says:

"The main ideas of IWW-ism—certainly of the IWW-ism of the first few years after 1905—were of American origin, not French, as is commonly supposed. These sentiments were brewing in France, it is true, in the early Nineties, but they were brewing also in this country and the American brew was essentially different from the French. It was only after 1908 that the *syndicalisme révolutionnaire* of France had any direct influence on the revolutionary industrial unionist movement here." (Brissenden, p. 53.)

The IWW brand of syndicalism, which its proponents insisted on calling "industrialism," never acknowledged French origination, and had no reason to. The IWW doctrine was *sui generis,* a native product of the American soil. And so was its chief author, Vincent St. John. St. John, as all the old-timers knew, was the man most responsible for shaping the character of the IWW in its heroic days. His public reputation was dimmed beside the glittering name of Bill Haywood, and this has misled the casual student of IWW history. But Vincent St. John was the organizer and leader of the cadres.

Haywood himself was a great man, worthy of his fame.

He presided at the Founding Convention, and his magnificent utterances there have already been quoted in the introductory paragraphs of this article. The "Big Fellow" conducted himself as a hero of labor in his celebrated trial in Idaho, and again called himself thunderously to public attention in the great IWW strikes at Lawrence, Paterson and Akron. In 1914 he took over from St. John the office of General Secretary of the IWW, and thereafter stood at its head through all the storms of the war and the persecution. There is historical justice in the public identification of Bill Haywood's name with that of the IWW, as its personification.

But in the years 1906–1914, the years when the character of the IWW was fixed, and its basic cadres assembled, it was Vincent St. John who led the movement and directed all its operations. The story of the IWW would not be complete and would not be true if this chapter were omitted.

St. John, like Haywood, was a miner, a self-educated man who had come up to national prominence the hard way, out of the violent class battles of the western mining war. If "The Saint," as all his friends called him, borrowed something from the writings of others, and foreigners at that, he was scarcely aware of it. He was not a man of books; his school was his own experience and observation, and his creed was action. He had learned what he knew, which was quite a lot, mainly from life and his dealings with people, and he drew his conclusions from that.

This empiricism was his strength and his weakness. As an executive leader in practical situations he was superb, full of ideas—"enough to patch hell a mile"—and ready for action to apply them. In action he favored the quick, drastic decision, the short cut. This propensity had yielded rich results in his work as a field leader of the Western Federation of Miners. He was widely renowned in the western mining camps and his power was recognized by friend and foe. Brissenden quotes a typical report about him by a mine-owners' detective agency in 1906:

"St. John has given the mine owners of the [Colorado mining] district more trouble in the past year than any twenty men up there. If left undisturbed he would have the entire district organized in another year."

In dealing with people—"handling men," as they used to say—Vincent St. John had no equal that I ever knew. He "sized up" men with a quick insight, compounded of simplicity and guile, spotting and sifting out the phonies and the dabblers—you had to be serious to get along with The Saint—and putting the others to work in his school of learning by doing, and getting the best out of them.

"Experience," "decision" and "action" were the key words in St. John's criteria. He thought a man was what he did. It was commonplace for him to pass approving judgment on an organizer with the remark, "He has had plenty of experience," or "He'll be all right when he gets more experience." And once I heard him say, with a certain reservation, of another who was regarded as a comer in the organization: "He's a good speaker, but I don't know how much decision he has." In his vocabulary "experience" meant tests under fire. "Decision" meant the capacity to think and act at the same time; to do what had to be done right off the bat, with no "philosophizing" or fooling around.

St. John's positive qualities as a man of decision and action were contagious; like attracted like and he created an organization in his own image. He was not a backslapper but a leader, with the reserve that befits a leader, and he didn't win men by argument alone. In fact, he was a man of few words. The Saint lived his ideas and methods. He radiated sincerity and integrity, and unselfishness free from taint or ostentation. The air was clean in his presence.

The young men who fought under his command—a notable cadre in their time—swore by The Saint. They trusted him. They felt that he was their friend, that he cared for them and that they could always get a square deal from him, or a little better, as long as they were on the square with the organization. John S. Gambs, in his book, *The Decline of the IWW*, a postscript to Brissenden's history, remarks: "I have heard it said that St. John, among outstanding leaders, was the best loved and most completely trusted official the IWW have ever had." He heard it right.

The IWW, as it evolved under the influence of St. John, scornfully rejected the narrow concept of "political action" as limited to parliamentary procedures. St. John understood the class struggle as a ruthless struggle for power. Nothing less and no other way would do; he was as sure of that as Lenin was. He judged socialist "politics" and political parties by the two examples before his eyes—the Socialist Party bossed by Berger and Hillquit and the Socialist Labor Party of De Leon—and he didn't like either of them.

That attitude was certainly right as far as it went. Berger was a small-bore socialist opportunist; and Hillquit, although slicker and more sophisticated, wasn't much better. He merely supplied a little radical phraseology to shield the cruder Bergerism from the attacks of the left.

De Leon, of course, was far superior to these pretentious pygmies; he towered above them. But De Leon, with all his great merits and capacities; with his exemplary selflessness and his complete and unconditional dedication to the workers' cause; with the enemies he made, for which he is entitled to our love and admiration—with all that, De Leon was sectarian in his tactics, and his conception of political action was rigidly formalistic, and rendered sterile by legalistic fetishism.

In my opinion, St. John was completely right in his

hostility to Berger-Hillquit, and more than half right in his break with De Leon. His objections to the parliamentary reformism of Berger-Hillquit and the ultra-legalism of the SLP contained much that must now be recognized as sound and correct. The error was in the universal opposition, based on these poor and limited examples, to all "politics" and all political parties. The flaw in his conceptions was in their incompleteness, which left them open, first to exaggeration and then to a false turn.

St. John's cultivated bent to learn from his own limited and localized experience and observations in life rather than from books, and to aim at simple solutions in direct action, deprived him of the benefits of a more comprehensive theory generalized by others from the worldwide experiences of the class struggle. And this was true in general of the IWW as a movement. Over-simplification placed some crippling limitations on its general conceptions which, in their eventual development, in situations that were far from simple, were to prove fatal for the IWW. But this took time. It took the First World War and the Russian Revolution to reveal in full scope the incompleteness of the governing thought of the IWW.

5. THE LONG DETOUR

The IWW's disdain for parliamentarism, which came to be interpreted as a rejection of all "politics" and political organizations, was not impressed on a body of members with blank minds. The main activities of the IWW, in fields imposed upon it by the conditions of the time, almost automatically yielded recruits whose own tendencies and predilections had been shaped along the same lines by their own experiences.

The IWW plan of organization was made to order for modern mass production industry in the eastern half of the country, where the main power of the workers was concentrated. But the power of the exploiting class was concentrated there too, and organizing the workers against the entrenched corporations was easier said than done.

The IWW program of revolution was designed above all to express the implicit tendency of the main mass of the basic proletariat in the trustified industries of the East. The chance for a wage worker to change his class status and become an independent proprietor or a small farmer, was far less alluring there than on the western frontier, where such class transmigrations still could, and in many cases actually did, take place. If the logic of the class struggle had worked out formally—as it always does in due time—those workers in the industrial centers east of the Mississippi should have been the most class conscious and the most receptive to the IWW appeal.

But that's not the way things worked out in practice in the time when the IWW was making its strongest efforts. The organization never succeeded in establishing stable unions among the workers in modern machine industry in the industrially developed East. On the contrary, its predominant activity expanded along the lines of least resistance on the peripheral western fringes of the country, which at that time were still under construction. The IWW found a readier response to its appeal and recruited its main cadres among the marginal and migratory workers in that region.

This apparent anomaly—which is really nothing more than the time lag between reality and consciousness—has been seen many times in international experience. Those workers most prepared for socialism by industrial development are not always the first to recognize it.

The revolutionary movement recruits first, not where it chooses but where it can, and uses the first recruits as the cadres of the organization and the carriers of the doctrine. Marxist socialism, the logical and necessary answer to developed capitalism, got its poorest start and was longer delayed in England, the pre-eminent center of world capitalism in the time of Marx and Engels, while it flourished in Germany before its great industrialization. The same Marxism, as developed by Lenin in the actual struggle for power—under the nickname of Bolshevism—is the program *par excellence* for America, the most advanced capitalist country; but it scored its first victory in industrially backward Russia.

The economic factor eventually predominates, and the class struggle runs its logical course everywhere—but only in the long run, not in a straight line. The class struggle of the workers in all its manifestations, from the most elementary action of a union organization up to the revolution, breaks the chain of capitalist resistance at the weakest link.

So it was in the case of the IWW. Simply having the right form of organization did not provide the IWW with the key to quick victory in the trustified industries. The founders, at the 1905 Convention, had noted and emphasized the helplessness of obsolete craft unionism in this field; that was their stated motivation for proposing the industrial-union form of organization. But, for a long time, the same concentrated power that had broken up the old craft union in modern industry was also strong enough to prevent their replacement by new unions in the industrial form.

The meager success of the IWW in establishing revolutionary industrial unions in their natural habitat was not due to lack of effort. Time and again the IWW tried to crack the trustified industries, including steel, but was beaten back every time. All the heroic attempts of the IWW to organize in this field were isolated and broken up at the start.

The employers fought the new unionism in dead earnest. Against the program of the IWW and its little band of agitators, they brought up the heavy guns of their financial resources; public opinion moulded in their favor by press and pulpit; their private armies of labor spies and thugs; and, always and everywhere, the police power of that "political state" which the IWW didn't want to recognize.

In all the most militant years of the IWW the best it could accomplish in modern mass production industry were localized strikes, nearly all of which were defeated. The victorious Lawrence textile strike of 1912, which established the national fame of the IWW, was the glorious exception. But no stable and permanent union organization was ever maintained anywhere in the East for any length of time—not even in Lawrence.

From the formulation of the industrial-union program of the IWW at the 1905 Convention to its eventual realization in life in the mass production industries, there was a long rough road with a wide detour. It took 30 years of propaganda and trial-and-error effort, and then a mass upheaval of volcanic power generated by an unprecedented economic crisis, before the fortresses of mass production industry could be stormed and conquered by industrial unionism. But the time for such an invincible mass revolt had not yet come when the IWW first sounded the call and launched its pioneering campaigns.

Meantime, defeated and repulsed in the industrialized East, where the workers were not yet ready for organization and the corporations were more than ready to prevent it, the IWW found its best response and concentrated its main activity in the West. It scored some successes and built up an organization primarily among the seasonal and migratory workers there.

6. THE WOBBLIES AS THEY WERE

There was no such thing as "full employment" in the time of the IWW. The economic cycle ran its normal ten-year course, with its periodic crises and depressions, producing a surplus labor army squeezed out of industry in the East. Unemployment rose and fell with the turns of the cycle, but was always a permanent feature of the times. An economic crisis in 1907 and a serious depression in 1913–1914 swelled the army of the jobless.

Many of the unemployed workers, especially the young, took to the road, as those of another generation were to do again in the Thirties. The developing West had need of a floating labor force, and the supply drifted toward the demand. A large part of the mobile labor population in the West at that time, perhaps a majority, originated in the eastern half of the continent. Their conditions of life were pretty rough.

They were not the most decisive section of the working class, that resided, then as now, in the industrial centers of the eastern half of the continent. But these migrants, wherever they came from, responded most readily to the IWW program for a drastic change in the social order.

The IWW was right at home among footloose workers who found casual employment in the harvest fields—traveling by freight train to follow the ripening of the grain, then back by freight train again to the transportation centers for any kind of work they could find there; railroad construction workers, shipping out for temporary jobs and then shipping back to the cities into unemployment again; lumberjacks, metal miners, seamen, etc., who lived in insecurity and worked, when they worked, under the harshest, most primitive conditions.

This narrow stratum of the unsettled and least privileged workers came to make up the bulk of the membership of the IWW. It was often said among the Wobblies, only half facetiously, that the name of their organization "Industrial Workers of the World," should be changed to "Migratory Workers of the World."

The American political system offered no place for the participation of this floating labor force of the expanding West. Very little provision of any kind was made for them. They were overlooked in the whole scheme of things. They lacked the residential qualifications to vote in elections and enjoyed few of the rights of political democracy accorded to settled citizens with a stake in their community. They were the dispossessed, the homeless outcasts, without roots or a stake any place in society, and with nothing to lose.

Since they had no right to vote anyway, it took little argument to persuade them that "political action"—at the ballot box—was a delusion and a snare. They had already been convinced, by their own harsh experiences, that it would take more than paper ballots to induce the exploiters to surrender their swollen privileges. The IWW, with its bold and sweeping program of revolution by direct action, spoke their language and they heard it gladly.

The IWW became for them their one all-sufficient organization—their union and their party; their social center; their home; their family; their school; and in a manner of speaking, their religion, without the supernatural trimmings—the faith they lived by. Some of Joe Hill's finest songs, it should be remembered, were derisive parodies of the religious hymns of the IWW's rivals in the fight for the souls of the migratory workers milling around in the congested Skid Row sections of the western and midwestern cities.

These were not the derelicts who populate the present-day version of the old Skid Row. For the greater part, they were the young and venturesome, who had been forced out of the main industries in more settled communities, or had wandered away from them in search of opportunity and adventure. They had been badly bruised and beaten, but not conquered. They had the courage and the will to fight for an alleviation of their own harsh conditions.

But when they enlisted in the IWW it meant far more to them than joining a union to promote a picayune program of immediate personal needs. The IWW proclaimed that by solidarity they could win everything. It gave them a vision of a new world and inspired them to fight for the general good of the whole working class.

These footloose workers, recruited by the propaganda and action of the IWW, became the carriers of its great, profoundly simple message wherever they traveled—the message expressed in the magic words: Solidarity, Workers' Power, One Big Union and Workers' Emancipation. Wherever they went, they affirmed their conviction that "there is power in a band of working men," as stated in the singing words of Joe Hill—"a power that must rule in every land."

They felt themselves to be—as indeed they were—the advance guard of an emancipating army. But it was an advance guard separated from the main body of troops in concentrated industry, separated and encircled, and compelled to wage guerrilla actions while awaiting reinforcements from the main army of the proletariat in the East. It was a singing movement, with confidence in its mission. When the Wobblies sang out the swelling chorus of "Hold the Fort," they "heard the bugles blow" and really believed that "by our union we shall triumph over every foe."

Recruits enlisted in the main from this milieu soon came to make up the main cadres of the IWW; to provide its shock troops in all its battles, east and west; and to impress their own specific ideology upon it—the ideology which was in part the developed result of their own experiences, and in part derived from teachings of the IWW. These teachings seemed to formulate and systematize their own tendencies. That's why they accepted them so readily.

Many a worker recruited to the IWW under those conditions was soon on the move again, carrying his red card and his newly found convictions with him and transmitting them to others. All the progressive and radical sections of the labor movement were heavily influenced by the IWW in the years preceding the First World War.

The left-wing socialists were ardent sympathizers of the IWW, and quite a few of them were members. The same was true in large measure of the more militant trade unionists in the AFL. "Two-card men" were fairly numerous—those who belonged to the AFL unions for bread and butter reasons and carried the "red card" of the IWW for the sake of principle.

The IWW struck a spark in the heart of youth as no other movement in this country, before or since, has done. Young idealists from "the winds' four corners" came to the IWW and gave it all they had. The movement had its gifted strike leaders, organizers and orators, its poets and its martyrs.

By the accumulated weight of its unceasing propagandistic efforts, and by the influence of its heroic actions on many occasions which were sensationally publicized, the

IWW eventually permeated a whole generation of American radicals, of all shades and affiliations, with its concept of industrial unionism as the best form for the organization of workers' power and its program for a revolutionary settlement of the class struggle.

It was a long way from the pioneer crusade of the IWW among the dispossessed migratory workers on the western frontier, in the second decade of our century, to the invincible picket lines and sit-down strikes of the mass production workers in the eastern centers of concentrated industry, in the Thirties. A long way and not a straight one. But that's the route over which the message of industrial unionism eventually reached those places where it was most applicable and could explode with the greatest power.

7. THE TURNING POINT

The whole record of the IWW—or at any rate, the best part of it, the positive revolutionary part—was all written in propaganda and action in its first 15 years. That is the enduring story. The rest is anticlimax.

The turning point came with the entrance of the United States into the First World War in the spring of 1917, and the Russian Revolution in the same year. Then "politics," which the IWW had disavowed and cast out, came back and broke down the door.

These two events—again coinciding in Russia and America, as in 1905—demonstrated that "political action" was not merely a matter of the ballot box, subordinate to the direct conflict of the unions and employers on the economic field, but the very essence of the class struggle. In opposing actions of two different classes the "political state," which the IWW had thought to ignore, was revealed as the centralized power of the ruling class; and the holding of the state power showed in each case which class was really ruling.

From one side, this was shown when the Federal Government of the United States intervened directly to break up the concentration points of the IWW by wholesale arrests of its activists. The "political action" of the capitalist state broke the back of the IWW as a union. The IWW was compelled to transform its principal activities into those of a defense organization, striving by legal methods and propaganda, to protect the political and civil rights of its members against the depredations of the capitalist state power.

From the other side, the same determining role of political action was demonstrated positively by the Russian Revolution. The Russian workers took the state power into their own hands and used that power to expropriate the capitalists and suppress all attempts at counter-revolution. That, in fact, was the first stage of the revolution, the precondition for all that was to follow. Moreover, the organizing and directing center of the victorious Revolution had turned out to be, not an all-inclusive union, but a party of selected revolutionists united by a program and bound by discipline.

The time had come for the IWW to remember Haywood's prophetic injunction at the Founding Convention in 1905: that the American workers should look to Russia and follow the Russian example. By war and revolution, the most imperative of all authorities, the IWW was put on notice to bring its theoretical conceptions up to date;

to think and learn, and change a little.

First indications were that this would be done; the Bolshevik victory was hailed with enthusiasm by the members of the IWW. In their first reaction, it is safe to say, they saw in it the completion and vindication of their own endeavors. But this first impulse was not followed through.

Some of the leading Wobblies, including Haywood himself, tried to learn the lessons of the war and the Russian Revolution and to adjust their thinking to them. But the big majority, after several years of wavering, went the other way. That sealed the doom of the IWW. Its tragic failure to look, listen and learn from the two great events condemned it to defeat and decay.

The governing role of theory here asserted itself supremely, and in short order. While the IWW was settling down in ossification, converting its uncompleted conceptions about the real meaning of political action and political parties into a sterile anti-political dogma, the thinking of others was catching up with reality, with the great new things happening in the world. The others, the young left-wing socialists, soon to call themselves Communists, lacked the battle-tested cadres of the IWW. But they had the correct program. That proved to be decisive.

The newly formed Communist Party soon outstripped the IWW and left it on the sidelines. It was all decided within the space of two or three years. By the time of its fifteenth anniversary in 1920 the IWW had already entered the irreversible road of decline. Its strength was spent. Most of its cadres, the precious human material selected and sifted out in heroic struggles, went down with the organization. They had borne persecution admirably, but the problems raised by it, and by all the great new events, overwhelmed them. The best militants fell into inactivity and then dropped out. The second-raters took over and completed the wreck and the ruin.

The failure of the main cadres of the IWW to become integrated in the new movement for the Communist Party in this country, inspired by the Russian Revolution, was a historical miscarriage which might have been prevented.

In action the IWW had been the most militant, the most revolutionary section of the workers' vanguard in this country. The IWW, while calling itself a union, was much nearer to Lenin's conception of a party of professional revolutionists than any other organization calling itself a party at that time. In their practice, and partly also in their theory, the Wobblies were closer to Lenin's Bolsheviks than any other group in this country.

There should have been a fusion. But, in a fast-moving situation, a number of untoward circumstances, combined with the inadequacy of the American communist leadership, barred the way.

The failure of the IWW to find a place in the new movement assembling under the banner of the Russian Revolution, was not the fault of the Russians. They recognized the IWW as a rightful part of the movement they represented and made repeated attempts to include it in the new unification of forces. The first manifesto of the Communist International specified the American IWW as one of the organizations invited to join. Later, in 1920, the Executive Committee of the Communist International addressed a special Open Letter to the IWW, inviting its cooperation.

The letter explained, in the tone of brothers speaking to brothers, that the revolutionary parliamentarism of the Communist International had nothing in common with the ballot-box fetishism and piddling reformism of the right-wing socialists. Haywood says of that letter: "After I had finished reading it I called Ralph Chaplin over to my desk and said to him: 'Here is what we have been dreaming about; here is the IWW all feathered out!'" (*Bill Haywood's Book*, p. 360.)

In war-time France Trotsky had found his best friends and closest collaborators in the fight against the war among the syndicalists. After the Russian Revolution, in a notable series of letters, published later as a pamphlet, he urged them to join forces with the communists. The theses adopted by the Communist International at its Second Congress recognized the progressive and revolutionary side of prewar syndicalism, and said it represented a step forward from the ideology of the Second International. The theses attempted to explain at the same time, in the most patient and friendly manner, the errors and limitations of syndicalism on the question of the revolutionary party, and its role.

Perhaps the chief circumstance operating against a patient and fruitful discussion, and an orderly transition of the IWW to the higher ground of Bolshevism, was the furious persecution of the IWW at the time. When the Russian Revolution erupted in the victory in November, 1917, hundreds of the IWW activists were held in jail under excessive bail, awaiting trial. Following their conviction a year later, they were sentenced to long terms in the Federal Penitentiary.

This imprisonment cut them off from contact with the great new events, and operated against the free exchange of ideas which might have resulted in an agreement and fusion with the dynamically developing left-wing socialist movement headed toward the new Communist Party. The IWW as an organization was compelled to divert its entire activity into its campaign to provide legal defense for its victimized members. The members of the organization had little time or thought for other things, including the one all-important thing—the assimilation of the lessons of the war and the Russian Revolution.

Despite that, a number of IWW men heard the new word from Russia and followed it. They recognized in Bolshevism the rounding out and completion of their own revolutionary conceptions, and joined the Communist Party. Haywood expressed their trend of thought succinctly, in an interview with Max Eastman, published in *The Liberator,* April 1921:

"'I feel as if I'd always been there,' he said to me. 'You remember I used to say that all we needed was fifty thousand real IWW's, and then about a million members to back them up? Well, isn't that a similar idea? At least I always realized that the essential thing was to have an organization of *those who know.*'"

As class-conscious men of action, the Wobblies, "the real IWW's," had always worked together as a body to influence the larger mass. Their practice contained the essential idea of the Leninist conception of the relation between the party and the class. The Bolsheviks, being men of theory in all their action, formulated it more precisely and developed it to its logical conclusion in the organization of those class-conscious elements into a party of their own.

All that seemed clear to me at the time, and I had great hopes that at least a large section of the Wobblies would recognize it. I did all I could to convince them. I made especially persistent efforts to convince Vincent St. John himself, and almost succeeded; I didn't know how close I had come until later, when it was too late.

When he was released from the Federal Penitentiary at Leavenworth on bond—I think it was in the early part of

1919—The Saint stopped over in Kansas City and visited me. We talked about the Russian Revolution night and day. I believe he was as sympathetic at that time as I was. The revolution was an *action*—and that's what he believed in. But he had not yet begun to grapple with the idea that the Russian way would be applicable to this country, and that the IWW would have to recognize it.

His hostility to a "party" and "politicians," based on what he had seen of such things in this country, was the fixed obstacle. I noted, however, that he did not argue back, but mainly listened to what I had to say. A year or so later we had several other discussions in New York, when he was still out on bail before he was returned to prison in the fall of 1921. We talked a great deal on those occasions; or rather, I did, and The Saint listened.

In addition to my proselytizing zeal for communism in those days, I had a strong personal motivation for trying to win over Vincent St. John to the new movement. Coming from the syndicalistic background of the IWW, with its strong anti-intellectual emphasis, I had been plunged up to my neck in the internal struggles of the young Communist Party and association with its leading people. They were nearly all young intellectuals, without any experience or feel for the mass movement and the "direct action" of the class struggle. I was not very much at home in that milieu; I was lonesome for people of my own kind.

I had overcome my own "anti-intellectualism" to a considerable extent; but I knew for sure that the Communist Party would never find its way to the mass movement of the workers with a purely intellectualistic leadership. I was looking for reinforcements for a proletarian counter-balance on the other side, and I thought that if I could win over St. John it would make a big difference. In fact, I knew it.

I remember the occasion when I made the final effort with The Saint. The two of us went together to have dinner and spend the night as guests of Carlo Tresca and Elizabeth Gurley Flynn at their cottage on Staten Island beach. We spent very little time looking at the ocean, although that was the first time I had ever seen it. All through the dinner hour, and nearly all through the night, we discussed my thesis that the future belonged to the Communist Party; and that the IWW militants should not abandon the new party to the intellectuals, but come into it and help to shape its proletarian character.

As in the previous discussions, I did practically all the talking. The Saint listened, as did the others. There was no definite conclusion to the long discussion; neither expressed rejection nor acceptance of my proposals. But I began to feel worn-out with the effort and let it go at that.

A short time later St. John returned to Chicago. The officials in charge of the IWW center there were hostile to communism and were embroiled in some bitter quarrels with a pro-communist IWW group in Chicago. I don't know what the immediate occasion was, but St. John was drawn into the conflict and took a stand with the anti-communist group. Then, as was natural for him in any kind of a crisis, once he had made up his mind he took charge of the situation and began to steer the organization definitely away from cooperation with the communists.

Years later—in 1926—when Elizabeth Gurley Flynn herself finally came over to the Communist Party and was working with us in the International Labor Defense, she recalled that night's discussion on Staten Island and said: "Did you know you almost convinced The Saint that night? If you had tried a little harder you might have won him over." I hadn't known it; and when she told me that, I was deeply sorry that I had not tried just "a little harder."

The Saint was crowding 50 at that time, and jail and prison had taken their toll. He was a bit tired, and he may have felt that it was too late to start over again in a new field where he, like all of us, had much to learn. Whatever the reason for the failure, I still look back on it regretfully. Vincent St. John, and the IWW militants he would have brought along, could have made a big difference in everything that went on in the CP in the Twenties.

8. THE HERITAGE

The eventual failure of the IWW to remain true to its original self, and to claim its own heritage, does not invalidate its great contributions in propaganda and action to the revolutionary movement which succeeds it. The IWW in its best days was more right than wrong, and all that was right remains the permanent acquisition of the American workers. Even some of the IWW propositions which seemed to be wrong—only because the times were not ripe for their full realization—will find their vindication in the coming period.

The IWW's conception of a Republic of Labor, based on occupational representation, replacing the present political state with its territorial form of representation, was a remarkable prevision of the course of development which must necessarily follow from the victory of the workers in this country. This new and different form of social organization was projected at the Founding Convention of the IWW even before the Russian Bolsheviks had recognized the Workers Councils, which had arisen spontaneously in the 1905 Revolution, as the future governmental form.

The IWW program of *industrial* unionism was certainly right, although it came too early for fulfillment under the

IWW banner. This has already been proved to the hilt in the emergence and consolidation of the CIO.

The IWW theory of *revolutionary* unionism likewise came too early for general acceptance in the epoch of ascending capitalism in this country. It could not be realized on a wide scale in the time of the IWW. But *reformist* unions, in the present epoch of imperialist decay, have already become anachronistic and are confronted with an ultimatum from history to change their character or cease to be.

The mass industrial unions of workers, by the fact of their existence, instinctively strive toward socialism. With a capitalist-minded leadership, they are a house divided against itself, half slave and half free. That cannot stand. The stage is being set for the transformation of the reformist unions into revolutionary unions, as they were projected by the IWW half a century ago.

The great contradiction of the labor movement today is the disparity between the mass unions with their organized millions and the revolutionary party which still remains only a nucleus, and their separation from each other. The unity of the vanguard and the class, which the IWW tried to achieve in one organization, was shattered because the time was not ripe and the formula was inadequate. The time is now approaching when this antithetic separation must give way to a new synthesis.

This synthesis—the unity of the class and the socialist vanguard—will be arrived at in the coming period in a different way from that attempted by the IWW. It will not be accomplished by a single organization. The building of a separate party organization of the socialist vanguard is the key to the resolution of the present contradiction of the labor movement. This will not be a barrier to working class unity but the necessary condition for it.

The working class can be really united only when it

becomes a class *for itself,* consciously fighting the exploiters as a class. The ruling bureaucrats, who preach and practice class collaboration, constitute in effect a pro-capitalist party in the trade unions. The party of the socialist vanguard represents the consciousness of the class. Its organization signifies not a split of the class movement of the workers, but a division of labor within it, to facilitate and effectuate its unification on a revolutionary basis; that is, as a class for itself.

As an organization of revolutionists, united not simply by the immediate economic interests which bind all workers together in a union, but by doctrine and program, the IWW was in practice, if not in theory, far ahead of other experiments along this line in its time, even though the IWW called itself a union and others called themselves parties.

That was the IWW's greatest contribution to the American labor movement—in the present stage of its development and in those to come. Its unfading claim to grateful remembrance will rest in the last analysis on the pioneering role it played as the first great anticipation of the revolutionary party which the vanguard of the American workers will fashion to organize and lead their emancipating revolution.

This conception of an organization of revolutionists has to be completed and rounded out, and recognized as the most essential, the most powerful of all designs in the epoch of imperialist decline and decay, which can be brought to an end only by a victorious workers' revolution. The American revolution, more than any other, will require a separate, special organization of the revolutionary vanguard. And it must call itself by its right name, a party.

The experimental efforts of the IWW along this line remain part of the permanent capital of those who are undertaking to build such a party. They will not discard or discount the value of their inheritance from the old IWW; but they will also supplement it by the experience and thought of others beyond our borders.

The coming generation, which will have the task of bringing the class struggle to its conclusion—fulfilling the "historic mission of the working class," as the "Preamble" described it—will take much from the old leaders of the IWW—Debs, Haywood, De Leon and St. John, and will glorify their names. But in assimilating all the huge experiences since their time, they will borrow even more heavily from the men who generalized these experiences into a guiding theory. The Americans will go to school to the Russians, as the Russians went to school to the Germans, Marx and Engels.

Haywood's advice at the Founding Convention of the IWW still holds good. The Russian way is the way to our American future, to the future of the whole world. The greatest thinkers of the international movement since Marx and Engels, and also the greatest men of action, were the Russian Bolsheviks. The Russian Revolution is there to prove it, ruling out all argument. That revolution still stands as the example; all the perversions and betrayals of Stalinism cannot change that.

The Russian Bolsheviks—Lenin and Trotsky in the first place—have inspired every forward step taken by the revolutionary vanguard in this country since 1917. And it is to them that the American workers will turn for guidance in the next stages of their evolving struggle for emancipation. The fusion of their "Russian" ideas with the inheritance of the IWW is the American workers' prescription for victory.

Part 4

A critical review of Theodore Draper's history

First issue of *The Militant*, published in November 1928 after Cannon's expulsion from the Communist Party.

1. 'The Roots of American Communism'

The Roots of American Communism, by Theodore Draper. Viking Press, New York, N.Y. 498 pp. 1957. $6.95.

I

In the present turmoil of American radicalism, churned up by the Khrushchev revelations and the Polish and Hungarian revolts against Stalinism—with clear indications of more of the same to come—this serious work about the beginnings of communist history in this country arrives at a good time to get the attention it deserves. After a yearlong crisis, during which thousands of formerly devoted party members have been voting against it with their feet, and the old taboo on free discussion has been broken, the climate is more favorable for the circulation of unofficial

Reprinted from International Socialist Review, *Summer 1957.*

literature. Theodore Draper's book is an important contribution to the discussion now going on in all circles of the more or less socialist-minded.

The Roots of American Communism is the first volume of a projected series of studies now in progress by a team of scholars who are undertaking to write a complete history of the Communist Party. It is announced that Draper is to bring the story down to 1945; David A. Shannon is at work on a history of the party in the post-war years; and, in addition to that, a number of other scholars, exploring the party's record in various areas, will "attempt to assess the influence of communism in American life." The whole enterprise is backed by the Fund for the Republic which was set up by the Ford Foundation. There is irony in the circumstance that this rather formidable exploration of one aspect of American history has been made possible by an appropriation from money left behind by the rich eccentric who, for his part, once stated his conviction that "history is bunk."

In this first volume Draper tells the story of the Communist Party up to the end of 1922. Several introductory chapters provide the necessary background by tracing the evolution of the "historic" American left-wing movement out of which came the initiating forces for the new movement of communism in this country. American communism was directly inspired by the Russian Revolution; there is no doubt about that. But Draper's concise but graphic and factually accurate introductory chapters give conclusive proof at the start—if such proof is needed—that the Communist Party, formally organized in 1919, did not appear out of thin air; the new party had deep roots in the earlier movements of American labor radicalism, and found its originating troops and leaders in the ranks of older organizations.

Draper, as he relates in his introduction, started to gather his material five years ago as an independent endeavor, and he has been working at it ever since. And, to judge by what he came up with, he must have put in a lot of overtime. The book itself is evidence of a stupendous labor of investigation and research into all aspects of the germinal days of American communism, a decisively important period that has long been misunderstood, obscured and even falsified. On this score the author's work must command the admiration and even the awe of those who consider the history of the workers' movement important in all its aspects, and value the scholarship that digs up the facts and reports them honestly.

The Communist Party, or what is left of it at the present time, still bears the name of the original organization. But everything else is different. The party, at its inception, had grave faults which were in the main the hangovers from the American radical tradition, supplemented by its own groping ignorance and inexperience. But it was an honest party and it meant what it said. "There was a time," says Draper, "when everything was new, fresh, and spontaneous. Every crisis was the first crisis. Every move was unrehearsed." There was none of the cynical lying and weaseling double talk which have characterized the party in later years. In the formative period of the American communist movement "there was a minimum of mystery and reticence. . . . Oppositions functioned more or less freely. Communists were more contemptuous of outside opinion in the conduct of their own discussions. They were so confident of the future that they felt little need for mental reservations. In fact, they believed that the more frankly they made known their views, the sooner would they win over the masses of workers."

In its early period the party commanded the respect and

support of the great majority of radical American workers, and eventually came to hold a virtual monopoly of leadership in this sphere, before the credit of its original integrity finally ran out. The story of the transformation of the Communist Party is a story the disillusioned communist workers will have to know and understand before they can even begin to see daylight in the dark jungle of frustration and discouragement that surrounds them at the present time. By the same token, a new generation of social rebels, aspiring to create a new revolutionary political movement without previous experience of their own, will certainly need to inquire why and how the last one failed so ignobly. Such people can profit by a study of this book by Theodore Draper, which tells the truth about the communist pioneers and the movement they created.

It doesn't tell the whole story of the Communist Party, only the beginning; but the beginning is a good place to start the study of the whole story. As its name implies, *The Roots of American Communism* deals only with the background, origin and formative period of the Communist Party. But within that framework, it is a faithfully accurate account of what really happened in the early years when American communism was first taking shape, who the people were and what kind of people they were. Many who have tended to carry their own revulsion against the Communist Party to the point of repudiating communism, will have ample reason to reconsider that hasty and erroneous judgment when they read the story of what honest communists were actually like, and what the word communism signified, in the first years of the movement, as told by the author of this book.

The Communist Party has been around for almost 40 years, but very few of its active participants of later times have known much about the origin and history of their own organization; and most of the little they have known isn't true. Since the Twentieth Congress of the Soviet CP and the publication of Khrushchev's revelations at one of its secret sessions, the world has been pretty well informed that, among its other crimes, such as frame-ups, "confessions" extracted by torture, and wholesale murders of the old Bolsheviks, the Stalin regime was also guilty of the systematic falsification of the history of the Russian Revolution and the Soviet Communist Party—a crime against the inquiring youth.

The leaders of the American CP, who stuffed up the brains of several generations of young party members with Stalin's falsified version of Soviet party history, now piously confess Stalin's "mistakes"—in Russia; but they haven't said anything yet about their own "mistake" in falsifying the history of American communism. Foster's *History of the Communist Party of the United States* is just as crooked as Stalin's *History of the Communist Party of the Soviet Union*. Draper's book, in contrast, stands out as a truly remarkable work of honest scholarship which is certain to be the primary source for every serious student who really wants to know where the American communist movement came from and what happened in its formative years. In passing, with the back of his hand, Draper knocks Foster's tendentious and falsified "History" into the waste basket.

The author of *The Roots of American Communism* does not conceal his own bias, which leads him to an interpretation that I cannot share and to which I will return later in this review. But when it comes to a recitation of the facts of American communist history from 1917 to 1923, no one will ever dare to challenge him; he tells what really happened with the objectivity of a conscientious scholar and nails down his story with documentary proof at every point. Even those who went through all the battles of the pioneer days without fully knowing or remembering everything they did, will stand amazed at the exhaustive thoroughness of his research and the journalistic skill with which he has recreated the events of that time.

II

Especially illuminating is the fourth chapter on the "Influences and Influencers" which operated in the first years of the American communist movement. The Bolshevik Revolution of 1917 was the *action* that brought the American communist movement into existence. Everybody knows that, and it is usually taken for granted that the *ideas* of the Russian Bolsheviks shaped the new movement from the start. Draper proves conclusively—and this is one of his major contributions to an understanding of the period—that this was not really the case. It took quite a while for the influence of Bolshevik ideas to come up even with the authority of their action.

Other ideas were present, and even predominant, in the first fumbling years of the new movement. The half-baked theories, the fantastic unrealism, the sectarian tactics carried to the point of absurdity in the early days—which are all mercilessly listed and documented by Draper—were not imported from Russia. These flowers were home-grown—with some Dutch cultivation.

American communism grew directly out of the new left wing of the Socialist Party which took shape in the struggle against the First World War, with some reinforcements from the IWW, the Socialist Labor Party and the anarchist groups, all of which had been shaken up, first by the war and then by the Bolshevik Revolution in 1917. The strong points of all the forces in this new "regroupment," which was eventually to become the Communist Party, were their revolutionary spirit and opposition to the war; their firm stand on the principle of the class struggle against the reformist wing of the Socialist Party; and their support of industrial unionism, as against the conservative craft exclusiveness of the Gompersite labor aristocracy. This was a good start, but only a start, on the road to a rounded-out political program for a revolutionary party. Beyond that the American movement was not able to go on its own theoretical resources.

The "historic" American left wing had been dominated by syndicalist and semi-syndicalist conceptions. Even the "politicals" thought of the party mainly as a propaganda agency and an auxiliary to the unions in the economic struggle, rather than as the leading organization of the working class in all aspects of its struggle for socialism. The new left wing in its early years carried over this tradition. The traditional left wing had been pronouncedly sectarian, strongly influenced by De Leon's theories, even though De Leon's SLP was outside the main stream of the movement. The new left wing, even after it emerged as the Communist Party in 1919, carried over this tradition too, for several years.

The old American movement had been predominantly isolationist; it was too "American" for its own good. Then, when it began to be influenced by ideas from abroad during the First World War, the first of such importations to make a strong impression on the movement came, not from the Russian Bolsheviks but from the Dutch theoreticians, Anton Pannekoek and Herman Gorter, who were at the same time influential in the left wing of the German Social Democratic Party. These Dutch leaders were revolutionary in their opposition to the First World War and to the role of the Second International in it. But their conceptions in general were also semi-syndicalist and sectarian.

The American left wing found their ideas congenial; and their articles in the *International Socialist Review* and the *New Review,* the two left-wing organs of the time, did much to shape the ideology of the Americans. The Dutch theorists made a particularly deep mark on the young American writer who was to become the chief ideologist and propagandist of the American left wing turning toward communism, and by all odds, the single person most responsible for the founding of the American Communist Party. That man was Louis C. Fraina whom Foster, in his *History of the Communist Party of the United States,* forgot to mention even once. Maybe he never heard of him.

Fraina, who had been influenced first by De Leon, then by the Dutch theorists, and then later by Lenin and Trotsky, combined elements of all three influences in his own thinking. And he decisively put his own stamp on the American left wing, and on the Communist Party at the time of its formal organization.

The ideas of the Russian Bolsheviks, as they eventually began to break through in the American press, primarily in some of the writings of Lenin and Trotsky, became known in America somewhat later. But it didn't take long for these ideas to make their way. The power the Russians exerted over the American movement in that early time was ideological, not administrative. They changed and reshaped the thinking of the young American communists by explanation and persuasion, not by command; and the effect was clarifying and enlightening, and altogether beneficent for the provincial American movement.

The traditional sectarianism of the Americans was

expressed most glaringly in their attempt to construct revolutionary unions outside the existing labor movement; their refusal to fight for "immediate demands" in the course of the class struggle for the socialist goal; and their strongly entrenched anti-parliamentarism, which was only slightly modified in the first program of the Communist Party. All that hodgepodge of ultra-radicalism was practically wiped out of the American movement in 1920–21 by Lenin. He did it, not by an administrative order backed up by police powers, but by the simple device of publishing a pamphlet called *Left-Wing Communism: An Infantile Disorder*. (This famous pamphlet was directed in part against the Dutch theoreticians who had exerted such a strong influence on the Americans and a section of the Germans.)

The "Theses and Resolutions" of the Second Congress of the Comintern in 1920 also cleared up the thinking of the American communists over a wide range of theoretical and political problems, and virtually eliminated the previously dominating influence exerted by the sectarian conceptions of De Leon and the Dutch leaders.

The old sectarianism, which by 1922 had been driven out of the other fields, finally took refuge, with dwindling support, in the theory of "undergroundism in principle." But by that time a strong group of native American leaders had taken the cure, and they waged a determined struggle to rout the old sectarianism from its last stronghold. It was a tough fight, and it needed the intervention of the Russian leaders of the Comintern for the victory at the end of 1922. To be sure, this time there was a Comintern decision. But it was a decision taken after the most thoroughgoing discussion in which the great majority of the American communists were convinced. The result was the unification of the movement for a new period of expanding activity in the class struggle, with realistic tactics adapted to the American conditions of the time.

III

Draper's monumental study of the early years takes on all the more interest and liveliness because it is not the work of a library researcher cataloguing facts about a subject for which he has no feel. The author himself was deeply involved in the Communist Party during the tragic era when Browder ruled as the proconsul of Stalin, and the revolutionary party of the Twenties was transformed into its opposite. Draper belonged to that betrayed generation of rebellious college youth who faced graduation in the midst of the economic crisis of the Thirties with the prospect of no place to go.

These student rebels were different from the majority of their generation in that they were social-minded, fully committed and careless of personal consequences. These qualities of youth, which in my book are the best, propelled them toward the Communist Party, behind which they saw the image of the Soviet Union and the Russian Revolution. Mistaking Stalinism for communism, they streamed into the party and made their careers in its service.

They were the young dynamos who found places in the party apparatus, staffed the publications, or became functionaries in the innumerable front organizations. A surprisingly large number of these recruits from the campus played leading parts in the CIO organizing campaigns and wound up as officials, of high and low degree, in the unions controlled and manipulated by the Communist Party.

Draper was one whose youth was consumed in a career

as a party journalist. Such an experience could not fail to leave its mark. He writes now, not as a mere observer of the movement but as a wounded participant. For all that, if one is to judge by the scholarly objectivity and scrupulous fairness with which he now records the history of a movement to which he no longer pays allegiance, he came out of the experience with his integrity intact. In that he is exceptional, for the apparatus of Stalinism has been a devourer not only of men but also of character.

Unfortunately, as his present work seems to testify, Draper finally recoiled against Stalinism without correcting the original error of identifying it with Bolshevism. This identification, which has no foundation in reality, blurs his political judgment and inspires an interpretation—in fact, a thesis, clearly intimated in his introduction and in his concluding paragraph—which cannot stand up under serious examination. (Stalin had to frame-up and murder the old Bolsheviks before the specific regime of *Stalinism* could be consolidated.) The result is a contradictory book, which is beyond praise as a source of authentic information, but without value as a political guide in the study of its meaning. The degeneration of the Communist Party took a long time, and it did not come about automatically. Those who want to get to the heart of the mystery will have to evaluate the factual information by a different criterion than Draper's.

IV

Draper's thesis is that the American Communist Party's course was determined and its doom was sealed when it first yielded to Russian influence, and sought and secured Russian help in the solution of the American problems which the party had not been able to solve by itself; that the seeds of its destruction as an authentic expression of American radicalism were planted in the early years. He begins his book with an introductory statement that "the essential character of the movement was shaped at the beginning." And in his last chapter, which tells how the difficult task of lifting the party out of its underground isolation, and turning it toward the workers' mass movement, was accomplished with the help of the Russian leaders of the Comintern in 1922, he concludes that the victory thus gained cost more than it was worth.

The American party's dependence on the Russian leaders for political advice and help in the Lenin-Trotsky time of the Comintern was to lead—unavoidably, he seems to say—to the later subservience to Stalin in all respects. Thus, "something crucially important did happen to this movement in its infancy. It was transformed from a new expression of American radicalism to the American appendage of a Russian revolutionary power. Nothing else so important ever happened to it again."

V

An attempt to give an exhaustive answer to this oversimplified assumption would take us far afield. Innumerable articles, pamphlets and a shelf full of books have been devoted to the subject of Stalinism and Bolshevism—the most difficult and probably the most important theoretical and political problem of our time. Students who want to read a serious political meaning into the factual information assembled by the scholars will do well to include this analytical literature in their studies.

But here I believe it would be worth while and timely

to touch on one aspect of this world-wide problem, as it relates to the current discussion in this country. It is the liveliest discussion, and it is due to go on for a long time. And again it must be pointed out, for the benefit of people who have decided late in life to swear off all things Russian, that the Russians started all the commotion this time too.

The Twentieth Congress of the Soviet CP, and Khrushchev's revelations about some of the horrors and monstrosities of the Stalin regime in Russia, have stirred up almost as much interest, discussion and reappraisal in all circles of American radicalism as did the revolution of the Bolsheviks—an action of a different kind, but still a Russian action—in 1917. The reaction of many people, in their first shock of disillusionment, is to ask, this time, for a purely "American" party which will go it alone and erect customs barriers against the importation of foreign ideas and influences, including the Russian and especially the Russian.

Pathetic as this first reaction is in this day and age, and fleeting as it is bound to be, it nevertheless has created a temporary market for some fast-talking advocates of a new American socialist movement, somewhat on the pattern of what we had in this country "in the time of Debs." Leaving aside the fact that this idea is a half century out of date, it was not adequate even for the time of Debs, which was also the time of Berger and Hillquit, and the IWW, and the anarchists, and the Socialist Labor Party of De Leon. They did the best they could with what they had, but they didn't have enough. None of them, nor all of them together, were good enough for their own time, and a recreated movement of that kind wouldn't begin to fit the needs of the present time.

The fact of the matter is that the socialist and radical movement in this country, as in all other countries outside

Russia, came to a dead end in 1914. When the largest and strongest socialist parties of Europe, along with the movements of the anarchists and syndicalists, collapsed under the test of the First World War, a question mark was put over the perspectives of socialism everywhere. Socialists everywhere groped in darkness, questioning their previous assumptions.

Light came finally from the East. The Bolshevik party of Russia was the one party that demonstrated in action its capacity to cope with the problems of war and revolution. For that reason it became the inspiring center for a revival and regroupment of the revolutionary workers in all countries of the globe, including the United States whose previous movement had been the most primitive, isolationist, and politically backward of them all.

The young Communist Party of the United States arose as the expression of a new socialist hope, generated by the Russian example. It was this party, and no other, that took root, grew and expanded, and commanded the allegiance of virtually the entire generation of newly awakening rebel youth in the shops and in the schools. It is true, the Communist Party later succumbed to Stalinism—which also came from Russia—and ended up as a horrible caricature of its original self. This shows that bad things as well as good can be imported and that it is necessary to discriminate between them. But what happened to those organizations, groups and tendencies which rejected the influence of the Russian Revolution and the Bolsheviks in the first place? What have they to show for their isolationist wisdom?

The Socialist Party, even while Debs was still alive, became a hollow shell of futility which the new generation of labor militants passed by; and it is poorer, feebler, and less attractive now than ever, unless one feels an attraction to "State Department socialism." The Socialist Labor Party withered on the vine. The IWW, despite its heroic tradition and its magnificent cadres of working-class militants, declined into an impotent sect which was scarcely able to notice, still less to lead, the great upsurge of industrial unionism in the Thirties. The anarchists, who had played a role not without honor in opposition to the First World War, declined and finally disappeared from the scene in a shabby reconciliation with American imperialism in the Second World War.

There is not much in that record to build on for the future; not much to inspire a new generation to struggle for the socialist goal as the realistic perspective of their own time. If we are to look to the past for some inspiration in the present, the tradition of the young Communist Party, as it was before it succumbed to the corruption of Stalinism, has more to offer than any other party. Allowing for all the mistakes and inadequacies of its leadership, the party that responded to the Russian Revolution was the first genuinely revolutionary political party in this country.

The pioneer communists proclaimed their belief that this country, too, needs a social revolution and a party fit to lead it; and that the sooner such a party is started on its way the better. These propositions are still valid, and they are the necessary starting point for any regroupment in a new revolutionary party worthy of the name. The new party of revolutionary socialism, which will emerge in a regroupment of forces out of the present upheaval in all circles of American radicalism, will undoubtedly acknowledge the Communist Party, of the heroic formative years, as its true ancestor.

The predominant characteristic of the Communist Party in its later years of degeneration—and the basic cause for its degeneration—has been its implicit repudiation of the revolutionary program and perspective for America which the party stood for in its formative years. This is the rotten fruit of the Stalinist theory of "Socialism in One Country." This is the big "mistake" which has to be corrected before the damage can be repaired and a new start made. The Russian Bolsheviks who staked their lives in the fight against the Stalinist degeneration in the Soviet Union, fought under the slogan: "Back to Lenin." The American translation of that same slogan is a call to go back to the pioneer revolutionary period of American communism and begin again and build from there.

Of course, there can be no question of simply going back to the past. Much has happened in the world and in this country in the intervening years. All these great events and experiences have to be studied and interpreted, conclusions must be drawn and incorporated in the new program. But, in my opinion, these conclusions will not be a substitute for the basic theses of the original Communist Party, but rather a supplement to them, a development and a continuation.

The evidence to support this contention is amply provided in Theodore Draper's book. It belongs in the library of every socialist militant.

2. 'American Communism and Soviet Russia'

American Communism and Soviet Russia, by Theodore Draper. Viking Press, New York, N.Y. 558 pp. 1960. $8.50.

When Theodore Draper set out in 1952 to write the history of the American Communist Party he didn't know what he was getting into.

He had assumed, as he says in the introduction to the present volume, that "the 'real' history of American communism had begun with the economic depression of the early Nineteen-thirties," and that the first ten years could be given short shrift. "Originally I conceived of writing the whole story in one volume, of which the opening chapter would briefly outline the party's 'pre-history' from 1919 to 1929." It didn't work out that way.

The writing of this "pre-history" turned out to be a formidable chore because the first ten years stubbornly

Reprinted from International Socialist Review, *Winter 1961.*

refused to yield to summary treatment, and information about them was not easily found. The historical reports of others, Stalinist and anti-communist alike, proved to be inadequate and unreliable; superficial jobs, tendentiously slanted and even grossly falsified. Draper explains the problem that upset his original plans with polite restraint, as follows: "I found scholarly exploration almost completely lacking, sources uncollected and often unknown, and most of the available material encrusted with personal bias and political propaganda."

He had to undertake a basic research of original sources never assembled before. He soon discovered that he had to dig deep for the true story. And, once started, and lured on by its unfolding interest, he kept at it, year after year, until he had piled up a mountain of material and sorted it out into a coherent pattern.

Now, eight years and two thick and richly documented volumes later, he hasn't been able to get farther than the "opening chapter," as he at first had conceived it. That simple fact, standing by itself, is testimony to the significance and interest of the first ten years of American communism, and also to the seriousness of the first historian to report it with factual accuracy in scope and detail.

Draper's first volume, *The Roots of American Communism*, published in 1957, could carry the story only up to 1923. His second volume, *American Communism and Soviet Russia*, recently published, ends in the year 1929. His projected third volume, dealing with the Stalin-Browder era, which he had originally conceived to be the "real" story, has had to wait until the first ten years of the party's evolution, which eventually prepared the necessary conditions for the Browderian monstrosity, had been thoroughly explored and reported.

Serious students of American communism, and of its first ten years in particular, will be grateful for Draper's remarkable work of exploration and discovery. His two imposing volumes give the first and only detailed, rounded and connected account of the facts of American communist history, from its inception as a revolutionary movement inspired by the Russian Revolution until it succumbed to Stalinism in 1929. By that time, the American party, gradually yielding to conservative domestic pressures on the one side and to the deep-going reaction in the Soviet Union on the other, had undergone a profound transformation.

How this transformation was eventually brought about is related, step by step, in Draper's story. It seems simple and clear and easy as you read the flowing narrative from chapter to chapter—until you study the voluminous reference notes and reflect that it took the author eight years of hard labor to assemble them; and reflect further that the research relates to living people in action all the time.

Along the way, the party lost its character as a self-governing organization; its internal democracy was gradually reduced until it was completely strangled in 1929; and the great majority of the strongest and most independent leaders, who had founded the party and led it through the first ten years, were eliminated in one way or another.

All that took time. It took ten years. And they were not quiet, easy years. They were years in which living people—the pioneers of American communism—fought long and hard against insuperable odds to create the first revolutionary workers' party in this country. They failed, but they didn't fail easily. Some of them died, and some fell by the wayside in the exhausting struggle; some changed and deteriorated under the harsh pressures of time and circumstance, and were different people when the showdown came; and some were defeated standing up and had to make a new start.

And even then, the year before Stalin took over the party lock, stock, and barrel in 1929, saw two explosions in the leadership. The Trotskyists had to be expelled in the fall of 1928 and the Lovestoneites in the summer of 1929.

All that had to happen, in drawn-out, unceasing turmoil and conflict, before the party itself could be transformed into an entirely different party, as it is shown to be at the end of its first decade, at the end of Draper's second volume of party history. The American Communist Party met the economic crisis touched off by the stock market crash in October, 1929 with the same name and the same formal program as in the previous decade. But it was not the same party.

The thesis of Draper's book is implicitly stated in its title: *American Communism and Soviet Russia*. He thinks the trouble with the American Communist Party began at the beginning when it tied itself to the Russian Revolution and the Russian leaders, and that this initial mistake—the party's original sin, so to speak—led it inexorably, from one calamity to another, and to eventual defeat and disgrace.

His dim view of this original sin is carried over into his extensive report and passing comments on the activities of the sinners and the movement they created or tried to create, and—perhaps unconsciously—it seems to permeate everything he says about them. This deprecatory appraisal is implied, more than explicitly stated, in his style and tone. This style and tone dominate the absorbing narrative from start to finish.

He seems to think, if we take his attitude for his opinion, that the whole thing was a bloody mess, as our English cousins would say, and the people concerned were rather a bad lot, free from any trace of the odor of sanctity. This history is definitely not a work of hagiology. The only actors in the big cast of characters who escape with a few kind words—and this strikes me as an unintended comic touch—are those who dropped out or got themselves expelled.

Draper's bias is unconcealed. But he manifests it in a manner absolutely unique in anti-communist historical writing. His cocksure interpretations and summary judgments are woven into every page of his writing, from his introduction to his concluding sentence, but he does not twist his evidence to bolster them. He relates the facts as he found them, without prejudicial selection, or deliberate omission, or falsification.

He shows that Russian influence, which began with the influence of the ideas of the Russian Revolution in the Lenin-Trotsky time, culminated at the end of the first ten years in the complete domination of the American party by the Stalin regime in all respects, even to the extent of selecting, removing, and rearranging the party leadership, without regard to any prior decisions or preferences of the party membership.

Draper proves all that from the record, citing chapter and verse every time. Then he assumes and concludes that this Russian influence was strictly no good from start to finish. But he doesn't prove that.

This question is directly related to the world historical significance of the Russian Revolution of 1917; and to the long and deep reaction, with all its complexities, that followed the vernal period of the revolution but failed to cancel it out, and the effect of this reaction on all the communist parties of the world, including the American, and including the Russian. This is a world problem and the most complicated and difficult problem of modern times. It has to be seen in the light of Soviet Russia's isolation in a capitalist world. It does not admit of a simple, off-hand interpretation on national grounds, either Russian or American.

Draper's account, from a factual standpoint, is unassailable. He tells us what really happened in the American Communist Party, and how it happened. The why and the wherefore, and what it signifies for the future, is another matter; the critical reader will have to answer that for himself. By and large, the answer will depend on one's basic point of view about where the world, and America with it, are heading. The pioneers of American communism and their endeavors, their original aspirations and later disappointments, their achievements and defeats, can only be judged by how they fit into the general perspective.

It's an either-or proposition, as I see it. If it is assumed that American capitalism has solved, or is on the way to solving, its basic contradictions; and if it is assumed further that our great and blameless country, together with its allies, and with a clean-cut, All-American boy at the helm as president, will soon begin to reverse the trend of history started by the Russian Revolution of 1917—don't laugh!—then the doings and mis-doings of the pioneer American communists, who hitched their wagon to the Russian star, are irrelevant to the present and the future.

Their history, then, is the history of an off-beat adventure—of interest only to curious scholars and still more curious readers, similar to those who like to write and read about the various utopian colonies and bizarre cults of the past. This is a very limited audience which, moreover, is not likely to excite itself to controversy about the meaning of it all. What difference does it make anyway?

On the other hand, if the historical trend set off by the Russian Revolution is seen as virtually irreversible now, and strong enough to shake off the Stalinist deformations, becoming cleaner, freer and more democratic as it rolls along; and if America, too, is seen as inexorably destined for its own revolution on the Russian model—then the first attempt to organize a revolutionary party in this country was a soundly motivated and heroic undertaking which has a profound meaning and practical interest for the present and the future.

Those who see the future this way, and identify themselves with it by purposeful activity, stand in the direct line of succession to the original American communists who were inspired by the same vision forty years ago, and need to know all about them. The times were against the communist pioneers in this country, and their own timing was off, and they committed other mistakes and even some absurdities, and eventually most of them lost their way. But all that is secondary.

Their original vision of the future was true, and that's the main thing. It invests the ten-year story of their endeavors, and their defeat, and the new beginning in 1928, with a continuing interest for the upcoming generation of rebel youth.

Those who study Draper's history will note that the handful of American communists who revolted against the corruption of Stalinism and made a new beginning did not look for a new revelation. They called for a return to the basic ideas of the Russian Revolution which the

Stalinists had betrayed.

Draper devotes a chapter to a report of this revolt and new beginning in the fall of 1928 and concludes—with implied disapproval—that Trotskyism could not give us "the means of finding a new revolutionary road; at best it promised to lead back to an old one." This raises the question of what a revolutionary party is, where it starts, and what it lives on.

A revolutionary party begins with ideas representing social reality, and cannot live without them. And such ideas, like money, do not grow on trees. They have to be taken where they can be found and valued for their own sake, regardless of their point of origin. A would-be revolutionist who doesn't recognize this had better quit before he starts.

The original ideas of the modern socialist movement in all countries of the world, including Russia, had to be taken from Marx and Engels, who happened to be Germans. The continuation and development of these "German" ideas into revolutionary action and victory was the work of Russians, Lenin and Trotsky in the first place, who were internationalists and avowed disciples of the great originators. Revolutionary parties which sprang up in all countries of the world after the First World War were inspired by the original German ideas, which had become Russian ideas and actions, and lived on them in their early years.

The same is true of the entire historical period since the death of Lenin in 1924. The analysis of the new and complicated problem of Stalinism, fascism and the Second World War, and the programmatic ideas for a revolutionary opposition, all came again from the Russians, in this case Trotsky and his collaborators in the Soviet Union.

Of course, it might be flattering to one's personal conceit and sense of national pride—if one is bothered by such anachronistic absurdities at this hour of the clock—to organize a brand new "American" party with homegrown American ideas, new or old. But no such ideas—none that were any good, that is—were to be found in the United States when the first attempt to organize a revolutionary party in this country was made in 1919. They were not to be found when a handful of us made a new beginning in 1928. And they have not been found in the intervening 30-odd years.

To be sure, there have been numerous attempts to improvise a purely American party but they all melted away like last year's snow. That's the way it had to be, for there is no American road separate and apart from the international road. America has produced some great technologists, engineers and professional baseball players, and experts in other fields. But, so far, no creative political thinkers for the age of internationalism.

In this age of internationalism, those who have seriously wanted to build a revolutionary party in this country have had no choice but to look elsewhere for programmatic ideas. Draper says that our espousal of the Trotskyist program in 1928 "helped to perpetuate the dependence of all branches and off-shoots of the American communist movement on the Russian revolution and Russian revolutionaries." That's true. But what of it?

The famous bandit, Willie Sutton, was once asked by a reporter why he specialized exclusively on robbing banks. Willie, a thinking man's thief, answered right off the bat: "Because that's where the money is." In the entire historical period since the collapse of the international socialist movement in the First World War up to the present, revolutionary national parties in every country have had to look to the Russian Revolution and its authentic leaders. That's where the ideas are.

Index

Abern, Martin, 85, 152, 159, 170, 187, 199, 275
A Long Way From Home (Claude McKay), 85
American Commission of the Communist International
  At the 4th Congress (1922), 85–86, 88–89
  At the 8th Plenum (1927), 223, 227
  At the 6th Congress (1928), 250, 259–62
American Communism and Soviet Russia (Theodore Draper), 16, 398, 400–401
"American exceptionalism," 181, 228–29
American Labor Alliance, 56
American Federation of Labor (AFL), 123, 131–33, 139–41, 155, 175–80, 200, 203–5, 240, 245–46, 251, 290–91, 305–6, 325, 344, 365
American question (at the Comintern), 163
  At the 4th Congress (1922), 85
  At the 4th Plenum (1924), 160
  In 1927, 163, 208, 212–13, 223, 227, 252–54
  At the 6th Congress, 254–55
American Railway Union, 309, 346, 351
American Socialist Movement, The, 1897–1912 (Ira Kipnis), 120–21, 315

Amter, Israel, 71, 94
Anarchism
  Anarchists, 122–26, 203–4
  Anarchist groups, 386, 393–95
Anglo-Russian Committee, 243
Appeal to Reason, The, 312–14, 319–21, 323
Ashkenudzie, George, 88

Ballam, John J., 58, 208, 220–21, 230
Basky, Louis, 225–26
Batt, Dennis E., 70–71
Bedacht, Max, 68, 78, 84, 87, 89, 143–44, 167
Bending Cross, The (Ray Ginger), 289, 316
Berger, Victor, 289–90, 319, 324–26, 357–58, 393
Berkman, Alexander, 125, 137
Beuhler, A.A. ("Shorty"), 138
Billings, Warren K., 203
Bittelman, Alexander, 56, 58, 67, 69, 71, 94, 114–15, 119–20, 126–30, 141, 143–45, 149, 152, 157, 159, 162–63, 167–69, 186, 244–47, 258, 261, 263, 265–68, 277
Bolshevism, 22, 360, 370–71, 391–92
Bolsheviks, 21, 33–34, 59, 63, 83, 292–93, 331, 335–38, 369, 371, 374, 377, 385–88, 391, 393–94

Bolshevik Revolution, 128, 386
  See also Russian Revolution
Brandler, Heinrich, 223
Bridgeman Convention (1920), 55
  (1922), 72, 92–93
Brissenden, Paul F., 343, 349, 354, 356
British Communist Party, 75
British General Strike (1926), 243
British Labor Party, 74–75
Browder, Earl, 72, 111, 125, 136–39, 141–43, 151–54, 157–59, 163, 170, 247, 261, 263, 265–67, 275, 390
Brown, John, 317
Bukharin, Nikolai, 81–82, 84, 89, 161, 164, 183, 223, 244, 249, 251–53, 257–61, 270
Bulletin No. 1 (Konikow Group), 237
Butte Daily Bulletin, 233

Calverton, V.F., 61–62
Canadian Communist Party, 231, 255, 274
Cannon, James P., 9, 11–13, 130, 149, 151–53, 157–58, 167, 242, 249, 261
  Cannon group, 262
  Cannonites, 229, 267
  See also Foster-Cannon faction
Centralia prisoners (IWW), 203
Chaplin, Ralph, 370
Chicago Federation of Labor, 76, 79, 108–9, 132, 151
Christian Socialism, 319, 327
CIO. *See* Congress of Industrial Organizations

Class Struggle, The, 128
Coleman, McAlister, 316
Communist, The, 74, 77, 246, 248
Communist International
  Congresses of
    (2nd), 287, 370, 389
    (3rd), 74
    (4th), 76–78, 84, 106
    (5th), 239–41
    (6th), 33, 141–42, 163, 182–84, 225, 231, 234, 242–43, 248–51, 254, 257–63, 269–70, 274–75
  Degeneration of, 37
  Early role of, 22
  "Pan American Agency" of, 59
  "Parity Commission" of (1925), 166–69
  Plenums of
    (Feb.–March 1922), 78
    (June 1922), 80–81, 84
    (1924), 159–60, 162
    (1925), 164
    (1926), 176–77
    (1927), 253
  Senioren Konvent, 258
  See also "American Commission" *and* "American Question"
Communist Party of the United States
  Central Committees of, 69, 96–97, 130, 138, 165, 167, 169–70, 208–9, 211, 223, 226, 252–54
  Central Control Commission of, 276
  Conventions of
    (1925), 159, 162, 166–71, 184–186, 207, 218

Communist Party of the United States
Conventions of (*continued*)
(1927), 181, 214, 216–18, 220–21, 223, 227, 230
(1929), 183
Plenums of
(1927), 215, 252
(Feb. 1928), 227–30, 242, 274
(May 1928), 242, 244–46, 248
Political Committees of, 61, 110, 114–16, 149, 167, 171, 209–10, 276
See also Workers Council, Workers Party
Communist Unity (Alexander Bittelman), 144
Conference for Progressive Political Action (Feb. 1922), 78–79
Congress of Industrial Organizations, 31, 140, 155, 205, 297, 305–6, 308, 342–43, 347, 375, 390
Cooperative League of America, 137
Corey, Lewis. *See* Louis Fraina
Coutts, David, 135
Criticism of the Draft Program (of the Communist International) (Leon Trotsky), 33, 163–64, 249, 254–55, 262, 265, 268, 279
Criminal syndicalism laws, 203, 328

Daily Worker, The, 78, 157–58, 161, 219, 241

"Dawson" (J.P. Cannon), 246
Debs, Eugene Victor, 111, 121–22, 238, 289, 305–10, 319, 321–22, 325, 328–37, 339, 342–43, 345–48, 351, 377, 393–94
Decline of the IWW, The (John S. Gambs), 357
De Leon, Daniel, 342–43, 345, 348, 353, 357–58, 387–88, 393
Democratic Party, 48, 52, 319
Diary in Exile, 1935 (Leon Trotsky), 284
Dirba, Charles, 58
Don, Sam, 219
Dozenberg, Nicholas, 241
Draper, Theodore, 9, 13, 15–16, 381–86, 390–91, 396–405
Dubner, A. (Jakira), 239
Dunne, Grant, 234
Dunne, Margaret, 234
Dunne, Miles, 234
Dunne, Vincent R., 234
Dunne, William F. (Bill), 152, 157, 159, 169, 187, 230, 233–34, 246–47, 249, 261, 268
Dutch leaders and theoreticians, 386–89

Eastman, Max, 57, 85–88, 226, 236, 371
"Emancipation of Labor," 237
Engdahl, J. Lewis, 56, 157
Engels, Frederick, 31, 75, 360, 377, 404
Epstein, Melech, 56
"Europe and America" (speech by Leon Trotsky), 243–44
Ewart, (Braun), 223, 227

Farmer-Labor Party, 75–76, 108–9, 162
  Conventions of
    (1923), 79–80, 107–9, 122, 151
    (1924), 162
Federated Farmer-Labor Party, 65, 99, 107, 110, 113, 116, 146–47, 149
Finnish leaders (CP), 119
First Five Years of the Communist International (Leon Trotsky), 74
First International, 31
Fischer, Ruth, 223
Fisher (South Slavic Federation), 187
Fitzpatrick, John, 79, 107–9, 131–32, 134, 140–41, 146, 151, 271–72
Five Year Plan, 270
Flynn, Elizabeth Gurley, 373
"Ford-Dubner Thesis," 239
Forging of American Socialism, The (Howard H. Quint), 315
Foster, William Z., 68, 72, 159–60, 258–59, 271–72, 388
  In the AFL (also Trade Union Education League), 130–37, 139–41, 177, 187, 240, 245–46
  Chairman, CPUSA, 157–58
  Foster-Browder relationship, 141–43
  Foster-Cannon faction, 78, 99, 108–9, 115–20, 146, 149–51, 155, 157–59, 161–63, 169–72, 182–83, 186–87, 207, 218, 224–25, 239, 254, 261–62

Foster, William Z. (*continued*)
  Fosterites, 135–37, 141–42, 176–77, 186–88, 191–92, 197, 219, 222–23, 229, 246–49, 251, 262–68, 277–78
    on Trotskyism, 277–78
  Foster-Weinstone-Cannon, 214, 252–53
  As an independent (pre-1923), 110–11
  Trade union leader, 93, 95, 98
Fourth International, 17, 46, 120, 122, 181, 244
Fox, Jay, 135
Fraina, Louis (Lewis Corey), 58–64, 69–70, 74, 77, 388
Freiheit, 113–15

Gambs, John S., 357
Garvey, Marcus, 295
Gates, John, 273
Gebert, 187
German Communist Party, 164, 223
German Social Democratic Party, 387
Ginger, Ray, 289, 316
Gitlow, Benjamin, 53, 55, 68, 70–71, 94, 115, 176, 180–81, 197, 210, 239, 260
Goldman, Emma, 125, 137
Gomez, M., 187, 249, 261
Gompers, Samuel, 27, 122, 131–34, 140–41, 271–72, 310, 343
"Goose Caucus," 71–72, 80, 93, 181, 239
Gorter, Herman, 387
Green, P. (Gusev), 166–68, 171, 218
Gusev (P. Green). *See* above entry

Hammersmark, Sam, 136
Hansen, Reba, 16
Hapgood, Hutchins, 122–23
Hardman, J.B.S. (Salutsky), 56
Hathaway, Clarence, 187, 249, 257, 261
Haymarket martyrs, 125, 346
Haywood, William D., 122, 199, 201–3, 328, 342–45, 348, 354–55, 367–68, 370–71, 377
Bill Haywood's Book, 370
Hearst, William Randolph, 180–81
Herndon case, 294–95
Hervé, Gustave, 133
Hill, Joe, 363–64
Hillquit, Morris, 324, 357–58
  Hillquit-Berger Wing of Socialist Party, 121, 358
History of American Trotskyism (James P. Cannon), 33, 46, 58–59, 86, 164, 181, 230, 250, 254–55, 275, 278, 281–82
History of the Communist Party of America, The (Alexander Bittelman), 126–28, 144
History of the Communist Party of the United States (William Z. Foster), 135, 139, 385, 388
Hook, Sidney, 61
Houdek, Julia, 16
Hourwich, Nicholas I., 53, 69–70, 88
  Hourwich Group, 63, 130, 145
Hungarian Communist Party, 96
Hungarian Federation, 226
Hungarian uprising, 381

I Confess (Benjamin Gitlow), 176, 180–81, 217–18

Industrial Workers of the World (IWW, "Wobblies"), 33, 38, 54, 120, 124–25, 127, 132–33, 137–39, 141, 177, 199–200, 203–4, 238, 241, 245, 249, 280, 290, 322, 328, 341–55, 357–77, 386, 393–95
  Conventions
    Founding (1905), 341–47, 354, 360–61, 367, 374, 377
    (1906), 348–49, 351
    (1908), 353–54
International Labor Defense (ILD), 123, 198–204, 229, 241–42, 373
International Left Opposition, 264–65
International Socialist Review (pre-war organ of Socialist Party), 320, 331, 388
International Socialist Review (theoretical organ of the Socialist Workers Party), 17, 282, 381
Investigation of Strike in Steel Industry: Hearings before the Committee on Education and Labor, U.S. Senate—66th Congress, 1st session, 131–32, 140
IWW, The History, Structure and Methods (V. St. John), 348
IWW: A Study of American Syndicalism (Paul F. Brissenden), 343

Jakira, Abraham (Dubner), 239
Jewish Federation, 113, 115, 119
Jewish Labor in the U.S.A. (Melech Epstein), 56

Johannsen, Anton, 122–23
Johnson, Charles ("Scott"), 59–60
Johnson, Oakley C., 268–69
Johnstone, Jack, 85, 135–36, 141, 152, 157–59, 170, 261, 266–67
Jones, Mother, 346

Kansas City Central Labor Union, 123
Kaplan, David, 123
Karsner, David, 316
Karsner, Rose, 16–17, 199
Katayama, Sen, 59
Katterfeld, L.E., 70–71, 78, 84, 89, 94, 97, 239
Kautsky, Karl, 310
Keracher, John, 70–71
Khrushchev, Nikita S., revelations of, 381, 385, 393
King, Rev. Martin Luther, 299
Kipnis, Ira, 120–21, 290, 292, 315, 322, 326–27
Knights of Labor, 312, 346
Konikow, Dr. Antoinette, 236–38
Konikow, Edith, 237
Krumbein, Charles, 152, 159, 170, 219
Kucher, 240
Kutcher, James, 206

Labor Defender, The, 123, 199, 201
Labor Herald, The, 158
Labor party
  Labor party policy, 73–80, 107, 161–63, 165–66
  Labor party question, 73–80, 87–88, 146–47, 164–65
  La Follette–labor party question, 160, 235

Larkin, James Joseph, 70–71
Left Opposition in the Russian party, 33–34, 226, 232, 243–44, 258–59, 270
  See also Russian Opposition
Left-Wing Communism: An Infantile Disorder (V.I. Lenin), 75, 389
Lenin, Vladimir I., 28, 35, 74–77, 160, 232, 250, 260, 297, 300, 334–41
  Leninist Letts, 241
  Leninist type of party, 51, 334–35, 338–39
  Lenin School in Moscow, 249
Lewis, John L., 139
Lewis-Hillman-Murray, 51
Liberator, The, 59, 137, 371
Lindgren, Edward I., 71, 239
"Liquidators," 72, 76, 80, 83–85, 91, 94, 97–98
Lore, Ludwig, 119–20, 162, 226, 234–37
Losovsky, A., 180, 246–51, 260, 265
Lovestone, Jay, 55, 58, 68–69, 78–79, 98, 106, 110, 119, 143–44, 151, 153, 161, 167, 181–83, 193–96, 198, 209–11, 214–16, 218, 227–30, 240, 244–45, 249, 250–54, 259–60
Lovestone-Cannon combination, 67–69, 71, 94–95
Lovestone faction, 182–83, 191–92, 197–98, 212–14, 216–22, 225–30, 242–45, 248, 250–54, 258–61, 267, 275, 277, 400
Lovestone regime, 230, 244, 246, 263

Magil, A.B., 241–42f
Manley, Joe, 135–36
Marx, Karl, 31, 35, 360, 404
Marxism, 36, 310, 350, 360
Maslow, Arkadi, 223
McKay, Claude, 85
McNamara, J.B., 123–24
Memories of Lenin (Krupskaya), 336
Michigan Group, 128–30
  See also Proletarian Party
Militant, The, 131, 183, 202, 226, 237, 256, 277
Minneapolis trial, 256, 276
  See also Smith Act trial, 1941
Minor, Robert, 71, 94
Mooney, Tom, 125, 203
  Mooney Defense Committee, 125, 137
Morgan, Jeanne, 16
Moyer-Haywood case, 279, 312–13
Muste, A.J., 62
My Life (Leon Trotsky), 128

National Association for the Advancement of Colored People, 290
Nearing, Scott, 183
Neumann, Heinz, 164–65
New Review, The, 388
Notebook of an Agitator (James P. Cannon), 284
Novy Mir, 128

O'Flaherty, Tom, 187, 199
Olgin, Moissaye J., 56, 113–15, 119
One Step Forward, Two Steps Back (V.I. Lenin), 336

Opposition in the Communist Party of the United States (1927–28), 182–84, 215–17, 220–21, 261–64
  See also "Right Danger in American Party, The"—July 1928 Opposition Platform

Packinghouse workers' organizing drive (1917–18), 139, 151
Pages from Party History (Jay Lovestone), 182–83
Parity Commission (of the Comintern) (1925), 166–69
Parsons, Lucy, 346
Passaic strike (1926), 175–80, 246
  United Front Committee (Passaic), 175–79
People's Front, 52, 271, 275
Pepper, John (Pogany), 65, 68, 73–74, 77, 79, 95–101, 107, 110, 114–18, 146–49, 151–54, 157, 161, 163–64, 181, 183, 196, 220, 224, 235, 239–40, 244–45
  Pepperism, 146, 234
  Pepper majority, 112
  Pepper regime, 98–100, 107, 112–14, 117–19, 149
Pioneer Publishers, 74, 81, 257
Plekhanov, George, 237
Polish Communist Party, 91–92
Political Affairs, 268
Populist Party, 321
Populists, 312
Pravda, 281
Profintern, 234
  Congresses of
    (1921), 136, 139
    4th (1928), 247
  See also Red International of Labor Unions

Proletarian Party, 38, 58, 70–71, 128–29
See also Michigan Group

Quint, Howard H., 315

Radek, Karl, 81, 84, 89
Rakosi, Matyas, 85–86
Real Situation in Russia, The (Leon Trotsky), 226
Red International of Labor Unions (RILU), 82
See also Profintern
Reed, John, 53, 55, 59, 70–71
Reinstein, Boris, 96
Retail Clerks Union, 173–74
Revolutionary Age, The, 59, 74, 137–38
Reynolds, Bud, 187
Right Danger in the American Party, The (July 1928 Opposition Platform), 182–83, 261
Ripsaw, The, 320
Roosevelt, Franklin D., 48, 51–52
Roots of American Communism, The (Theodore Draper), 16, 381–82, 384, 398
Russian Communist Party, 25, 35, 37, 40, 88–89, 128, 160–61, 163, 190, 401–2
Central Committee of, 88
Russian Federation, 63–64
Russian Opposition (Trotskyist), 32–34, 226, 232, 249–50, 277, 280–81
Russian Revolution, 21–22, 33–34, 54, 59, 64, 125, 127, 137, 147, 159, 193, 290–93, 297–300, 329, 331, 333, 335–37, 341, 358, 366–72, 382, 385, 390, 394–95, 399, 401

Russian Revolution (1905), 341–42, 374
Russian Revolution, The (James P. Cannon), 81
Russian Revolution, The Fifth Year of (James P. Cannon), 106
Russian Social Democratic Party, 336
Ruthenberg, Charles E., 10, 55, 59, 63–64, 68–72, 79, 93–95, 97, 101, 106, 110, 145, 147, 151, 153–54, 157–58, 167, 182, 206–7, 215, 227–29, 241–42
Ruthenberg group, 161–62, 164–71, 175, 196–97, 207–8, 218, 228–29
Ruthenberg-Pepper-Lovestone faction, 167, 187, 191, 193, 198, 215–16, 225
"Ruthenberg-Pepper thesis," 149, 153
Rykov, 257, 270

Sacco and Vanzetti, 203–4
Sacco-Vanzetti case, 201
Sacco-Vanzetti Committee, 201, 241
Salutsky, J.B. (Hardman), 56
Schlesinger, Arthur, Jr., 315
Schmidt, Matt, 123, 203
Schmidt-Kaplan case, 123, 137
Schneiderman, William, 187
"Scott," Charley (Johnson), 241
Scottsboro case, 294–95
Second International, 36–37, 235, 370, 387
Shachtman, Max, 152, 170, 187, 199, 275–76

Shannon, David, 290, 292, 315, 322–23, 329, 382
Sherman, Charles O., 348–49
Shoaf, George H., 312
Siskind, G., 261
Smith Act, 205, 276
   Smith Act trial (Socialist Workers Party, 1941), 276, 300
Social Democratic Herald, The, 289
Social Democrats, 205, 234–35, 319
"Socialism in One Country"—theory of, 29, 33, 47–48, 103, 396
Socialist Labor Party, 38, 237, 318, 346, 353, 357, 386–87, 393, 395
Socialist Party (*see* Part III), 21, 36–37, 53–56, 63, 69, 120–21, 128–29, 136–38, 159, 237–38, 289, 298, 306, 309–10, 315–16, 318–34, 337–38, 346, 357, 386–87, 394–95
   Conventions of
      (Unity Convention), 310, 318
      2nd (1904), 324
      (1912), 327–28
      (1919), 53–54, 129
   Left Wing, 20–21, 54–56, 121, 127–28, 136, 159, 324–25, 327–29, 331, 338, 386–88
   Left Wing National Conference (June 1919), 53, 55, 59, 63, 69–70, 111, 129
   National Committee of, 335
Socialist Party of America, The (David Shannon), 315
Socialist Reconstruction of Society (Daniel DeLeon), 345
Socialist Workers Party, 174, 206
Solidarity, 322
Solntsev, 236–37
South Slavic Federation, 187, 219
Spanish Revolution, 125
Spector, Maurice, 230–31, 255, 263–64, 273–75
Spirit of Labor, The (Hutchins Hapgood), 122–23
St. John, Vincent (The Saint), 127, 348–51, 353–58, 371–74
   See Part III
Stachel, Jack, 219–20, 277
Stalin, Joseph, 25, 84, 142, 151, 160–61, 165, 195–96, 232, 243–44, 251, 253–54, 257–61, 267, 270, 278, 297, 300, 385, 390–93, 400
Stalin-Bukharin bloc, 253
Stalin-Hitler pact, 48
Stalinism, 19, 27, 30–32, 47, 103, 157, 234, 264, 271–73, 284, 377, 381, 390–92, 399, 403–4
Stalinists, 30, 48, 196, 204–6, 296, 298, 300–302, 404
"State Department Socialism," 395
Steel strike of 1919, 131–32, 139–40, 207
Steel workers organizing drive, 139–40
Stokes, Rose Pastor, 84
Stoklitzky, Alexander, 88
Swabeck, Arne, 84, 152, 159, 169, 187
Syndicalism, 126, 136–37, 318
Syndicalists, 127, 136–38, 318, 338, 370, 387, 394

Syndicalism (*continued*)
Syndicalist Wing of Pre-War Radical Movement (IWW), 126–27.
See also Industrial Workers of the World
Syndicalism, French, 140, 354
Syndicalism (William Z. Foster), 132–33

Thalheimer, August, 223
Third International. See Communist International
"Third Period," 269–71, 275, 296
Third Period of the Comintern's Mistakes, The (Leon Trotsky), 271
Toiler, The, 55
Tomsky, Mikhail, 257, 270
Trachtenberg, Alexander, 85
Trade Union Educational League (TUEL), 93, 110–11, 136, 141, 148, 158, 207, 247
Trade Union Unity League (TUUL), 180, 247
Tresca, Carlo, 373
Trial of the Stalinist Leaders, The (James P. Cannon), 202
Trotsky, Leon, 28, 32–33, 61–62, 74, 84–88, 128, 160, 163, 172, 189, 225–26, 231–32, 235–36, 243–44, 255, 263, 265, 270–71, 275, 279–80, 284, 339, 370, 377, 388, 404
"Trial for Trotskyism," 276–77
Trotskyist faction (American), 66, 276
Trotskyism, 183, 225, 232, 234, 264–65, 274–76, 278–81
Trotskyist movement, 232, 237

Trotsky, Leon (*continued*)
Trotskyists, 39–40, 205, 298, 400

United Communist Party, 55, 246
United Opposition Bloc, 221–23
United Toilers, 58, 85

Valetski, H., 84, 91–92, 95–96
Volkzeitung, 236

Wagenknecht, Alfred, 70–72, 94, 239
Walling, William English, 290
Walsh, U.S. Senator, 134–35
Washington, Booker T., 294
Wayland, J.A., 319
Weinstone, William W., 55, 58, 67, 71, 94, 192–93, 196–98, 209, 211–12, 214, 217–23, 230
Weisbord, Albert, 175–78
Weiss, Murry, 124
Weiss, Myra Tanner, 124
Western Federation of Miners, 312, 344, 346, 349, 355–56
Whither England? (Leon Trotsky), 243
Wicks, Harry, 58
Wilkins, Scott, 322
Williams, Albert Rhys, 85
Williamson, John, 152, 187
Wilshire's Magazine, 320
Winitsky trial, 69
Wolfe, Bertram D., 143–44, 182–83, 193, 195–96, 216, 219–20, 227–28, 230, 244–45, 259–60
Worker, The, 77, 79, 109, 150
See also Daily Worker

Workers Council, 56–58, 85
　Formation of, 56
　Fusion into Workers Party, 56–57, 71–72, 113–14
　See also Communist Party, U.S.A., and Workers Party
Workers Party
　Conventions of
　　(Unity, 1921), 55, 67, 69, 71
　　(1923), 116–19, 149–50, 157
　Formation of, 113
　General references (before 1925 as "the party"), 56–58, 65, 68–69, 71, 78–80, 92–95, 98–100, 108, 147–49, 157–59
　Negotiations with Workers Council, 56–57
　Plenum of (1923), 116–17
　Political Committee of, 61
Workers World, The, 138, 233

Workmen's Circle, 237
World War I, 16, 20–21, 36, 103, 121–22, 125–27, 131, 137, 232, 290, 292, 294, 297, 310, 328–29, 358, 365–66, 368, 386–87, 395, 404–5
World War II, 51, 126, 300–301, 395, 404
Wortis, Rose, 85
Wright, John G., 231
Writings and Speeches of Eugene V. Debs, 315–16, 346–47

Zack, J., 247
Zelms, Robert, 241
Zimmerman, Charles, 162
Zinoviev, Gregory, 81–82, 84–85, 87, 89–90, 92, 160–61, 163, 165–66, 225, 231–33, 235, 253

ALSO BY JAMES P. CANNON

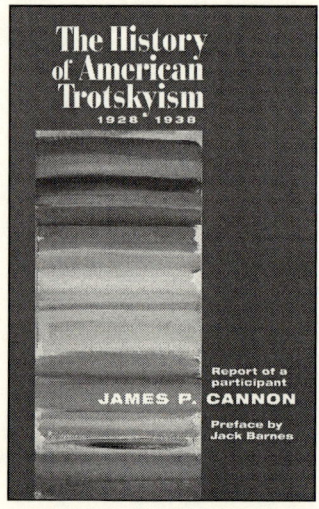

The History of American Trotskyism, 1928–38
Report of a Participant

"Trotskyism is not a new movement, a new doctrine," Cannon says, "but the restoration, the revival of genuine Marxism as it was expounded and practiced in the Russian Revolution and in the early days of the Communist International." Talks by a founding leader of American communism on building a proletarian party in the United States. $17. Also in Spanish and French.

The Struggle for a Proletarian Party

"The workers of America have power enough to topple the structure of capitalism at home and to lift the whole world with them when they rise," Cannon asserts. On the eve of World War II, a founder of the communist movement in the US and leader of the Communist International in Lenin's time defends the program and party-building norms of Bolshevism. $20. Also in Spanish and Farsi.

Letters from Prison
A Revolutionary Party Prepares for Post–WWII Labor Battles

The prison letters of a communist leader, jailed for his party's opposition to the US imperialist war effort in World War II. Cannon discusses organizing a revolutionary party in wartime and preparing its postwar political course. $20

The Socialist Workers Party in World War II, 1940–43

Preparing the communist workers movement in the United States to campaign against wartime censorship, repression, and anti-union assaults. $23

THE RUSSIAN REVOLUTION'S WORLD EXAMPLE

Lenin's Final Fight
Speeches and Writings, 1922–23
V.I. LENIN

In 1922 and 1923, V.I. Lenin, central leader of the world's first socialist revolution, waged what was to be his last political battle—one that was lost after his death. At stake was whether that revolution, and the international communist movement it led, would remain on the revolutionary proletarian course that brought workers and peasants to power in October 1917. $17. Also in Spanish, Farsi, Greek.

The History of the Russian Revolution
LEON TROTSKY

How, under Lenin's leadership, the Bolshevik Party led millions of workers and farmers to overthrow the state power of the landlords and capitalists in 1917 and bring to power a government that advanced their class interests at home and worldwide. Unabridged, 3 vols. in one. Written by one of the central leaders of that socialist revolution. $30. Also in French and Russian.

The Revolution Betrayed
What Is the Soviet Union and Where Is It Going?
LEON TROTSKY

In 1917 workers and peasants of Russia were the motor force of one of the deepest revolutions in history. Yet within ten years a political counterrevolution by a privileged social layer, whose chief spokesperson was Joseph Stalin, was being consolidated. The classic study of the Soviet workers state and its degeneration. $17. Also in Spanish, Farsi, Greek.

PATHFINDERPRESS.COM

BUILDING A PROLETARIAN PARTY

New!
The Fight against Jew-Hatred and Pogroms in the Imperialist Epoch
Stakes for the International Working Class

V.I. LENIN, LEON TROTSKY
FARRELL DOBBS
JAMES P. CANNON, JACK BARNES
DAVE PRINCE

Jew-hatred and pogroms—like Hamas carried out on October 7, 2023—are now part of the permanent social convulsions and wars of the imperialist epoch. That's why fighting Jew-hatred is of decisive importance to the working class and oppressed nations of the entire world. The authors answer the all-important question: *What is to be done to end it*—for all time. $10. Also in Spanish and French.

The Low Point of Labor Resistance Is Behind Us
The Socialist Workers Party Looks Forward

JACK BARNES
MARY-ALICE WATERS
STEVE CLARK

The global order imposed by Washington after its victory in World War II is shattering. A long retreat by the working class and unions has come to an end. The bosses and their government are stepping up attacks on our wages, conditions, and constitutional rights. This book highlights opportunities for building a mass proletarian party able to lead the struggle to end capitalist rule, opening a socialist future for humanity. $10. Also in Spanish and French.

CAPITALIST CRISIS AND THE FIGHT FOR WORKERS POWER

Are They Rich Because They're Smart?
Class, Privilege, and Learning under Capitalism

JACK BARNES

Exposes growing class inequalities in the US and the self-serving rationalizations of well-paid professionals who think their "brilliance" equips them to "regulate" working people, who don't know what's in our own best interest. $10. Also in Spanish, French, Farsi, Arabic, Greek.

The Clintons' Anti-Working-Class Record
Why Washington Fears Working People

JACK BARNES

What working people need to know about the profit-driven course of Democrats and Republicans alike over the last three decades. And the political awakening of workers seeking to understand and resist the capitalist rulers' assaults. $10. Also in Spanish, French, Farsi, Greek.

Teamster Rebellion
FARRELL DOBBS

The 1934 strikes that won union recognition for truckers and warehouse workers in Minneapolis and helped pave the way for the working-class social movement that built the industrial unions. The first of four volumes by a central leader of these battles. $16. Also in Spanish, French, Farsi, Greek.

PATHFINDERPRESS.COM

CUBA'S SOCIALIST REVOLUTION

New Edition!
Che Guevara on Economics and Politics in the Transition to Socialism
CARLOS TABLADA

It's essential for working people to win state power, said Ernesto Che Guevara. "Then there's the second stage, maybe more difficult than the first"—the transition from dog-eat-dog capitalism to socialism. That includes moving from work as a condition for survival, to voluntary social labor through which we express our common humanity. Includes Fidel Castro's 1987 speech "Che's Ideas Are Absolutely Relevant Today." New edition with substantially expanded selections from Guevara's writings. $17. Also in Spanish, coming in French.

Cuba and the Coming American Revolution
JACK BARNES

This is a book about the example set by the Cuban people that socialist revolution is not only necessary—it can be made. A book about the struggles of workers and other exploited producers in the imperialist heartland, and the youth attracted to them. About the class struggle in the US, where the revolutionary capacities of working people are as utterly discounted by the ruling powers as were those of the Cuban toilers. And just as wrongly. $10. Also in Spanish, French, Farsi.

Colombia: Fidel Castro on the Debate around Revolutionary Strategy and Lessons of the Cuban Revolution
FROM THE PAGES OF THE *MILITANT*

Fidel Castro describes the Cuban leadership's efforts to end decades of war between the FARC guerrilla movement and Colombia's brutal regime. He explains why Cuban revolutionaries, unlike FARC leaders, rejected taking hostages and organized Cuba's working people to win state power, not pursue a "prolonged people's war." $5. Also in Spanish.

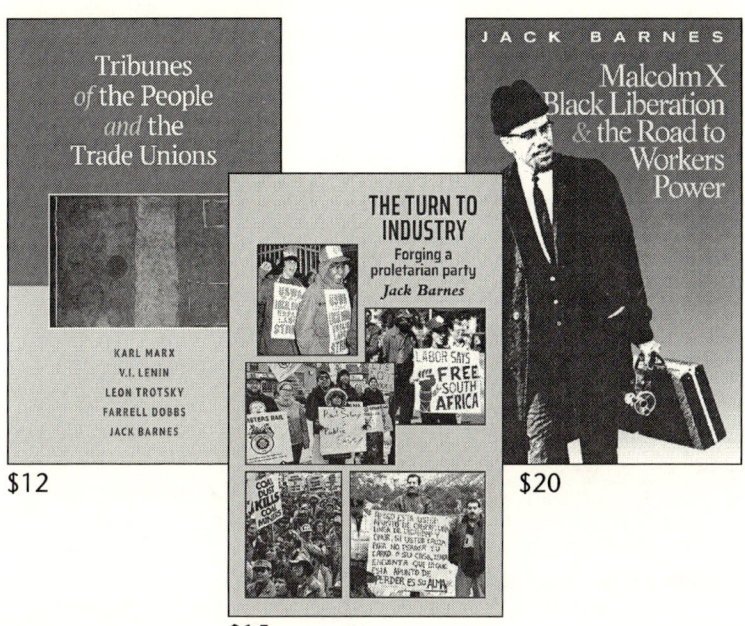

$12 $20

$15

Three books to be read as one…

about building a party that's working class in program, composition, and action. One that recognizes, in word and deed, the most revolutionary fact of our time…

… that working people have the power to create a different world as we act together to defend our own class interests—not those of the privileged classes who exploit our labor, not of those who fear us as "deplorables," or just plain "trash."

As we advance along a revolutionary course toward workers power, we will transform ourselves and awaken to our own worth. Also in Spanish, French, Farsi, Greek.

Special Offer!
All three $30

The Turn to Industry and Tribunes of the People and the Trade Unions $20

Either book plus Malcolm X, Black Liberation, and the Road to Workers Power $25

PATHFINDERPRESS.COM

WOMEN'S EMANCIPATION AND THE WORKING CLASS

Women in Cuba: The Making of a Revolution within the Revolution
VILMA ESPÍN
ASELA DE LOS SANTOS
YOLANDA FERRER

The integration of women in the ranks and leadership of the Cuban Revolution was intertwined with the proletarian course of the leadership of the revolution from the start. This is the story of that revolution and how it transformed the women and men who made it. $17. Also in Spanish, Farsi, Greek.

The Origin of the Family, Private Property, and the State
FREDERICK ENGELS

The emergence of class-divided society gave rise to repressive state bodies and the oppression of women to enable the ruling classes to pass along wealth and privilege. Engels discusses the consequences for working people of these class institutions—from their ancient forms to their modern versions. $15. Also in Spanish and Farsi.

Cosmetics, Fashions, and the Exploitation of Women
JOSEPH HANSEN, EVELYN REED
MARY-ALICE WATERS

How big business reinforces women's second-class status and uses it to rake in profits. Where does women's oppression come from? How has the entry of millions of women into the workforce strengthened the battle for emancipation, still to be won? $12. Also in Spanish, Farsi, Greek.

DEFENDING CONSTITUTIONAL FREEDOMS

50 Years of Covert Operations in the US
Washington's Political Police and the American Working Class
LARRY SEIGLE, FARRELL DOBBS STEVE CLARK

How class-conscious workers have defended constitutional freedoms and fought the capitalists' drive to build the "national security" state essential to maintaining their rule. $10. Also in Spanish and Farsi.

Socialism on Trial
Testimony at Minneapolis Sedition Trial
JAMES P. CANNON

The revolutionary program of the working class, presented in response to frame-up charges of "seditious conspiracy" in 1941, on the eve of US entry into World War II. The defendants were leaders of the Minneapolis labor movement and the Socialist Workers Party. $15. Also in Spanish, French, Farsi.

FBI on Trial
The Victory in the Socialist Workers Party Suit against Government Spying
MARGARET JAYKO

The record of a historic victory in the fight for political rights, including the 1986 federal court ruling against government spying and excerpts from trial testimony by SWP leaders Farrell Dobbs and Jack Barnes. $17

PATHFINDERPRESS.COM

EXPAND YOUR REVOLUTIONARY LIBRARY

Labor, Nature, and the Evolution of Humanity
The Long View of History

FREDERICK ENGELS, KARL MARX
GEORGE NOVACK
MARY-ALICE WATERS

Without understanding that social labor, transforming nature, has driven humanity's evolution for millions of years, working people are unable to see beyond the capitalist epoch of class exploitation that warps all human relations, ideas, and values. Only the revolutionary conquest of state power by the working class can open the door to a world free of capitalist exploitation, degradation of nature, subjugation of women, racism, and war. A world built on human solidarity. A socialist world. $12. Also in Spanish and French.

Thomas Sankara Speaks
The Burkina Faso Revolution, 1983–87

Under Sankara's guidance, Burkina Faso's revolutionary government led peasants, workers, women, and youth to expand literacy; to sink wells, plant trees, erect housing; to combat women's oppression; to carry out land reform; to join others worldwide to free themselves from the imperialist yoke. $20. Also in French.

The Communist Manifesto
KARL MARX AND FREDERICK ENGELS

Communism, say the founding leaders of the revolutionary workers movement, is not a set of ideas or preconceived "principles" but workers' line of march to power, springing from a "movement going on under our very eyes." $5. Also in Spanish, French, Farsi, Arabic.

The Jewish Question
A Marxist Interpretation

ABRAM LEON

The battle against reactionary forces aiming to exterminate the Jews remains central to world politics, as shown by the genocidal October 2023 pogrom in Israel. Why is Jew-hatred still raising its ugly head? What are its class roots? Why, as Abram Leon explains, is there no solution "independent of the world proletarian revolution"? Revised translation, new introduction, 40 pages of illustrations and maps. $17. Also in Spanish and French.

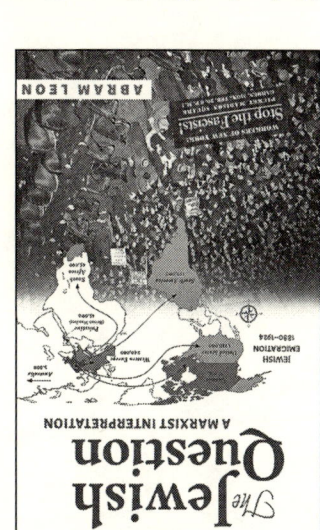

Malcolm X Talks to Young People

"The young generation of whites, Blacks, browns, whatever else—you're living at a time of revolution," said Malcolm in 1964. "And I for one will join with anyone, I don't care what color you are, as long as you want to change this miserable condition that exists on this earth." Four talks and an interview in the last months of Malcolm's life. $12. Also in Spanish, French, Farsi, Greek.

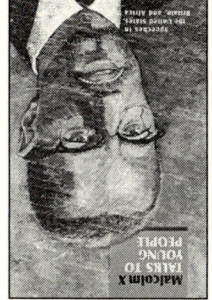

Pathfinder Press **accessible e-books** for the blind, those with low vision, or other challenges reading print books

For a list of current accessible titles, go to: pathfinderpress.com/collections/books-for-the-blind.

Visit bookshare.org for information on how to sign up.

PATHFINDERPRESS.COM

PATHFINDER AROUND THE WORLD

UNITED STATES
(and Caribbean, Latin America, and East Asia)
Pathfinder Books, 306 W. 37th St., 13th Floor
New York, NY 10018

CANADA
Pathfinder Books, 7107 St. Denis, Suite 204
Montreal, QC H2S 2S5

UNITED KINGDOM
(and Europe, Africa, Middle East, and South Asia)
Pathfinder Books, 5 Norman Rd.
Seven Sisters, London N15 4ND

AUSTRALIA
(and New Zealand, Southeast Asia, and the Pacific)
Pathfinder Books, Suite 2, First floor, 275 George St.
Liverpool, Sydney, NSW 2170
Postal address: P.O. Box 73, Campsie, NSW 2194

JOIN THE PATHFINDER READERS CLUB
BUILD YOUR LIBRARY!

$10 / YEAR
25% DISCOUNT ON ALL PATHFINDER TITLES
30% OFF BOOKS OF THE MONTH

Valid at pathfinderpress.com and local Pathfinder book centers

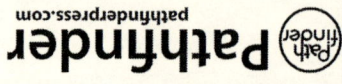

Pathfinder

Go to: pathfinderpress.com/
products/pathfinder-readers-club